T0358530

THE EVOLUTION OF
INTERNATIONAL BUSINESS
1800–1945

The Evolution of International Business 1800–1945
Selected and with a new Introduction by Mark Casson

Rippy, J.F. – *British Investments in Latin America, 1822–1949*

Spence, C.C. – *British Investments and the American Mining Frontier, 1860–1901*

Jackson, W.T. – *The Enterprising Scot: Investors in the American West after 1873*

Cameron, R.E. – *France and the Economic Development of Europe, 1800–1914*

Bagchi, A.K. – *Private Investment in India, 1900–1939*

Southard, F.A. Jr – *American Industry in Europe*

Phelps, D.M. – *Migration of Industry to South America*

Hou, Chi-ming – *Foreign Investment and Economic Development in China, 1840–1937*

Other titles in the series, *The Rise of International Business 1200–1800*

The Emergence of International Business 1200–1800
Selected and with a new Introduction by Mark Casson

Dollinger, P. – *The German Hansa*

de Roover, R. – *Money, Banking and Credit in Medieval Bruges*

Rabb, T.K. – *Enterprise and Empire*

Chaudhuri, K.N. – *The English East India Company*

Davies, K.G. – *The Royal Africa Company*

Davis, R. – *Aleppo and Devonshire Square*

Klein, P.W. – *De Trippen in de 17eeuw*

The Hegemony of International Business 1945–1970
Selected and with a new Introduction by Mark Casson

Dunning, J.H. – *American Investment in British Manufacturing Industry*

Islam, M. – *Foreign Capital and Economic Development*

Safarian, A.E. – *Foreign Ownership of Canadian Industry*

Brash, D.T. – *American Investment in Australian Industry*

Kidron, M. – *Foreign Investments in India*

Vernon, R. – *Sovereignty at Bay*

Stonehill, A. – *Foreign Ownership in Norwegian Enterprises*

Stubenitsky, F. – *American Direct Investment in the Netherlands*

THE EVOLUTION OF INTERNATIONAL BUSINESS 1800–1945

Volume 8

Foreign Investment and Economic Development in China, 1840–1937

Chi-ming Hou

London and New York

First published 1965 by Harvard University Press
This edition reprinted 2000 by Routledge
2 Park Square, Milton Park, Abingdon, Oxfordshire OX14 4RN

Simultaneously published in the USA and Canada
by Routledge
711 Third Avenue, New York, NY 10017

Routledge is an imprint of the Taylor & Francis Group, an informa business

© 1965 The President and Fellows of Harvard College

Typeset in 10/12pt Times by Graphicraft Limited, Hong Kong

British Library Cataloguing in Publication Data
A catalogue record for this book is available from the British Library

Library of Congress Cataloging in Publication Data
A catalogue record for this book has been requested

ISBN 13: 978-0-415-19007-7 (Set)
ISBN 13: 978-0-415-19015-2 (Volume 8)
ISBN 13: 978-0-415-52965-5 (POD Set)

Publisher's Note
The publisher has gone to great lengths to ensure the quality of these
reprints, but wishes to point out that certain characteristics of the
original copies will, of necessity, be apparent in reprints thereof.

Acknowledgements
The publishers would like to thank Harvard University Press for permission
to reprint Chi-ming Hou, *Foreign Investment and Economic Development in China,
1840–1937*, Harvard University Press, 1965.

Foreign Investment and
Economic Development in China

1840–1937

Chi-ming Hou

HARVARD UNIVERSITY PRESS

CAMBRIDGE · MASSACHUSETTS

1965

Preface

The subject of this book is the role of foreign investment in China's economic development before 1937. This is, of course, a highly controversial subject, and it would be beyond expectation that I should settle the controversy. I will be satisfied if, by examining and testing a number of hypotheses, I can put the entire matter in a clearer and less subjective perspective; and if, by casting doubts on the validity of certain conventional arguments, I can stimulate further inquiry into the process of economic modernization in China. For it is my firm belief that such investigation into the Chinese economy will contribute significantly to a better understanding of the complexities of social change not only in China but also in other underdeveloped or developing countries.

I should like to express my deep gratitude to the following scholars who have read my manuscript in its entirety and made many valuable suggestions: Professors Simon Kuznets and Dwight Perkins of Harvard University, Professor Everett E. Hagen of M.I.T., and Dr. Richard Moorsteen of the RAND Corporation. My sincere thanks are also due to those who have either read the manuscript or discussed its contents with me at various stages and made substantive suggestions, among them: Professor James W. Angell of Columbia University, Professor Theodore Herman of Colgate University, Professor K. C. Liu of the University of California, Davis, Professors Raymond Vernon and L. S. Yang of Harvard University, and Professor and Mrs. Y. C. Yin of the University of Southern California. Needless to say, I alone am responsible for any shortcomings that may have remained undetected.

My acknowledgments of indebtedness would be notably incomplete without special reference to Professor Franklin L. Ho and the late Professor Ragnar Nurkse, both of whom first encouraged me to write my Ph.D. dissertation on this subject at Columbia

University, and gave me invaluable guidance and advice. Though this book differs substantially from my dissertation in scope, approach, and major conclusions, it incorporates much of the material from the dissertation.

I did the research for this book and wrote it in the fall of 1959, the fall of 1962, and the summers of 1959–1962 at Harvard University's East Asian Research Center, without whose financial support I could never have finished it. I am deeply grateful to the Center for its aid and especially to its director, Professor John K. Fairbank, who has never failed to give me encouragement and good counsel. I also want to express my thanks to Mrs. Virginia Briggs of the Center and her secretarial staff for their assistance in typing and related matters.

All those who have made use of the Harvard-Yenching Library know what a distinctive contribution it makes to Chinese studies in the United States and how generous and helpful are its librarian, Dr. K. M. Chiu, and his staff. Throughout the progress of this work, I have been able to count upon their cooperation and courtesy.

My gratitude is also due to the Lucius N. Littauer Foundation, whose grants-in-aid (through the Research Council at Colgate University) were very helpful in the early stages of my research.

Mrs. Elizabeth Matheson, Mrs. Virginia LaPlante, and Mrs. Dorothy Sickels have, by their intelligent editing, done much for the form and style of the manuscript. To them too, my warm thanks.

Chi-ming Hou

December 3, 1964
Hamilton. New York

Contents

Tables

APPENDIX

Introduction

Few would deny that one of the most important factors shaping the Chinese economy over the past one hundred years or so has been economic contact with the West. This external economic confrontation has been widely regarded by the Chinese as detrimental to the development of their economy — as an instrument used by the Western powers to control the Chinese economy so as to serve their own interests. It has been regarded as economic imperialism practiced by the West for the purpose of converting China into a colony or a semicolony.

I do not plan to discuss here all of the arguments that have been advanced in connection with this proposition. The following points are the most frequently mentioned in condemning foreign economic intrusion in China. First, it is argued that foreign economic intrusion — that is, foreign trade and investment in China — upset the economy by ruining the handicraft industries and disrupting agriculture. Second, foreign trade and investment are alleged to have drained the economy of its wealth because of the secularly unfavorable balance of trade and the large amount of income that was made or remitted to their home countries by Western enterprises. Third, it is maintained that foreign enterprises in China were so effective in their competitive power or enjoyed so many advantages secured by their respective governments that the Chinese-owned modern enterprises were utterly and hopelessly oppressed and had little, if any, chance to grow.

It is not easy to establish which of these arguments has been more prevalent, or to identify the most influential advocates of each at any particular period, for all of them have gained wide acceptance in China throughout her modern history, and almost every critic of foreign economic influence has noted them with varying degrees of emphasis. Among the critics, who have included people from all walks of life, officials and scholars have been particularly active.

In evaluating the consequences of the penetration of foreign capitalism, Mao Tse-tung admits that it accelerated the development of the "commodity economy" in China, in both town and countryside.[1] However, he regards it as a disintegrating force in the sense that it destroyed the foundation of China's "self-sufficing natural economy" and "disrupted her handicraft industries in both the cities and peasant homes." At the same time, he charges that foreign imperialism conspired with the Chinese feudal forces (compradors, merchant usurers, landlords) to arrest the development of Chinese capitalism. The imperialist powers attempted to transform China into a semicolony or colony. The establishment of many light and heavy industries in China by the imperialist powers directly exerted "economic pressures on China's own industries and hampered the development of her productive forces."[2]

While Mao's comments reflect the line of thinking of the Chinese Communists on foreign trade and investment in China, Chiang Kai-shek's comments represent the attitude of the Nationalists. Like Mao, Chiang has only criticism for its effects on the Chinese economy or Chinese society as a whole. He argues that the rights enjoyed by foreigners to navigate Chinese inland waters, engage in coastal trade, open mines, issue bank notes, etc., crippled the national economy and caused the economic life of the people to degenerate into an "abnormal condition."[3] The new industrial and commercial system developed in the treaty ports under the protection of the unequal treaties was extended, through railroads and steamship lines, to the Chinese interior, causing "the bankruptcy of our existing handicraft industries and the decline of our agriculture."[4] Furthermore, argues Chiang, foreign economic penetration based on the unequal treaties also had undesirable social, moral, and psychological effects. The degeneration of Chinese social life and morality, reflected in insincerity, procrastination, frivolity, deceit, irresponsibility, and indolence, was in no small degree influenced and shaped by the moral tone prevailing in the foreign concessions. All of the traditional Chi-

nese virtues "were swept clean by the prevalence in the concessions of the vices of opium-smoking, gambling, prostitution, and
robbery."[5]

Chiang's criticisms are, however, only a continuation of those
of Dr. Sun Yat-sen. Sun regarded economic oppression by foreign
powers as even more severe and harmful to China than political
oppression.[6] In addition to attributing the decline of the rural
sector to foreign economic penetration, he ascribed the huge
drain of money out of China (some Chinese $1,200 million a year)
to the "invasion of foreign goods," "invasion of foreign paper
money," freight charges, and all other profits or income collected
by foreigners. Sun concluded: "While foreign imperialism backs
up this economic subjugation, the living problems of the Chinese
people are daily more pressing, the unemployed are daily increasing and the country's power is, in consequence, steadily
weakening."[7] However, Sun (like many other Chinese officials)
did not object to the use of foreign capital per se, for he clearly
needed it (in cooperation with the Chinese government) to carry
out his ambitious industrial plans for China.[8]

Arguments against foreign economic intrusion did not begin
with the era of the republic. They were widely held in the closing
decades of the Manchu dynasty.[9] Indeed, it would be difficult
to find a high official who did not find fault one way or another
with the effect of foreign trade and investment. In addition to
the fear that economic penetration such as the building of railroads and inland navigation might lead to foreign military penetration of the Chinese interior, the other economic arguments
were recurrently noted, such as the disruptive effect on handicrafts and the oppression of Chinese-owned industries. Perhaps
the most frequently mentioned argument was the *lou-chih* (drain)
argument, a mercantilist theory that any profit to foreign traders
and investors was made at the expense of the Chinese and a drain
of wealth from China.

It is clear that the views of the Chinese officials were extremely
critical of foreign economic intrusion. When the views of the
scholars of modern Chinese economic history are examined, it
is found that they differ little from the official attitudes. Statements like the following are typical:

The Chinese people by and large considered foreign capital in China as dominating and oppressive, not merely because of its large share in the various sectors of the Chinese economy, but because of the special background against which it was possible for foreign capital to grow to such mammoth proportions . . . With their superior technology, managerial efficiency and financial backing, foreign enterprises in China waged an easy competition with native industries which before the 1930's never had had a chance to establish themselves, for they were deprived of tariff and other proper protections . . . It is, therefore, not an exaggeration to say that the destiny of Chinese national economy was not in the hands of the native Chinese but in those of the many grasping Powers with conflicting interests. The entire economy was in an orderless state, each Power pursuing its own economic end in China in utter disregard of the healthy development of the general economy.[10]

How valid are the arguments summarized above? It will be the purpose in the following pages to present a framework against which these charges may be clearly scrutinized and tested whenever data permit.

Furthermore, China was not the only country subject to foreign economic penetration. The Age of Mercantilism and the Age of Imperialism were world-wide phenomena, and there is abundant literature on the impact on the underdeveloped economies of the mercantilist trade policies and the colonial type of international investment. Due to the world-wide attention focused on the economic future of the underdeveloped or low income countries since the Second World War, some of the major themes concerning the consequences of international trade and investment have made their reappearance — especially those developed by Hobson and Lennin.[11]

In attempting to explain the phenomenon that the gap between rich countries and poor has become larger than ever during the last century or so, Singer, Prebisch, and Myrdal — among others — have suggested that the economic intercourse between these two groups may have contributed greatly to the growing inequality of the distribution of their income and wealth.[12] Specifically, they argue that the poor countries have not benefited much, if at all, from trade with the rich countries, for the secular terms of trade have been against them. Neither have they benefited much from foreign investments, for such investments have been merely economic outposts of the rich countries and have helped the poor countries little in the way of generating external economies or producing cumulative effects leading to economic development. On the contrary, such investments may even have been harmful, for the export development that resulted in the poor countries may have absorbed what little native entrepreneurial initiative and domestic investment there was and thereby prevented the countries from developing what are called the "growing points." Whatever benefit derived from export development was absorbed by the investing countries. In brief, this is the essence of the now familiar Singer-Prebisch-Myrdal thesis, which may be conveniently called the "absorption" thesis.

The absorption thesis has been widely criticized, especially by Haberler, for it is not in accord with traditional international trade theory.[13] Of course, there is nothing inconsistent with traditional theory in the contention that trade or capital movement may result in an uneven distribution of benefits to the participants. However, it is inconsistent to contend that trade or capital movement may actually do harm to any of the participants. Thus, Haberler has categorically stated that international trade (presumably investment, too) has made a tremendous contribution to the development of less developed countries in the nineteenth and twentieth centuries and can be expected to make an equally big contribution in the future, if it is allowed to proceed freely.[14] Apart from the static gains dwelt upon by the traditional theory of comparative cost, external trade is believed to bestow significantly what Mill used to call the "indirect benefits." (In other words, trade results not only in a movement along the production possibility curve but also in a shift of the curve outward.)

Specifically, Haberler argues that trade provides material means that are indispensable for economic development but are unavailable at home. Trade is the means and vehicle for the dissemination of technical knowledge, the transmission of ideas, and the importation of know-how, skills, managerial talents, and entrepreneurship. Trade is also the vehicle for the international movement of capital, especially from the developed to the underdeveloped countries. Furthermore, free trade is the best antimonopoly policy and the best guarantee for the maintenance of a healthy degree of free competition.[15]

A full-scale testing of the Singer-Prebisch-Myrdal thesis against Haberler's criticisms would involve a careful study of the processes of development or the lack of it in a number of underdeveloped countries — a task that is obviously beyond the scope of this study.[16] What will be presented is the more limited objective of describing and analyzing the influence of external trade and foreign investment upon certain aspects of the Chinese economy. Such an analysis should shed some light on the controversy.

This study is divided into nine chapters. Chapter 1 presents a general picture of foreign investment in China before 1937: how much was made, when, where, by whom, in what form, and in what fields. Chapter 2 concentrates on the foreign borrowings of the Chinese government: the amounts and the terms of foreign loans, how the funds were utilized, and whether it profited the government to borrow abroad. Chapter 3 gives a detailed account of the history, institutional background, amounts, and fields of foreign direct investment in China. A statement on the framework of analysis of the effects of foreign investment on the Chinese economy is presented in Chapter 4. Chapter 5 raises the question as to why foreign investment in China was never large in amount. (This is an unorthodox question to ask, for conventionally it is put the other way around: Why was foreign investment in China so large?)

The question asked in Chapter 6 is, was there any modernization in the Chinese economy before 1937, and if so, did foreign trade and investment contribute to such a development? The often-asked question whether foreign trade and investment retarded the development of Chinese-owned modern enterprises is also critically examined in Chapter 6. The question whether Chinese handicrafts and agriculture were adversely affected by foreign economic forces is taken up in Chapter 7. Some external aspects of the Chinese economy, such as the matter of lopsided export development and external instability, the movement of the terms of trade, and foreign investment servicing, are discussed in Chapter 8. Finally, a summary of the major findings and conclusions of this study is presented in Chapter 9.

Chapter 1

A General Picture of Foreign Investment in China

China has had trade relations with other countries since the time of the Roman Empire, but it was not until the middle of the nineteenth century, when she was forced to open more ports to foreign traders, that her external trade began to assume any importance. It is true that her external trade had increased greatly before that time. Trade with England and India, her principal partners, increased from about 1.5 million taels a year in the 1760's to about 17 million taels in the 1830's.[1] Except for Spanish trade at Amoy, however, Chinese external trade was carried on only at Canton, which had been the one port open to foreigners since 1757.

The Treaty of Nanking of 1842, which concluded the Opium War, permitted foreigners to trade with the Chinese at five ports along the coast and opened a new chapter of history between China and the West. Foreign merchants, having had an opportunity to learn more about China and to make a handsome profit in trade, became interested in expanding their economic activities. Apart from shipping, insurance, and banking, which were necessary to promote trade, they began to establish factories in the treaty ports, and to take advantage of Chinese labor and raw materials. Quite naturally, their manufactures were first in the fields of ship repairing, shipbuilding, and processing for exports. For example, as early as the 1860's some Russian tea merchants had set up factories to process tea for export in a location deep in the interior — more than a hundred miles from Hankow. In the 1880's, a number of foreign concerns were established in the treaty ports to manufacture such products as matches, paper, soap, and drugs, which had previously been imported.

All this was done illegally, of course. Not until 1895 were foreigners permitted by the Chinese government to establish factories in the Chinese territory. The Treaty of Shimonoseki of 1895, which brought to an end the Sino-Japanese War, permitted the Japanese to undertake manufacturing in the open ports. Article 6 of the treaty stipulated that "all Japanese subjects may freely engage in any sort of manufacturing industry in the open ports of China." All of the other powers shared this advantage by virtue of the most-favored-nation clause; consequently, more and more foreign factories were founded in the Chinese ports that were open to foreigners.

Foreign merchants in China were also the first ones the Chinese government turned to for loans. As an emergency measure to meet the financial crisis caused by the Taiping rebels, a provincial governor was forced to seek imperial approval to borrow 300,000 taels from foreign merchants in 1861, marking the beginning of foreign borrowing by the Chinese government. More loans were contracted before 1895 from foreign firms in China, especially the British, largely for military purposes such as coastal defense, expeditions against the Mohammedans in the Northwest, and the controversy with France over Tongkin and Formosa.[2]

No comprehensive estimates have been made of total foreign investments in China before 1895. One source estimates that by about 1850 America had approximately US$3 million invested in Canton in fields associated with trade.[3] Foreign merchants required not only property and equipment to conduct business, but a considerable amount of silver as well. Of the above US$3 million, five sixths are estimated to have been in the form of silver stock. American investments in China are estimated to have reached a total of US$7 million in the 1870's.[4]

British investments in China must have been many times the American total and were probably considerably greater than those of all the other countries put together. There is little doubt that in the nineteenth century Great Britain was the foreign power of greatest importance in China. A census of Canton factories taken in 1836 — shortly after the East India Company lost its monopoly of British trade — showed that over half of the foreign residents were British and that three fourths of the foreign firms, excluding the Indian, were British. From 1818 to 1833 probably half of the ships calling at Canton were under the British flag, and more than half of the trade was with Great Britain. In 1887 there were 420 foreign firms in China, of which 252 were British. In 1892, of all the foreign steamers and sailing vessels calling at Chinese ports or navigating Chinese inland waters, nearly 85 percent were British.[5] In the field of foreign banking in China, Great Britain enjoyed a monopoly until 1890.

The right to manufacture in the open ports did not result in any spectacular movement of foreign investment. Apart from continuous investment in processing for exports, only a few cotton textile mills were founded in Shanghai by foreign merchants in 1897, and these had little success. As late as 1913 there were only eight foreign cotton mills in China, with about 339,000 spindles and 2,000 looms.[6]

Although no single field became a special target for investment, a wide range of manufactures received the attention of the foreign investor. In 1914, foreign investment in manufacturing amounted to US$111 million.[7]

The largest field of foreign investment between 1895 and 1911 was in railroads, which were constructed through special negotiations with the Chinese government. A notorious scramble for concessions took place from 1896 to 1903. The French Yunnan Railway, the Russian Chinese Eastern Railway, and the German Kiaochow-Tsinan Railway were built during this period. The foreign loans that the Chinese government received from 1894 to 1911 totaled nearly £92 million; of this amount, about £36 million were used to build railroads, and the rest was used for indemnity payments to Japan.[8]

Although it never attracted a large amount of foreign capital, mining was another field to receive serious attention by foreign powers during 1895–1911. The Fushun colliery and the K'ailan mines, the two largest coal mining enterprises in pre-1937 China, were under Japanese and British control respectively.

After 1891 a period of extensive expansion in foreign banking began in China. The British lost their monopolistic position as German, Japanese, Russian, French, Belgian, American, and

Dutch banking interests entered the Chinese scene. Public utilities were also developed by foreign capital in the open ports where foreigners resided.

Politically, the period from 1912 to 1926 is known as the Peking government period. It was a time of political chaos and civil war. From the very beginning the republic was confronted with serious financial difficulties and had to resort to foreign loans. The large Reorganization Loan was contracted in 1913; amounting to £25 million, it was used almost entirely for general administrative purposes. The notorious Nishihara loans from Japan, also contracted in this period, were used primarily for waging civil wars and handling other general administrative purposes.

Foreign direct investments for the purpose of domestic consumption increased during this period. The decline in imports, which was due both to the First World War and to the upward revisions of Chinese tariffs, presented a good opportunity for foreign capital to be employed in cotton textiles in China. The opportunity was particularly seized by the Japanese, who also made impressive progress in the field of banking in China.

When the National government was founded in 1927, it was very careful in floating foreign loans, partly as a result of the intention to improve the then extremely low national credit position, partly because of the reluctance to contract loans with political implications, and partly because of the increasing opportunities to float internal debts. Not until the last two years of the period from 1927 to 1937 were substantial railroad loans contracted from foreign sources. As for foreign direct investments, little progress was made, although Japanese investment in Manchuria witnessed an increase after the latter was taken over by Japan in 1931. In China proper, the new field of commercial aviation was developed by foreign investors, with both the United States and Germany participating prominently in cooperation with the Chinese government.

Remer's Estimates

The most comprehensive and authoritative estimates on foreign investments in China before 1931 were made by C. F. Remer. In *Foreign Investments in China*, Professor Remer estimated the total amount of foreign investment for the years 1902, 1914, and 1931. He defined foreign investment as a source of income owned by a foreigner or a non-Chinese who may live either in or outside of China. A foreigner could be an individual, a firm, or a government. Geographically he included Hong Kong in China, although the latter was ceded to Great Britain in 1842. Many British firms that were situated in Hong Kong actually conducted business in China.

Remer's definition of foreign investment differs from that used by the Department of Commerce of the United States or by the International Monetary Fund. According to them, foreign investment includes only those investments made by nonresidents. Residency is not the same as nationality; a foreigner is a resident if he resides in the home country. By this definition a great deal of what Remer reported as foreign investment in China would not be accepted, since it was made by foreigners who never lived anywhere except in China. Obviously Remer's figures can not be easily used to calculate the inflow of capital for balance of payment purposes. An important justification for Remer's definition, however, is the fact that all foreigners in China were immune from Chinese law, retained their identity, and were regarded as foreigners in the eyes of the general public. Moreover, Remer claimed that this was the only definition with which he could make estimates from the data.

Remer made the customary distinction between loans and direct investment. Foreign loans were made either to the Chinese government or to private individuals and business firms — although those to the latter never became significant. Foreign loans were estimated on the basis of principal outstanding plus interest in arrears.

Direct investment included those investments that remained under foreign ownership and control. While the method of estimation is not fully explained, it seems that direct investments were estimated on the basis of the market value of the physical property of the foreign firms in China, as well as the market value of other assets owned by them. Claims by foreign firms in China against the Chinese government were included, however, in foreign loans of the Chinese government. The value of the physical property was the approximate market value of land holdings, equipment, and stocks of goods. An allowance for good will was not included. In some cases, the sum of the paid-up capital, surplus, and undistributed profits was used to estimate the value of firms. In the case of Sino-foreign concerns, which figured significantly in mining, only the foreign shares were included.

It can be suggested that in measuring foreign direct investment, one should include the total assets of foreign enterprises. This method has the advantage of measuring the economic influence that foreign enterprises have in a country in terms of the amount of assets under foreign control and management. However, if one is interested in the share of an economy that is financed by foreign capital, the "total assets approach" is obviously an exaggeration. Total assets of foreign enterprises may be financed partly by domestic funds if the enterprises borrow from domestic sources. Therefore, from the viewpoint of financing, foreign direct investment should be measured by the difference between total assets of foreign enterprises and their total liabilities to domestic sources. The difference is the amount of capital contributed by foreign sources. This approach may be called the "claim approach."

In using either of the above two methods, double-counting has to be avoided when there are inter-firm claims among the foreign enterprises. Both methods face the difficult problem of valuation of assets. The book value of assets may be materially different from their replacement or market value, not only because of changes in price levels but also because of depreciation policies.

It is not possible to ascertain the extent to which Remer made use of the two approaches mentioned above. Most likely his estimates were in the main based on the total assets approach. He attempted to eliminate double-counting; for instance, in measuring foreign investment in banking and finance, he included only the actual physical property of the banking and financial corporations together with advances to Chinese. Advances to foreign enterprises in China are presumably reflected in the assets of these concerns (assuming they borrowed for the purpose of acquiring assets). In the field of banking and finance he explicitly rejected the idea that the funds supplied to foreign banks in China by Chinese depositors should not be included in total foreign investment in banking. His reasons were that foreign banks were income-producing enterprises and that the income went to foreign owners who were usually outside of China.[9] In this particular field he explicitly rejected the claim approach.

Remer's estimates are presented in Table 1. At current prices foreign capital in China doubled between 1900 and 1914 and redoubled between 1914 and 1931. While it is doubtful that any price index can be used as an appropriate deflator, the following

Table 1. Foreign investments in China, 1902–1936 (US\$ millions; percent in parentheses).[a]

Type of investment	1902	1914	1931	1936
Direct investments	503.2 (64)	1067.0 (67)	2493.2 (78)	2681.7 (77)
Obligations of Chinese government[b]	284.7 (36)	525.8 (33)	710.6 (22)	766.7 (22)
Loans to private parties	0.0	17.5 (1)	38.7 (1)	34.8 (1)
Total	787.9 (100)	1610.3 (100)	3242.5 (100)	3483.2 (100)

Source: For 1902, 1914, and 1931, see Remer, *Foreign Investments,* pp. 69, 76, 82, 124. British investment in Hong Kong in 1931 amounted to about US\$94 million. For 1936 (excluding Manchuria but including Hong Kong), see Tōa kenkyūjo, *Rekkoku tai-Shi tōshi to Shina kokusai shūshi,* pp. 2, 72–73, 131, 200. Because there was no significant change in price levels for 1931 and 1936, Remer's 1931 figures were added to the institute's figures as follows: British and French direct investments in railroads — US\$39.8 million; British, French, and American investments in real estate — US\$232.5 million. (*Ibid.*, p. 76.) A total of US\$150 million was deducted from the institute's figure, which mistakenly included the total capital of Lever Brothers (the soap-making company), whose head office was in London and which had a capital of £30 million. This deduction is made in view of the output data on foreign soap-making enterprises in China as estimated by Ou Pao-san, "*So-te* hsiu-cheng," p. 132, and in view of the information given by Yang Ta-chin, *Hsien-tai Chung-kuo shih-yeh chih;* and China: Ministry of Industries, *Chung-kuo shih-yeh chih.*

For Japanese investments in Manchuria in 1936, see *Japan Yearbook 1943–1944,* p. 965. At an exchange rate of US\$1 = ¥3.45 they amounted to US\$829.9 million. For other countries' investments (amounting to US\$10.3 million), see *Chinese Yearbook, 1936–1937,* p. 135. These figures refer, however, only to investments in Northern Manchuria in 1937.

[a] Hong Kong and Manchuria included. Percentages may not total 100 because of the rounding of numbers.

[b] The Boxer indemnity is omitted because it did not exist in 1902 and was insignificant in 1931 and 1936. Moreover, it has always been regarded in a different light from the other obligations. The total outstanding on the indemnity at the end of 1913 was US\$309.2 million; if it was included under government obligations, the figures for 1914 would show business investments to be 56.5 percent of the total and government obligations to be 43.5 percent.

indices may be suggestive. Franklin L. Ho's wholesale price index moved up from 93 in 1902 (1900–1904 average) to 102 in 1914 (1912–1914 average), with 1913 as the base year.[10] Nankai's Tientsin wholesale price index increased from 67 in 1914 (1913–1914 average) to 112 in 1931 (1927–1931 average), with 1926 as the base year.[11] If Ho's index for 1900–1914 and Nankai's index for 1914–1931 are used as deflators, it appears that foreign investments in China, as measured in constant prices, probably increased by 87 per cent for the twelve years from 1902 to 1914 and increased only about 21 percent for the seventeen years from 1914 to 1931.[12] The picture does not change significantly if we convert Remer's figures into Chinese dollars (at the exchange rates Remer used) and then deflate these amounts. There was a slightly greater increase from 1902 to 1914, but a slightly smaller increase from 1914 to 1931.

Foreign direct investment in China, always predominant, became increasingly so as time went on. In 1931 no less than 78 percent of total foreign investment in China was direct investment. The steadily increasing importance of direct investment was accompanied by a decline in foreign borrowing by the Chinese government. Foreign borrowing by private individuals and firms remained negligible.

The total direct investments of Great Britain, Japan, Russia, and the United States accounted for more than 90 percent of all foreign direct investments in 1931 and was distributed geographically as follows: 46.4 percent (US$1,049.9 million) in Shanghai, 36 percent (US$812 million) in Manchuria, and 17.6 percent (US$399.0 million) in the rest of China.

Japanese Estimates

The figures for 1936 in Table 1 (Manchuria excluded) are primarily the estimates of the East Asia Research Institute, Tokyo.[13] For Manchuria, the estimates were also made by Japanese institutions. The East Asia Research Institute's estimates were based on the total assets approach, but no attempts were made by the institute to eliminate double counting, even in the field of banking. The institute was primarily interested in the economic influence or controlling power that foreign enterprises enjoyed in China, which according to the institute, were best indicated by the amount of their total assets. Consequently, the institute's estimates have an upward bias as compared with Remer's.[14]

As for investments in Manchuria, it is impossible to say to what extent the estimates for 1931 and 1936 are comparable, for it is not known how the estimates for 1936 were made. Remer estimated that in 1931 Japanese direct investments in Manchuria amounted to US$550 million and Russian direct investments in Manchuria amounted to US$262 million, making a total of US$812 million. (Other countries were insignificant.) In 1936 Japanese direct investments, which accounted for virtually all foreign direct investments in Manchuria, increased to US$830 million. After allowing for the purchase of the Russian-owned Chinese Eastern Railway in 1935 (valued by Remer at US$211 million in 1931), the increase of US$280 million would have left very little for the development of other fields. Since Japan actually paid only ¥170 million (or about US $50 million at the exchange rate of US$1 = ¥3.45) for the railroad in 1936, there would of course have been a substantially larger amount available for the development of other industries. Information is not available as to how the railroad was valued in 1936. At any rate, the increase in Japan investments in Manchuria from 1931 to 1936 did not seem too large.[15]

It is clear that in attempting to compare the amounts of foreign investment in China in 1931 and 1936, one should realize that the figures may not be entirely comparable. Nevertheless, the closeness of Remer's and the East Asia Research Institute's total estimates seems to justify the belief that at any time in the first half of the 1930's foreign investments in China were most probably in the neighborhood of US$3 to 3.5 billion.[16]

Distribution by Use and by Country

The fields in which foreign capital was put were also estimated by Remer for the years 1914 and 1931. They are presented in Table 2. Useful as they are, these figures do not reflect how the government loans were utilized, since the loans were repaid in previous years and were not outstanding in 1914 or 1931. Therefore, it is necessary to separate government loans from direct in-

Table 2. Foreign capital in China by use (US$ millions; percent in parentheses).

Use	1914	1931
Government administration	330.3 (20.5)	427.7 (13.2)
Transportation	531.1 (33.0)	846.3 (26.1)
Communications and public utilities	26.6 (1.7)	128.7 (4.0)
Import-export trade	142.6 (8.8)	483.7 (14.9)
Banking and finance	6.3 (0.4)	214.7 (6.6)
Mining	59.1 (3.7)	128.9 (4.0)
Manufacturing	110.6 (6.9)	376.3 (11.6)
Real estate	105.5 (6.5)	339.2 (10.5)
Miscellaneous	298.2 (18.6)	282.8 (8.7)
Obligations of foreign municipalities	0.0	14.2 (0.4)
Total	1610.3 (100.0)	3242.5 (100.0)

Source: Remer, *Foreign Investments*, p. 70.

vestment. While the purposes for which government loans were contracted will be discussed in detail in the next chapter, it may be noted here that they were primarily used for railroad construction, indemnity payments, and general administrative purposes. Very little went to industrial development. The fields in which foreign direct investments were employed are shown in Table 3.

Table 3. Foreign direct investments in China by industry (US$ millions; percent in parentheses).

Industry	1914	1931	1936
Import-export trade	142.6 (13.4)	483.7 (19.4)	450.2 (16.8)
Banking and finance	6.3 (0.6)	214.7 (8.6)	548.7 (20.5)
Transportation	336.3 (31.5)	592.4 (23.8)	669.5 (25.0)
Manufacturing	110.6 (10.4)	372.4 (14.9)	526.6 (19.6)
Mining	34.1 (3.2)	108.9 (4.4)	41.9 (1.6)
Communications and public utilities	23.4 (2.2)	99.0 (4.0)	138.4 (5.1)
Real estate	105.5 (9.9)	339.2 (13.6)	241.1 (9.0)
Miscellaneous	308.2 (28.9)	282.9 (11.3)	65.3 (2.4)
Total	1067.0 (100.0)	2493.2 (100.0)	2681.7 (100.0)

Source: For 1914 and 1931, see Remer, *Foreign Investments*, pp. 70, 135, 441, 512. For 1936, see Table 1, notes. Japanese direct investments in Manchuria are distributed according to the percentages given in Table 5. The investments of other countries in Manchuria are included under Miscellaneous.

It can readily be seen that foreign capital in China was primarily used in transportation (chiefly railroads) and fields associated with foreign trade (import and export trade, banking and finance). A reasonable amount went into manufacturing (especially cotton textiles). Very little was used for mining (chiefly coal and iron), and practically none went into agriculture or plantations.

The principal foreign investors in China were the British, Russians, Germans, and French in the last century and the British and Japanese in the 1930's. Table 4 shows the distribution of

Table 4. Foreign investments in China by country, 1902–1936
(US$ millions; percent in parentheses).

Country	1902		1914		1931		1936	
Great Britain	260.3	(33.0)	607.5	(37.7)	1189.2	(36.7)	1220.8	(35.0)
Japan	1.0	(0.1)	219.6	(13.6)	1136.9	(35.1)	1394.0	(40.0)
Russia	246.5	(31.3)	269.3	(16.7)	273.2	(8.4)	0.0	
United States	19.7	(2.5)	49.3	(3.1)	196.8	(6.1)	298.8	(8.6)
France	91.1	(11.6)	171.4	(10.7)	192.4	(5.9)	234.1	(6.7)
Germany	164.3	(20.9)	263.6	(16.4)	87.0	(2.7)	148.5	(4.3)
Belgium	4.4	(0.6)	22.9	(1.4)	89.0	(2.7)	58.4	(1.7)
Netherlands	0.0		0.0		28.7	(0.9)	0.0	
Italy	0.0		0.0		46.4	(1.4)	72.3	(2.1)
Scandinavia	0.0		0.0		2.9	(0.1)	0.0	
Others	0.6	(0.0)	6.7	(0.4)	0.0		56.3	(1.6)
	787.9	(100.0)	1610.3	(100.0)	3242.5	(100.0)	3483.2	(100.0)

Source: For 1902–1931, see Remer, *Foreign Investments*, p. 76. For 1936, see Table 1, notes.

foreign investments in China by country for 1902, 1914, 1931, and 1936.[17]

Britain remained the most important investor in China throughout this period, both in absolute amounts of investment and in relative share. Like the investment by other countries, British investment consisted primarily of direct investment, although loans to the Chinese government figured very importantly in the last century. Direct investment formed respectively, 58 percent, 66 percent and 81 percent of the total British investment for 1902, 1914, and 1930, while loans to the Chinese government constituted 42 percent, 34 percent, and 19 percent respectively for the same years. Of the direct investment in 1931, 50 percent was in fields directly associated with trade: import, export, and general trading, 25 percent; banking and finance, 12 percent; and transportation (predominantly shipping), 14 percent. The remaining half was distributed among real estate (21 percent), manufacturing (18 percent), public utilities (5 percent), mining (2 percent), and miscellaneous (3 percent). Geographically, 77 percent of British investment in China in 1929 was located in Shanghai, 9 percent in Hong Kong, and 14 percent in the rest of China.[18]

Japan, the second largest investor in China by the 1930's, was rather late to enter the field. She began to have significant amounts of investment in China only after 1905, when Japan defeated Russia and acquired substantial interests in South Manchuria. In fact, Manchuria remained the central target of Japanese investment throughout the period. Of all Japanese direct investment in China, 69 percent and 63 percent respectively were in Manchuria in 1914 and 1930. (Shanghai absorbed virtually all of the rest in 1914 and 25 percent in 1930.) An important fact was that 79 percent of Japanese direct investment in Manchuria in 1914 was owned by the South Manchuria Railway Company; the percentage was 60 percent in 1930. From the time that the company was formed in 1906, 50 percent of its capital stock was owned by the Japanese government, which completed its control over the company by appointing the principal officers. The company relied quite heavily upon borrowing in London, receiving loans amounting to £14 million from 1907 to 1911.

Japanese investment in China was principally in the form of direct investments, which accounted for 100 percent of the total in 1900, 98 percent in 1914, and 77 percent in 1931. Loans to the Chinese government were made principally during the era of the Peking government (1912–1927) and were mostly political loans. On December 31, 1930, the Chinese government owed the Japanese US$224 million of which only 37 percent were railroad obligations, 8 percent were obligations for communications other than railroad, and the rest were general administrative loans. Loans were also made to Chinese corporations (principally the Hanyehping Corporation) and formed respectively 9.6 percent and 3.8 percent of total Japanese investments in China in 1914 and 1930.

Japanese direct investments were mainly in transportation (chiefly South Manchuria Railway), which accounted for 36 percent of the total Japanese direct investment in 1914 and 23 percent in 1930. Imports and exports accounted for 22 percent in 1914 and 20 percent in 1930. Manufacturing, an insignificant 5.5 percent in 1914, rose to 18.6 percent in 1930, chiefly in cotton textiles. Mining was another important field, accounting for 15 percent in 1914 and 12 percent in 1930. Other fields included public utilities, banking and finance, and real estate.[19] It is interesting to note that even in Manchuria, Japanese investment in agriculture, as revealed in Table 5, remained negligible.

Table 5. Japanese direct investments in Manchuria, by industry, 1931–1936 (percent).[a]

Industry	1931	1935	1936
Agriculture and forestry	0.9	0.5	0.4
Fishery	0.0	0.1	0.1
Mining	0.3	2.5	2.1
Manufacturing	9.4	19.9	23.2
Transportation	81.9	67.9	64.1
Banking and commerce	5.8	4.1	4.5
Others	1.7	0.1	4.6

Source: Japan Manchoukuo Yearbook, 1939, p. 604. These percentages differ considerably from Remer's. His estimates for 1930 are as follows: transportation, 35.4 percent; public utilities, 2.8 percent; mining, 15.0 percent; banking and finance, 7.5 percent; real estate, 13.3 percent; import and export, 10.7 percent; miscellaneous, 6.4 percent. See Remer, *Foreign Investments*, p. 506. It might be that the *Yearbook* has included in transportation all of the South Manchuria Railway Company, which accounted heavily for total Japanese investment in mining and real estate in Manchuria. The company also had investments in other fields.

[a] Percentages may not total 100 because of the rounding of numbers.

Russian investments in China could easily be identified with the Chinese Eastern Railway, which was owned by the Russian government to a greater degree than was the South Manchuria Company by the Japanese government, although in both cases their operative control was complete. Russian investment in the railroad constituted respectively 81 percent, 70 percent, and 77 percent of the total investment in China in 1904, 1914, and 1930.[20] As a result of the railroad and other Russian interests in Manchuria and Outer Mongolia, Russian direct investments in China were almost all located in those two regions (98.8 percent in 1910, 98 percent in 1914, and 97.7 percent in 1930). Loans to the Chinese government never assumed important proportions, comprising only about 11 percent of total Russian investments in 1904 and 12 percent in 1914. As of 1930 a total of nearly US$14 million could be traced as Chinese obligations to Russia, although both the Russian and Chinese governments regarded these obligations as having been canceled or nonexistent.

French investments, unlike those examined above but like the Italian, Belgian, and Dutch investments, were characterized by the fact that loans to the Chinese government remained more than half of the total. Loans to the Chinese government formed respectively 68 percent, 65 percent, and 51 percent of the total for 1902, 1914, and 1930.[21] The French, in close cooperation with Russia and Belgium, were active in both general and railroad loans.

French direct investment was represented in part by the Yunnan Railway, which, though nominally owned by a corporation, was to a large degree under the control of the French government. Investment in this railroad constituted respectively 19 percent and 17 percent of total French investment in China in 1914 and 1931. An unusual feature of French investment was that a large fraction (21 percent) of her direct investment was represented by the property held for income by the Roman Catholic missions. The income was used for the support of mission activities in China, including work of an educational character.

German investments, which were less than 3 percent of all foreign investments in China in 1931, had once been the third largest, having accounted for 21 percent of total foreign investment in China in 1902. In 1914, they accounted for nearly 15 percent.[22] In those early days Germany, apart from being active in participating in loans to the Chinese government (which formed 48 percent of her total investment in both 1902–1904 and 1914), showed an increasing interest in the development of the Shantung province, because of her acquisition of Kiaochow in 1898 and the construction of the Tsingtao-Tsinan Railway. The First World War, however, liquidated most of the German assets and interests in China. Her total direct investment was estimated to be only US$35 million in 1921. Thereafter, although progress was made, German investments in China remained small.

American investments in China, which had reached some US$7 million in 1875 (half of which was invested in shipping and half in import-export trade and landholding), never grew large.[23] The China Trade Act of 1922, amended in 1925, which provided for the federal incorporation of American companies engaged in business in China and for certain exemptions from federal taxation, undoubtedly stimulated American direct investment in China. But American investments never formed more than 7 percent of total foreign investments in China before 1937.

Direct investments were the main form of American investment, constituting 89 percent of the total in 1900, 85 percent in 1914, and 79 percent in 1930. In 1930 as well as in previous years they were largely in fields associated with trade. Investments in import-export trade, banking, and finance constituted 49 percent of all American direct investments. Public utilities, primarily in Shanghai, accounted for 23 percent, real estate 6 percent, and transportation 7 percent. Manufacturing, chiefly of carpets in Tientsin and Peiping, absorbed 14 percent.

The American government made serious attempts to promote loans to China, but little was accomplished. The short-lived Hankow-Peking Railway loan in 1898, the Canton-Hankow Railway loan, which was canceled in 1905, and the abortive Knox Plan of 1909, which was intended to develop railroads in Manchuria, were victims either of international politics or of the unavailability of capital in the United States at the time. A change in administration in America led to her withdrawal in 1913 from the Old Consortium, a six-power group for making loans to China. The New Consortium, formed in 1918 under the initiative of the American government, was not accepted by the Chinese government for fear of international control of China's finance. It achieved nothing in the way of increasing American possession of Chinese government securities. American investment remained slight in the 1930's, even though it had increased since 1914. A large fraction of the securities went to American firms, primarily for railroad equipment.[24]

Chapter 2

Foreign Obligations of the Chinese Government

The Taiping Rebellion presented a two-sided financial problem to the imperial government: disruption of revenues in certain localities and an increase in urgent military expenditures. To meet the emergency, a provincial governor obtained the permission of the court to borrow from foreign merchants in China, and the first foreign loan was contracted in 1861, amounting to 300,-000 taels (£100,000).[1] Five more loans were subsequently made from 1862 to 1866.[2] All were obtained from foreign merchants in China by local authorities in the southeast provinces, were small in amount, and for short terms, and were primarily for military expenditures.

The western expedition of Tso Tsung-t'ang against the Mohammedans in the Northwest from 1867 to 1882 led to the conclusion of another series of loans from foreign merchants in China, notably from a British bank, the Hong Kong and Shanghai Banking Corporation. These loans were larger in amount and for longer terms than previously; the largest one was for 5 million taels (£1.5 million), contracted in 1877. The loans contracted by the local governors between 1883 and 1886, primarily from the above British bank and for the purpose of financing the struggle with France over Formosa and Tongking, were the last military loans before 1894. They amounted to some £11.2 million.

A total of £1.8 million was borrowed during the period 1861–1893 for nonmilitary purposes, £250,000 in 1887 for the construction of the famous Summer Palace, and 2 million taels (£462,-000) in 1888 to repair the Yellow River banks at Chengchow. The first foreign railroad loan was issued in 1887, when the Kaiping Railroad Company decided to extend the Tangshan-Hsukochwang railroad to Tientsin and thence to Peking. A loan of one million taels (£242,700) was issued and subscribed by British and German merchants in China.[3]

Practically all foreign loans contracted during the period 1894 to 1898 had to do with the Sino-Japanese War and the indemnity payments resulting from it. The war with Japan in 1894–1895 forced China to borrow £6,635,000 to meet war expenses (about £2 million were not used directly for the war but were used later for other military purposes).[4] When the war was over, an indemnity of 200 million Kuping taels was imposed on China. This sum, plus the expense of the Japanese garrison at Weihaiwei and the payment of 30 million Kuping taels for the retrocession of the Liaotung Peninsula, totaled some 250 million Kuping taels. Of this amount it was agreed that 50 million Kuping taels would be paid before September 1895, another 50 million Kuping taels before March 1896, and the balance in six equal annual installments before March 1901. Interest at 5 percent per annum on the unpaid balance was to be charged, but if China paid the whole indemnity within three years (that is, before 1898) the interest item would be waived.

The total sum of the indemnity was paid to the Japanese government between 1895 and 1898. However, the Chinese government was able to do this only by borrowing abroad. Three loans totaling £47.8 million were contracted between 1895 and 1898 for this purpose.[5] In addition, the first sizeable railroad loans were contracted in 1898: the Peking-Hankow railroad loan of £4,500,000 and the Peking-Mukden railroad loan of £2,300,000.

Nearly 90 percent of all the foreign loans contracted during the period 1899 to 1911 (disregarding the Boxer indemnity, which will be discussed later) were for the construction of railroads. The defeat by Japan in 1894 and the Russo-Japanese War of 1904–1905, which was fought in Manchuria, gave China a strong impetus to build railroads, if only for national defense. Despite efforts made by the public, the local governments, and the imperial government, a movement to build railroads with their own capital met with little success; the capital raised was too small even to carry out part of the plans. Foreign loans were sought, and no less than £27.3 million were floated during this period.

The foundation of the Chinese railroads was laid largely with these funds.

In addition to railroad loans, three telephone and telegraph loans totaling £758,000 were floated during the period.[6] Furthermore, 20 percent of the £5,000,000 Peking-Hankow railroad redemption loan of 1908 was devoted to the establishment of various industries. Loans for administrative purposes amounted to only £600,000.

With regard to the indemnity resulting from the Boxer Uprising in 1900, China had to agree to pay the powers 450 million Haikwan taels (or US$334 million). Because the Chinese government found it difficult to pay the amount at one time, it agreed to issue bonds in that amount with a 4 percent interest on the unpaid portion. The amortization of principal was to run from 1902 to 1940 with an increasing scale of annual payments, so that with interest the total amount of the indemnity paid by 1940 would amount to 982,238,150 Haikwan taels (or US$729 million).[7]

During the first three years the Chinese government paid the installments in silver because it was taken for granted that an indemnity of so many taels could be paid in taels. However, since the treaty stated that "capital and interest shall be payable in gold or at the rates of exchange corresponding to the dates at which the different payments fall due," the Protocol Powers succeeded in obtaining from China in 1904 a sum of about 8 million taels to make up for the "loss on exchange" that was brought about by the decline in the price of silver in terms of gold. This meant an additional charge not provided for by the customs and salt revenues and the provincial contributions that had been specifically allocated for the indemnity payment. Consequently, the Chinese government was compelled in 1905 to contract a loan of £1 million, known as the Exchange Adjustment Loan. This was the only loan floated to pay the Boxer indemnity.

China did not pay the powers all the principal and interest of the indemnity. With China's entry into the First World War, the Allied Powers (with the exception of Russia, which agreed only to suspend a portion of her indemnity payments) agreed to defer all payments of the indemnity for a period of five years. At the same time all payments of German and Austrian indemnities were suspended and were later canceled by the treaties of Versailles and St. Germain respectively. With the exception of Portugal, Spain, Sweden, and Norway, all the other countries remitted in subsequent years the outstanding portion of their shares.[8] Some abandoned every claim thereon, while others clearly stipulated the terms and fields (mostly cultural and educational) in which the remitted amounts should be employed. The total estimated amount of the remissions is shown in Table 6.

The period 1912 to 1926 began with the establishment of the republic and ended with the formation of the National government — a period of political instability and civil war. When the Republic of China was organized, one of the most difficult prob-

Table 6. Remissions of the Boxer indemnity (millions of Haikwan taels).[a]

Country	Original indemnity	Principal and interest by Dec. 31, 1940	Amount of remission[b]
Russia	130.4	284.6	65.8
Germany	90.1	196.6	136.4
France	70.9	154.7	101.8
Great Britain	50.6	110.5	74.6
Japan	34.8	75.9	0.0
United States	32.9	72.0	55.9
Italy	26.6	58.1	39.2
Belgium	8.5	18.5	12.5
Austria	4.0	8.7	6.1
Netherlands	0.8	1.7	0.0
Spain	0.1	0.3	0.0
Portugal	0.1	0.2	0.0
International claims	0.1	0.3	0.0
Sweden and Norway	0.1	0.1	0.0
Total	450.0	982.2	492.3

Source: For all countries except Great Britain, see Chia Shih-i, Ts'ai-cheng shih, IV, 49, 50, 56, 62, 66, 76, 81. For Great Britain, see Bank of China, Foreign Loan Obligations, p. 38.

[a] The following conversion rates of the various currencies were adopted by the Protocol of 1901: 1 Haikwan tael = 3.055 marks, 3.595 Austro-Hungarian crowns, 0.742 U.S. dollar, 3.750 francs, 3s. 0d Pound sterling, 1.407 yens, 1.796 Dutch florins, 1.412 gold rubles.

[b] Remissions were made in the following years: United States, 1908 and 1924; Great Britain, 1922; France, 1925; Russia, 1924; Belgium, 1928; Netherlands, 1933; Italy, 1925 and 1933.

lems facing the new government was the question of finance. The revolution had upset the administrative machinery, including the organization of tax collection. The new regime was compelled to resort to foreign loans, since internal borrowings were raised only with difficulty. The Reorganization Loan was contracted in 1913, amounting to £25 million. Of this total, over one half was to go for the repayment of debts and the remainder was to be used for general administrative purposes.[9]

The second largest loan contracted in this period was the series of so-called Nishihara loans, which has been defined as "a series of payments of Japanese funds to a group of Chinese officials — then in power — in exchange for agreements giving Japanese interests certain claims, particularly in Manchuria, and so advancing the policy of the Japanese government." [10] These loans were made for the most part in 1917 and 1918.[11] It has been widely believed that most of them were spent by the Peking government to carry on the military contest it was waging with the southern provinces. A number of railroad loans were also contracted at this time, totaling £31 million. Industrial loans totaling £12 million were principally for telephone and cable construction.

Foreign loans to China were at a standstill for a few years after the National government was established in Nanking in 1927. On the one hand, the credit standing of the Chinese government in the international market reached a new low after the mid-1920's, when most of its foreign debts went into default. On the other hand, the new government was reluctant to contract loans having political implications. It was not until 1931 that a loan of US$9.2 million, known as the wheat loan, was contracted from the United States for flood relief. Another loan from the United States, amounting to US$26.3 million and known as the cotton and wheat loan, was contracted in 1933.

The real revival of foreign loans did not take place until 1936 and 1937. In those two years no less than £21.4 millions of foreign loans were issued, almost exclusively for railroad construction. A striking feature was the fact that internal debts were also raised in the hope that the railroad materials would be financed by foreign investors and the local building expenses by domestic savings.

Distribution by Use and by Country

The above short sketch of the history of foreign borrowings by the Chinese government shows that before 1893 loans were raised almost exclusively for military purposes. The loans contracted from 1894 to 1898 were primarily for indemnity payments to Japan. Railroad loans dominated the years from 1899 to 1911. During the era of the Peking government, 1912–1926, while general administrative loans were dominant, railroad loans were also considerable. The latter overwhelmingly asserted their dominance under the National government, 1927–1937.

Table 47 shows the annual contraction, by use, of foreign loans to the Chinese government from 1861 to 1937. No claim can be made that it is a definitive or complete list. Discrepancies exist among the standard sources on the subject. They differ not only with regard to the amounts and dates of issue of certain loans but also as to whether certain loans were issued at all. This is particularly true about the so-called unsecured loans. For instance, the Japanese loans to China as reported by a Japanese source[12] do not entirely match those recorded in a Chinese source.[13] Nevertheless, the discrepancies are not too large to justify the belief that what is shown is fairly accurate.

Table 7 presents the distribution, by use, of foreign loans to the Chinese government at various periods as expressed in both current and constant prices. The deflator used is the Nankai's price index of China's imports. It is appropriate to the extent that the proceeds from foreign loans were used for imports from abroad, particularly in connection with railroad and industrial loans. Although some administrative loans involved no imports at all, the selected deflator may also be appropriate for them to the extent that the prices of imports did correspond broadly with domestic prices. Of course, all the shortcomings in the use of a deflator remain.

Table 7 shows that for the entire period from 1861 to 1937, 44 percent of foreign loans (expressed in constant prices) were for military and indemnity purposes, 20 percent for general administrative purposes, 5 percent for industrial purposes, and 31 percent for railroads. Of the indemnity loans, those contracted for pay-

Table 7. Distribution of foreign loans to the Chinese government by use, 1861–1937 (£ millions; percent in parentheses).

Period	Military and indemnity[a]	Adminis-trative	Railroad	Industrial	Total
		In current prices			
1861–1893	11.2 (86.3)	1.1 (8.5)	0.7 (5.2)	0.0	13.0
1894–1898	54.5 (88.9)	0.0	6.8 (11.1)	0.0	61.3
1899–1911	1.0 (3.3)	0.6 (2.0)	27.3 (89.0)	1.8 (5.7)	30.7
1912–1926	13.4 (11.4)	61.3 (51.9)	31.1 (26.4)	12.2 (10.3)	118.0
1927–1937	0.0	8.0 (23.4)	24.4 (71.0)	1.9 (5.6)	34.3
Total	80.1 (31.1)	71.0 (27.6)	90.3 (35.1)	15.9 (6.2)	257.3
		In 1913 prices			
1861–1893	29.1 (87.7)	2.5 (7.6)	1.6 (4.7)	0.0	33.2
1894–1898	80.2 (89.5)	0.0	9.5 (10.5)	0.0	89.7
1899–1911	1.2 (3.7)	0.7 (1.9)	29.5 (88.7)	1.9 (5.7)	33.3
1912–1926	10.6 (11.0)	46.6 (48.2)	27.9 (28.7)	11.6 (12.0)	96.7
1927–1937	0.0	4.8 (22.0)	15.9 (72.4)	1.2 (5.6)	21.9
Total	121.1 (44.1)	54.6 (19.9)	84.4 (30.7)	14.7 (5.3)	274.8

Source: See Table 47.

[a] Boxer indemnity not included. Loans contracted for the payment of indemnity to Japan after 1895 are included. If such loans were excluded, the percentage distribution for the entire period 1861–1937 would be as follows:

Prices	Military	Administrative	Railroad	Industrial
Current	12.7	35.0	44.5	7.8
1913	21.0	28.1	43.4	7.5

ment to Japan were predominant. These loans were of no direct value to the Chinese economy except that without them the Chinese government would have had to find the means internally to pay the indemnity. As for the military loans, they were largely used to pay the soldiers in the years before 1893, to finance the Sino-Japanese War of 1894–1895, to purchase some torpedo boats and torpedo-boat destroyers in 1914, to finance Chinese participation in the First World War, and to acquire some airplanes in 1919 and weapons and ammunition in the early 1920's. No substantial amount was ever raised to modernize the army or build up a military power.

It is difficult to ascertain the purposes for which the general administrative loans were used. Undoubtedly the greatest part was used to pay interest on previous foreign debts and to meet the general expenditures of the government. A small amount was contracted for a specific purpose: to pay tuition for Chinese students abroad, especially in the early 1920's; to finance certain schools; to build a shopping center in a city; to repair the Yellow river; or to buy wheat and cotton.

Telephone and telegraph loans constituted the largest part of industrial loans. Other industrial loans were used for a wide variety of purposes, such as streetcars, electricity and waterworks, sewers, paper manufacturing, ammunition making, coinage, cotton spinning, and salt producing. None of the industrial loans was large.

When the Chinese record of utilizing foreign loans is compared with that of other countries, the Chinese record is rather disappointing. Too great a proportion was used for nonproductive purposes. For instance, in 1930, 68 percent of the total foreign capital in India was represented by government loans; the remaining 32 percent was represented by direct investments and private borrowings, with direct investments being overwhelmingly predominant. A large proportion — perhaps more than 80 or 90 percent — of India's foreign public borrowings was employed for productive purposes, notably railroad construction and irrigation projects.[14] In Africa, government loans were largely for the construction of railroads, harbors, roads, and telegraph lines.[15] In Japan, it has been said that it was the wise disposition of borrowed funds by the Japanese government that gave foreign capital an important role in Japan's economic development from 1864 to 1914.[16] However, there are some South American countries that compare rather poorly with China; for instance, at least 60 percent of the money borrowed abroad by the Argentine government between 1922 and 1927 was used for nonproductive purposes.[17]

As noted before, foreign loans before 1893 were supplied to China principally by foreign merchants in China. After 1894 when the amount of loans grew large, loans were floated in the foreign money markets through foreign banks in China. Great Britain, Germany and France were the main sources of supply of loans to the Chinese government before 1914. Thereafter, Japan became the leading lender. Most Japanese loans were made to the Peking government between 1912 and 1925. The holdings in dollar amounts of Chinese government obligations by various countries at various years are given in Table 45; the percentage distribution is given in Table 48; and the distribution of railroad loans by creditor is shown in Table 49.

Cost of Foreign Borrowing

The first important factor in determining the cost of borrowing is the rate of interest. The rate of interest on China's foreign loans varied a great deal because loans were contracted for different purposes and at different times. As shown in Table 8, the weighted rate of interest on all foreign loans was from 8 to 9 percent for 1864–1865 and 5.3 to 7 percent for 1886–1894. From 1895 to 1915, it ranged from 4.5 to 5.8 percent, with 5 percent being most common. From 1916 to 1929, China had to borrow at very high interest rates, generally from 7.5 to 9.5 percent. The interest rate came down in 1931–1937, with 5 to 6 percent being most common.

The interest rates given in Table 8 except for certain years of the railroad loans do not include the discount. The discount was the difference between the par value of the principal that China borrowed and was obligated to repay (that is, the redemption value) and the amount that was received by China and available for spending. The difference usually went to the issuing banks, although sometimes the bonds could be sold to the public at a price below par. Strictly speaking, discount is another form of interest charge and should be included in calculating the effective rate of interest. (The latter is the rate that equates the purchase price of a bond with the present value of the redemption value of the bond plus the present value of the annuity of bond interest payments.)

Data on the discount are not available for all the foreign loans contracted, but on those loans whose issuing prices are known, the discount was in most cases between 5 and 10 percent especially for railroad loans (that is, the issuing price was 90 to 95 percent of the par value).[18] When a loan of 30 years bears 5 percent but is contracted at 90 percent of par, the effective rate of interest becomes 5.7 percent. If it is contracted at 95 percent of par, the

Year	Military and indemnity	Administrative	Railroad[b]	Industrial	Total
1864	8.0	—[c]	—	—	8.0
1874	8.0	—	—	—	8.0
1877	8.0	—	—	—	8.0
1878	8.0	—	—	—	8.0
1884	9.0	—	—	—	9.0
1885	9.0	—	—	—	9.0
1886	6.0	7.0	—	—	6.2
1887	—	5.5	5.0	—	5.3
1888	—	7.0	—	—	7.0
1894	7.0	—	—	—	7.0
1895	4.5	—	—	—	4.5
1896	5.0	—	—	—	5.0
1898	4.5	—	5.0; 5.8	—	4.6
1900	—	—	—	5.0	5.0
1901	—	—	—	5.0	5.0
1902	—	—	5.0; 5.9	—	5.0
1903	—	—	5.0; 5.7	—	5.0
1904	—	—	5.0; 5.6	—	5.0
1905	5.0	—	4.8; 5.8*	—	4.8
1907	7.0	—	5.0; 5.4*	—	5.2
1908	—	—	5.0; 5.4	—	5.0
1909	—	5.0	5.0	—	5.0
1910	—	—	5.1; 5.4*	—	5.1
1911	—	7.0	5.0; 5.3	5.0	5.1
1912	10.0	5.1	6.9	—	5.8
1913	6.0	5.0	5.3; 5.6*	5.0	5.1
1914	6.0	5.1	6.4	—	5.3
1915	—	7.0	5.0; 5.3	7.0	5.5
1916	—	7.3	7.1	—	7.2
1917	8.0	7.0	5.0; 5.6	7.0	7.5
1918	8.0	7.9	8.0	8.0	8.0
1919	8.0	10.1	7.1	8.4	9.0
1920	18.2	10.9	8.0	8.2	8.3
1921	—	7.6	8.0	11.1	8.1
1922	—	13.1	7.3	6.1	7.3
1923	—	9.5	—	—	9.5
1924	—	12.3	—	—	12.3
1925	9.6	9.3	—	—	9.3
1926	—	9.5	—	—	9.5
1928	—	—	6.0; 8.2	8.0	6.3
1929	—	—	8.0	7.3	7.5
1931	—	4	—	—	4.0
1933	—	5	—	—	5.0
1934	—	—	7.0	7.0	7.0
1935	—	6	6.0; 7.2*	—	6.0
1936	—	—	6.3	—	6.3
1937	—	—	5.2	6.0	5.2

Source: See Table 47. Rates of interest are known for all but a small number of the loans included in Table 47, and these loans are small in amount. For effective rates, see Sprague, *Extended Bond Tables.*　[a] Discount included only under railroad loans.
[b] Figures following semicolons include the discount. Those without an asterisk

effective rate becomes 5.34 percent. Similarly, the effective rate of a 6 percent loan of 30 years is 6.8 percent if it is issued at 90 percent of par and 6.4 percent if it is issued at 95 percent of par.

The question should be asked why the rate of interest on China's foreign loans was considerably lower in 1895–1915 and 1931–1937 than in other periods. An answer is that in those periods China's foreign loans were principally floated in foreign money markets, where interest rates were low. For instance, it has been estimated that for Great Britain the yields on overseas government and railroad securities were 4.0 and 4.4 percent respectively for 1907–1908.[19] For 1900–1904 the rates of interest offered by British foreign borrowers on large issues averaged 5.39 percent; for 1905–1909, they averaged 4.97 percent. (The rates of interest offered by home borrowers in Great Britain averaged 3.18 percent for 1900–1904 and 3.61 percent for 1905–1909.)[20] From 1929 to 1934 the percentage return on British overseas government and municipal loans ranged from 4.6 to 4.1 percent.[21] Thus, the rate of interest that China had to offer in order to borrow from foreign money markets was only a little higher than that offered by other countries that borrowed from England.

On the other hand, interest rates in the periods 1864–1893 and 1916–1929 were very high because the loans were primarily made to the Chinese government by foreign banks in China that charged an interest rate prevailing in the Chinese money market. The loans in 1864–1893 were made primarily by foreign merchants in China and by the Hong Kong and Shanghai Banking Corporation. During 1916–1929 when China was in a period of civil war the loans obtained from Japanese banks had deep political implications. Furthermore, a number of the foreign loans contracted in this period were small in amount and were provided by foreign banks in China. Compared with interest rates prevailing in China, the interest rates on foreign loans did not appear high, but they were higher than those in foreign money markets. The yields on bonds in the United Kingdom and the United States during the 1920's are shown in Table 9.

When tabulated according to the different purposes of the loans, the interest rates on China's foreign loans do not seem to differ much in terms of weighted average. The weighted means of the

include all the loans. Those with an asterisk include the discount for half or more of the loans contracted. ° Dash: no loans contracted or the rate of interest not known.

Table 9. Interest rates in United Kingdom and United States, 1919–1929 (percents).

Year	U.K. yield on consols	U.K. weighted average of price of all new public overseas borrowing[a]	U.K. price of new foreign public borrowing	U.S. weighted average yield of new foreign bonds
1919	—	—	—	5.97
1920	—	—	—	7.69
1921	5.2	6.5	7.49[b]	7.54
1922	4.4	6.1	7.21	6.63
1923	4.3	5.6	6.96[b]	6.42
1924	4.4	6.1	7.57	6.56
1925	4.4	5.1	8.00[c]	6.51
1926	4.5	6.2	7.32	6.51
1927	4.6	5.5	7.07	6.14
1928	4.5	5.5	6.73	6.09
1929	4.6	5.2	7.20[b]	5.81

Source: For U.K., see Royal Institute of International Affairs, *International Investment*, p. 135. For U.S., see United Nations, *International Capital Movements*, p. 57.

[a] Public borrowing is defined as borrowing by dominion, colonial, and foreign governments, states, and municipalities. The price of new capital is determined by the yield to maturity at the price of issue.

[b] No municipal borrowing.

[c] No government borrowing.

rates of interest (discount not included) for the period 1864–1937 was 5.4 percent for military and indemnity loans, 6.3 percent for administrative loans, 6.1 percent for railroad loans, 6.6 percent for industrial loans, and 6.0 percent for all loans. However, such weighted averages should be regarded only as broad approximations, for they are computed on an undeflated basis. Since China's foreign loans contracted in 1895–1915 bore lower interest rates than in later years and since general price levels continued to go up, the weighted averages tend to have an upward bias.

The weighted averages also conceal the fact that because several large indemnity and administrative loans were contracted at low interest rates, they tend to overshadow the terms of other loans. For instance, the 37-year Franco-Russian loan of 1895, amounting to £15.8 million, was contracted at 4 percent with an issue price of 94 1/8 percent (or an effective rate of 4.32 percent). The 36-year £16 million Anglo-German loan of 1896 bore an interest rate of 5.0 percent with an issue price of 94 percent (or an effective rate of 5.3 percent). The 44-year £16 million Anglo-German loan of 1898 was contracted at 4.5 percent with an issue price of 83 percent (or an effective rate of 5.5 percent). The Reorganization Loan of 1913, totaling £25 million, was contracted at 5 percent.[22] Although intended for general nonproductive purposes, these loans were fully secured on the revenues of the Chinese government and hence were no riskier than railroad loans.

In calculating the cost of borrowing, factors other than interest should be taken into account. Most of the railroad and industrial loans gave the right of construction to the foreign agencies, thereby granting these agencies some degree of monopoly power in supplying materials for construction. The agencies often charged a 2 1/2 to 5 percent commission on the total cost of construction as payment for acting as purchasing and constructing agent. In most contracts it was agreed that the interest payments would be handled by the foreign banks or agencies concerned, and a 1/4 of 1 percent commission was charged.

Furthermore, some of the railroad contracts before 1907 granted foreign agencies the right to receive 20 percent of the net profit as long as the loans were not paid.[23] The practice of participation in net profit was terminated in 1908 by article 20 of the Tientsin-Pukow Railway Agreement, which stipulated that "in commutation of participation in net profits the Syndicate is granted the right to retain two hundred thousand pounds sterling out of the first issue of this loan," which amounted to £3 million.[24]

Most of the debt contracts called for payment to foreign banks in Peking, Shanghai, or other Chinese centers. The rate of exchange was fixed on the day payment was due, and the rate fixed was the opening rate quoted by the banks for ordinary commercial transactions. When a large payment of interest on amortization was to be made, there was an increased demand for sterling exchange and more silver had to be given for the pound sterling. The foreign banks were known to change their rates arbitrarily on the day when a large payment was to be made. There were times when a drop of a farthing in the sterling rate caused the Chinese government to pay 1/2 of 1 percent more silver than it would have had to pay under the current market rates for gold exchange.[25]

Control Clause

Almost all of the foreign loans that the Chinese government contracted before 1914 were "secured" loans. The unsecured loans were contracted primarily during the First World War and the years immediately following. For railroad loans the security consisted of a first mortgage upon the entire property and, in most cases, the net revenue of the railroad concerned.[26] In some cases railroad loans were also secured by a first charge upon taxes, such as likin, salt revenues, etc. Telephone, telegraph, and wireless revenues were pledged as security for most of the telegraph and telephone loans. For general loans, customs and salt revenues were the main resources to be pledged as security, since these two taxes were among the most important sources of revenue for the Chinese government. Other revenue, such as that from wine and tobacco taxes, likin, etc., were also sometimes pledged.[27]

Securities alone were not sufficient to guarantee the payment of principal and interest charges. Greater assurance was achieved by having the railroads and taxes directly controlled by the lender himself. The so-called control clause was designed to serve this purpose, apart from its other political implications.

As previously mentioned in the case of railroad loans, the right to construct the lines was granted in most cases to the lender. This right not only created an opportunity for profit, but was a guarantee that the loans were used for the purposes indicated in the contract. All railroad loans before 1908 placed the management of the railroads in the hands of the lender during the period of the loan. The appointment of the managing director, the chief engineer, the accountant, the auditor, and other high officials was made by the creditor. As a rule, foreigners were employed in such positions. The Tientsin-Pukow Railway Agreement of 1908 changed the pattern for the first time by stipulating that the construction and control of the railroad was to be entirely vested in the Chinese government. However, a foreigner was to be appointed as the chief engineer so that the creditor was not completely deprived of management.

The Maritime Customs Administration played a leading role in controlling the taxes that were pledged as security. The Maritime Customs of China was first administered by foreigners in 1853, when the Taiping Rebellion caused the breakdown of the previous system. Customs revenues were pledged as security for foreign loans as early as 1861, when China's first foreign loan was contracted. According to the loan contracts, customs receipts were placed in the custody of specified foreign banks, and not until the obligations of foreign debts had been met could the customs receipts be drawn upon by the Chinese government.

Salt revenues, which were first pledged as security for foreign loans in 1895, came under foreign control in 1913, when the Reorganization Loan was contracted. Article 5 of the agreement stipulated that the Chinese government should establish a Central Salt Administration at Peking, and that a foreign associate chief inspector should be appointed to superintend the issue of licenses and the compilation of reports and returns of revenues. It was also agreed that in each salt-producing district there would be a branch office of the chief inspectorate under one Chinese and one foreign district inspector, who would be jointly responsible for the collection and deposit of salt revenues.

No foreign control was imposed over the other taxes that were pledged as security. However, it was usually stipulated in the loan contracts that if there were any default in the payments, the pledged revenue would forthwith be transferred to, and administered by, the Maritime Customs for the account of, and in the interest of, the creditors.

Foreign Loans in Default

Amortization and interest charges on foreign railroad loans of the Chinese government were, on the whole, paid on time up to 1920.[28] During the twenties, however, especially after 1925, the railroads were unable to pay the charges, with the exception of a few lines. By the end of 1931 the total amount of foreign railroad debts in default (accrued amortizations and interest in arrears) reached silver $386.8 million (or US$110.5 million).[29] Since the total amount of foreign railroad loans outstanding was silver $973.9 million (or US$278.3 million),[30] this meant that nearly 40 percent of the total payments was in default. The default was due in part to the decline in business revenues of the railroads, which in turn had resulted from drought, flood, and the destruction caused by frequent civil wars.[31] It was also due to the appropriation of some of the railroad revenues for military use by the central government and the local warlords.

Loans for general purposes also went into default in increasing amounts in the 1920's, especially after 1924. Previously the amortization and interest charges had, on the whole, been paid. The economic effect of the civil wars became apparent when the salt revenues, which had been assigned for the payment of some foreign loans, were retained and used for military purposes by the warlords. As other revenues of the Chinese government declined and military expenditures rose, little was left for the servicing of foreign debts.[32] In addition, the price of silver in terms of gold continued to decline in the 1920's. Such a decline, though favorable to China's balance of payments, further aggravated its difficulty in servicing foreign debts for, as noted before, its revenues were in terms of silver while in most cases its payments of debts were in gold. The only foreign loans that the Chinese government managed to continue to service were those loans secured on Maritime Customs revenues, including the Anglo-German loan of 1898 (£16 million) and the Reorganization Loan of 1913.[33]

The increasing amount of foreign debts in default seriously impaired China's credit standing. Several attempts were made by the Chinese government to readjust the loans and restore the national credit standing in the foreign markets.[34] However, not until the early 1930's was real progress seen and the national credit standing gradually restored, as reflected in the rising quotations of Chinese government foreign bonds in London.[35]

The terms of readjustment generally consisted of reduction of the interest rate, abolition of the compound method of computing interest for a certain period, cancellation or reduction of the payment of interest in arrears, and postponement of the payment of principal. Although the terms of adjustment appear unfavorable to the bond holders, the assurance of the resumption of servicing debts certainly increased the confidence of creditors. The revival of contracts for new foreign railroad loans in 1936 and 1937 was largely a result of this effort.

The Benefits of Foreign Borrowing

How useful to China were the foreign loans of the Chinese government? Was it profitable for the Chinese government to borrow from foreign sources? Since the loans carried with them many political implications, as will be shown later, a simple answer to the above questions is not possible or meaningful. What follows is simply an attempt to discuss or evaluate the usefulness of these loans to the Chinese economy wherever data permit.

It is fairly obvious that beneficial links can be found between railroad loans and economic development. The railroad, which Max Weber considered the most revolutionary instrumentality known to history, certainly provided employment to many, reduced the cost of transportation, and stimulated the development of a variety of industries in China. For instance, in the Chinese National Railroads, which represented virtually all Chinese-owned railroads and were built chiefly with foreign loans, the number of employees increased from about 60,000 in 1916 to about 130,000 in 1936. Passenger kilometers increased from about 2 billion in 1915 to 4.3 billion in 1936; while metric-ton kilometers of goods carried increased from 2.3 billion in 1915 to 6.5 billion in 1936.[36] But the benefits of the railroads to the Chinese economy as a whole can hardly be quantified.

The figures in Tables 10 and 11 show some direct measurable results of the Chinese railroads: how much profit they made and whether it was sufficient to pay the interest charges.[37] To show approximately the rate of return on investment, the ratio of net profit to cost of roads and equipment (the largest asset item of the Chinese National Railroads) is computed. This ratio ranged from −1.7 to 8.6 percent, with a weighted average of 3.3 percent, for the period from 1917 to 1936. If the cost of roads and equipment was evaluated on the commonly used book value — that is, original cost minus accumulated depreciation — the "real" weighted ratio would be smaller than 3.3 percent, because the book value of the roads and equipment must have been smaller than their replacement value due to the generally rising price level during the period. However, it is difficult to make the necessary

Table 10. Statistics of the Chinese National Railroads, 1916–1936 (Chin$ millions).

Year	Cost of road	Net operating revenue	Interest payment on funded debts	Profit or loss	Remittances to government	Additions to properties
1916	414.0	33.9	—	—	—	—
1917	411.6	33.8	10.1	+20.8	—	—
1918	428.4	43.3	8.5	+34.7	—	—
1919	485.1	44.6	7.7	+40.2	—	—
1920	510.2	48.7	7.1	+44.1	—	—
1921	537.3	42.5	12.3	+31.4	13.1	17.0
1922	563.5	42.9	12.6	+27.0	10.1	10.7
1923	629.1	54.7	15.9	+36.2	17.4	10.8
1924	642.7	51.1	16.0	+32.8	0.0	9.4
1925	665.6	54.2	14.2	+32.8	0.0	11.2
1926	671.2	30.1	17.4	+0.9	8.0	4.5
1927	661.1	32.5	17.9	+4.7	22.0	5.8
1928	557.3	38.6	16.9	+13.2	0.0	2.7
1929	723.4	49.5	18.9	+21.4	11.3	3.3
1930	677.9	43.1	18.9	+13.0	18.5	4.6
1931	679.2	52.1	22.0	+0.3	0.5	3.0
1932	841.9	41.3	23.7	−14.5	4.1	2.0
1933	855.3	42.2	28.8	+3.1	25.1	2.0
1933/34	859.6	46.0	26.6	+9.8	24.8	2.1
1934/35	874.8	56.8	24.7	+37.6	31.4	5.8
1935/36	899.2	60.8	19.9	+45.4	17.6	5.5

Source: China: Ministry of Railways, *Statistics of Chinese National Railways,* various years.

adjustment, partly because there is no appropriate deflator available and partly because new roads and equipment were added from year to year, as Table 10 shows. The Nankai's wholesale price index at Tientsin shows a gradual rise from 80 in 1917 to 111 in 1936.

To answer the question as to whether the railroads made sufficient earnings to pay interest charges, the ratio of net operating revenue to the cost of roads and equipment is computed — a ratio capable of indicating the earning power of the railroads. Over the period of twenty-one years from 1916 to 1936 this ratio averaged 7.4 percent, with a marked fluctuation from a low of 4.0 percent in 1926 to a high of 10.2 percent in 1918. This seems to show that Chinese railroads were barely profitable enough, on the whole, to pay interest charges on the loans with which they had been built.

Table 11. Earning power of the Chinese National Railroads, 1916–1936 (percent).

Year	Ratio of net operating revenue to cost of road and equipment	Ratio of interest payments to net operating revenue	Ratio of net profit to cost of road and equipment
1916	8.4	—	—
1917	8.2	29.7	4.9
1918	10.2	19.7	8.1
1919	9.2	17.2	8.3
1920	9.5	14.5	8.6
1921	7.9	29.0	5.8
1922	6.9	29.3	4.8
1923	8.4	29.0	5.8
1924	7.2	31.2	5.1
1925	7.3	26.2	4.9
1926	4.0	26.0	0.1
1927	4.9	27.1	0.7
1928	7.1	43.9	2.4
1929	6.8	38.1	3.0
1930	5.5	43.9	1.9
1931	6.6	32.4	0.1
1932	4.2	57.3	−1.7
1933	4.6	68.3	0.4
1933/34	4.7	57.9	1.1
1934/35	6.2	43.4	4.3
1935/36	6.8	32.8	5.1
Weighted average	7.4	35.0	3.3

Source: Table 10.

The Chinese National Railroads did not honor all the interest payments. Interest payments from 1917 to 1936 represented, on the average, 35 percent of the net operating revenue or 2.6 percent of the cost of roads and equipment. While a considerable portion of the net operating revenue remained available after interest payments, the credit standing of the Chinese government was obviously impaired because of the default.

The profit rates of Chinese railroads compared very poorly with those of the South Manchuria Company. The profits made by the latter averaged 25.5 percent of the capital investment in the railroads for the period from 1907 to 1937.[38] The difference in profit rates between Chinese- and Japanese-controlled railroads cannot easily be accounted for. The locality, the efficiency of management, the political environment, and the accounting methods may all have contributed to it. It is interesting to note that Chinese railroads suffered most between 1925 and 1927, which were among the worst years of civil war, and again between 1932 and 1935, when the country was confronted with a general depression. It is also interesting to note that only Chin$100 million, or about 34 percent of the net profit of the railroads, were appropriated for addition to properties from 1921 to 1936. Twice as much went to the Chinese government, which often employed the funds of the railroads regardless of whether or not they made a profit. For instance, in the years of 1926, 1927, and 1930–1934, the government employed more than 50 percent of the total net operating revenues, an amount far exceeding that of current profit. As a former minister of railroads of China observed, this diversion of revenue was in part responsible for the defaults of Chinese railroad loans.[39]

While foreign railroad loans of the Chinese government were barely self-liquidating, in the sense that the earning ratio was close to the interest rate, other foreign loans were never used on a self-liquidating basis. The indemnity loans were imposed upon China and obviously did not contribute anything to China's productivity or economic development. Strictly speaking, they were not loans made to China but were unilateral payments from China to foreign countries. They were simply an arrangement whereby the indemnities were paid not at once but in a number of installments. As for administrative loans, most of them were used to pay interest charges on previous foreign loans, to meet general government expenditures, and to finance civil wars. Little was used in a way that resulted in a greater capacity of the government to service its foreign debts.

Financial Burden of Foreign Loans

The financial burden of China's foreign loans was severe. The loans contracted in the 1890's to pay the indemnity to Japan called for an immediate annual payment of more than 20 million taels for interest charges and amortization.[40] The annual payment of the Boxer indemnity to the Allied Powers amounted to another 19 million taels from 1902 to 1910.[41] Yet the normal annual revenue of the imperial government during this period was estimated to be no more than 90 million taels.[42] Thus, the total indemnity payments constituted about 43 percent of the total revenue of the imperial treasury. The Peking government was compelled to ask the provinces to contribute large sums against their will. For the payment of the Boxer indemnity, the provinces remitted to Peking from 1902 to 1910 no less than 21 million taels a year over and above their usual quotas.[43] In the closing decades of the nineteenth century, the total revenue collected by the provinces was probably around 200 million taels,[44] of which around 90 million was the normal contribution to Peking.

Annual payment on foreign loans after 1912 cannot be easily estimated from the available data. According to Remer, total foreign loans outstanding were US$526 million in 1914, which at the average rate of interest of 6 percent would have required an interest payment of US$32 million (or Chin$64 million). Remer's figure does not include the Boxer indemnity, which would have required an annual payment of £2,985,000 (or Chin$29.9 million) from 1911 to 1914, and £3,673,000 (or Chin$36.7 million) from 1916 to 1931.[45] A. G. Coons estimated that in 1925 the interest on all foreign debts and amortization of capital on secured loans amounted to Chin$150 million.[46] The Boxer indemnity was not included. In 1931 total foreign loans outstanding, according to Remer, were US$711 million, which at an interest rate of 6 percent would have required an annual interest payment of US$43 million (or Chin$142 million).[47] To interest payment should be added the amortization of principal which, assuming an average currency of forty years, would have amounted to US$13 million (or Chin$26 million) in 1914 and US$18 million (or Chin$59 million) in 1931.

When the above figures are compared with the revenues of the Chinese central government, as shown in Table 12, it is found that, even excluding the Boxer indemnity, the total payment on account of foreign debts (interest plus amortization) would have amounted to 25.2 percent of the budgetary revenue in 1914 and 36.3 percent of the actual cash receipts in 1931. For 1925 the required payment on foreign debt, as estimated by Coons, formed no less than 32.5 percent of the budgetary revenue of the Chinese

Table 12. Total revenue of the
Chinese central government
(Chin$ millions).

Year	·	Revenue[a]
1913		333.9
1914		357.4
1916		432.4
1922		235.9
1923		236.9
1924		233.9
1925		461.2
1928		332.5
1929		438.1
1930		497.8
1931		553.0
1932		559.3
1933		621.7
1934		776.0

Source: For 1913–1916, 1925–1933, see *Ts'ai-cheng nien-chien* 1935, I, 188–198. For 1922–1924, see Coons, p. 123. Coons's figures are the estimates of the Commission for the Readjustment of Finance; they refer to revenues for the central government, although not all of them were actually remitted to it by the provinces. Coons states that at most the actual receipts in those years did not exceed Chin$180 million a year (p. 128). For 1934, see *China Yearbook*, 1938, p. 471. Although the *Yearbook* gives the year 1935, this apparently means the fiscal year 1934–1935.

[a] Revenue from borrowings not included. For 1913–1916 and 1925, figures are budgetary figures. For 1922–1924 and 1928–1934, figures represent actual cash receipts.

central government. The actual payment (Chin$96 million) constituted 20.8 percent of the budgetary revenue in 1925, which was nearly twice as much as the actual revenue in 1924.

The large amount of foreign debt as compared to revenue was evidently the result of necessity. In the closing decades of the Manchu regime the total revenue of the imperial government was small, consisting primarily of the traditional land and salt taxes, the recently erected likin (an internal transit tax), and tariffs.[48]

Very little, if anything, was left after the ordinary expenditures were met which were mainly for salaries of officials and employees of the government and for upkeep of the court and the army.[49] When confronted with the demand for large amounts of funds for indemnity payments and railroad construction, and in the absence of fundamental reform of the fiscal system to raise revenue, the imperial government had no alternative but to borrow from foreign sources. It was found difficult to raise internal debts, as illustrated by an abortive attempt in 1894, when the "merchant's loan" was issued for the patriotic purpose of carrying on the war with Japan and only about 11 million taels were subscribed.[50] In 1898, another internal loan was attempted, and as an inducement to purchasers, official titles were offered to those who subscribed more than 10,000 taels. Again the result was disappointing: only a few million taels were subscribed out of the originally planned 100 million.[51]

When the Republic of China was founded in 1912, it started out on a shaky financial basis. Only the large Reorganization Loan of 1913 enabled the government to meet the bulk of its expenditures. The situation became worse after 1917, when military expenditures consumed a large part (perhaps 90 percent) of the dwindling total revenue. The local militarists retained much of the revenue belonging to the central government. Not until the 1930's was a degree of political stability finally achieved and fiscal reform launched under the Nationalist government.

The fiscal background of the Chinese government should be borne in mind when one attempts to evaluate the effect of the general administrative loans on the Chinese economy. What would have happened if China had been denied such loans? Possibly some of the activities of the Chinese government would have been curtailed — and such curtailment might have been beneficial to the development of the country, since a large part of the funds borrowed abroad were used to prolong civil wars. However, some of the administrative loans were used to service foreign loans, maintain internal order, finance education, or carry out ordinary government business. Without them, the government would have had either to curtail its already limited activities or to raise more taxes, which would perhaps have had to come from the newly developed industries.

International Politics

A striking feature of the foreign loans of the Chinese government was the interlocking relationship of such loans to international politics. Since the powers were interested in establishing spheres of influence in China, loans to the Chinese government by their citizens naturally became an important instrument to this end. While a full investigation into the intricate relationship between loans and diplomacy is beyond the scope of this study and the competence of the author, a few examples may suffice to reveal the nature of the problem.

When China faced the problem of finding means to pay the indemnity to Japan after 1895, there was a prospect that Sir Robert Hart, the British Inspector General of the Chinese Maritime Customs, would be appointed by the Chinese government to make arrangements for securing loans from foreign sources. Fearing that such an appointment would give the British too much power in the control of Chinese financial affairs and that the contemplated loans would be obtained largely from the British, Russia entered the competition and proposed a loan to China.[52] With the participation of a syndicate of six French banks and tour Russian banks, an agreement was finally reached with the Chinese government, and the Chinese imperial government's 4 percent gold loan of 1895, better known as the Franco-Russian loan, was concluded. Guaranteed by the Russian government, it amounted to £15,820,000, and was China's first large foreign loan. Article IV of the protocol of exchange of declarations concerning the loan stipulated: "in consideration of this loan the Chinese government declares its resolution not to grant to any Foreign Powers any right or privilege under any name whatsoever concerning the supervision or administration of any of the revenue of the Chinese Empire. But in case the Chinese government should grant to any one Power rights of this character, it is understood that from the mere fact of their being so granted, they should be extended to the Russian government." [53]

When the terms of the Franco-Russian loan became known, Great Britain and Germany pressed the Chinese government to negotiate with their respective nationals for loans. As a result, the British loan, known as the Cassel loan, and the German loan, known as the Nanking loan, were both concluded in 1895, each for the amount of £1 million.

When the second installment of the Japanese indemnity fell due in 1896, negotiations were already under way between the Chinese government and an Anglo-German banking group, which offered a loan with an interest of 5 percent and an issue price of 89 1/2 percent. Declaring these terms to be too severe, China turned to other sources. The French government, with the support of Russia, offered to guarantee a loan with a condition that the Chinese Maritime Customs (now under the inspector generalship of Sir Robert Hart) be turned over to the French and that France receive certain privileges in the three southern provinces of Kwangsi, Kwangtung, and Yunnan. The Anglo-German group counteracted by offering an even better issue price of 94 percent. A condition was stipulated, however, that "the administration of the Imperial Maritime Customs of China shall continue as at present constituted during the currency of this loan," which would mature in 1932. The Anglo-German loan of 1896 was finally concluded for the amount of £16 million.[54] In this case, China apparently benefited from the international competition with regard to the terms of the loan.

Immediately upon its establishment, the Republic of China had to ask the Four-Power Consortium for financial help. The consortium was first formed by British, French, and German banking interests to make railroad loans to China. It was joined in 1909 by an American banking group that, in accordance with the policy of their government, was interested in industrial and railroad development in Manchuria. Japan and Russia objected to the consortium's ambitions in Manchuria, but finally joined the group in 1912, making it the Six-Power Consortium, despite the fact that neither Russia nor Japan had the financial capacity to make loans to China. When making advances to the Chinese government in 1912, the consortium was given to understand that it would hold an option on the proposed comprehensive loan for general reorganization. The Chinese government, however, did not consider that this amounted to a monopoly on the part of the consortium and proceeded to conclude a loan from a Belgian syndicate. The consortium objected, and China finally agreed to cancel the Belgian loan contract. The agreement of the Reorganization Loan was not signed until 1913, after long and difficult negotiations over such matters as foreign supervision of expenditures, the terms of the loan, and the appointment of advisors. The consortium members reached an agreement on the last point only after a long delay. The American group withdrew from the consortium before the agreement was signed because of President Woodrow Wilson's change of policy toward China.

During the negotiations the Chinese government undertook to conclude a loan from the British firm of C. Birch Crisp and Company, which was independent of the consortium. It is of interest to note that the British government actually tried to stop the Crisp negotiations, and their intervention was partially successful, since only 40 percent of the £5 million of the loan offered in London was subscribed by the public.[55]

The political nature of the Nishihara loans was obvious. As noted previously, these loans were made by Japanese banks to a group of Chinese officials in exchange for certain privileges, especially in Manchuria and Mongolia. They were certainly used as an instrument to advance the policy of the Japanese government, which in 1926 decided to take over from the Japanese creditors their claims against the Chinese government in exchange for Japanese government bonds.[56]

If it is clear that China's foreign loans were inseparable from international politics, the consequences of such entanglements remain to be investigated, especially with regard to the amounts and terms of the loans.[57] On the one hand, the desire of the powers to promote loans to China for the purpose of advancing influence in China or achieving a certain degree of power equilibrium gave China an opportunity to play one group against another, resulting in larger foreign loans on more favorable terms. On the other hand, the struggle of the powers to extend their individual spheres of interest and their attempts to minimize international conflicts by organizing consortiums narrowed China's choices and thereby limited the amount and worsened the terms of her foreign loans.

China's own fear of foreign domination also limited her desire to raise foreign loans. There was frequent reluctance or even opposition by the gentry and provincial interests to accepting foreign participation.[58] Although the Chinese government evidently wanted to raise funds externally to modernize the country, the entanglement of international politics made the government extremely cautious in contracting such loans, especially at a time when it was feared that China might be divided up by the powers.[59]

Chapter 3

Foreign Direct Investments in China

Import and Export Trade

Long before 1842 foreign merchants had established trading ports (factories) in several Chinese ports along the Southeast coast. The Portuguese had had trade relations with China since 1511; the Spaniards, since 1575; the Dutch, since 1622; and lastly the British joined in the 1630's. In the nineteenth century, however, it was the British who were particularly active. In the 1830's and 1840's some of the largest British trading firms in China were founded, such as Jardine, Matheson & Co., David Sasson & Co., Harrison, King and Irwin, Ltd., Boyd & Co., and Dent & Co. In the 1860's were added such firms as Mackenzie & Co., the Bradly Co., Mustard & Co., Caldbeck, Macgregor & Co., Arnhold & Co. and Butterfield & Swire.[1] It is interesting to note that thirty-nine of the British trading firms founded in the nineteenth century were still in operation in 1936, as shown in Table 13. In general, the mortality rate of firms in this field was very high.

American trading firms in China also had a long history. Russell & Co. and Olyphant & Co. participated in China's external trade as early as the beginning of the nineteenth century. Only after the 1890's, however, did the American share in the handling of Chinese export and import trade begin to assume importance. The Standard Oil Co. (predecessor of Standard Vacuum Oil Co.), Getz Brothers & Co., Anderson, Meyer & Co., and Connel Brothers & Co. established branches in China at the turn of the twentieth century. The speed of the establishment of American firms accelerated after the First World War as did the establishment of Japanese and French trading firms.

In the field of external trade, the foreign trading firms in China displayed a high degree of pioneering spirit, introducing a number

Table 13. Number of foreign trading firms established in China, by period.[a]

Period	British	American	German	French	Total
1830–1839	2	0	0	0	2
1840–1849	6	0	1 ·	0	7
1850–1859	2	0	0	0	2
1860–1869	8	0	1	0	9
1870–1879	6	1	4	1	12
1880–1889	6	0	4	0	10
1890–1899	9	1	4	2	16
1900–1909	14	7	5	7	33
1910–1919	28	18	1	5	52
1920–1929	63	50	22	12	147
1930–1936	38	28	35	14	115
Total	182	105	77	41	405

Source: Tōa kenkyūjo, Shogaikoku no tai-Shi Toshi, I, 362, 552, 558, 601.

[a] Included are firms that were still in operation in 1936 (excluding Manchuria). In that year 214 other trading firms of the above four nations were in operation, but their dates of establishment are not known.

of Chinese products into the international market and opening the Chinese market for foreign products.[2] Undoubtedly they contributed a great deal to the growth of China's foreign trade. It has often been suggested, however, that because they handled most of China's external trade and enjoyed a high degree of monopoly power, they had a restrictive effect on China's foreign trade.[3] The exporting firms were able to manipulate prices at the expense of Chinese producers, with the result that low prices discouraged production. Likewise, the importing firms discouraged imports by charging higher prices than under pure competition.

How much monopoly power was actually enjoyed by foreign trading firms in China and how prices were determined are still questions to be investigated. A look at the lists of foreign firms suggests, however, that in general there was keen competition among them.[4] The number of firms was large, and in terms of capital (paid-up capital and surplus) none was large enough to overshadow the others. The situation did not even resemble that of an oligopoly, for the relatively large firms were far too many. However, there are no data available on the share of total trade handled by the largest trading firms.

Of course, the firms did not all necessarily take part in the trade of each and every article. In the trade of certain articles in certain localities there were only a small number of foreign trading firms participating, but even in these cases it is not entirely certain whether they enjoyed a high degree of monopoly power.[5] The tea trade is an example. The three leading treaty ports for the export of tea were Hankow, Foochow, and Shanghai. In the 1920's there were eighteen foreign trading firms in Hankow, twelve in Foochow, and twenty-two in Shanghai.[6] They did not buy tea for export directly from the sellers but through their Chinese purchasing agents. There were fewer of these agents because some represented more than one trading firm.

In Hankow in the early 1930's one British trading firm accounted for between 60 and 80 percent of all tea purchased for export.[7] In the same tea market, however, there were also a number of Chinese merchants buying for domestic distribution. The tea guild organized by them did not serve as a unifying force in price-fixing. Therefore, the foreign trading firms had to compete with the Chinese merchants. The marked fluctuations in prices hardly support the notion that there was a high degree of monopsony power on the demand side.[8] The fact that many a small Chinese seller suffered from an unfavorable market each year, early in the season, may be attributable to a number of factors, such as the lack of credit, and does not necessarily constitute evidence that he was the victim of a monopsony or oligopsony market [9]

Assuming that there was a certain degree of monopoly power held by foreign trading firms in China, it does not follow that these firms were to blame for the decline of certain Chinese exports, such as tea, as has been asserted. Monopoly power is perfectly consistent with a growing market; it will deter the growth of the market only when the degree of monopoly power deepens. In the case of Chinese tea export, the main cause of its secular decline was the increasing competition from India, Ceylon, and Java. No evidence has been presented to suggest that the tea market in China became more monopolized in the course of time.

Banking

The growing volume of external trade after the opening of the five ports in 1842 created a demand for the establishment of financial institutions in China to finance imports and exports. Chinese "native" banks never financed foreign trade, and Chinese "modern" banks were not yet in existence. Foreign banks moved in and began to establish branches in the treaty ports to meet the needs of their own nationals. In 1848 the British-chartered Oriental Banking Corporation opened a branch in Shanghai, having established a branch in Hong Kong in 1845.[10] It was the first foreign bank to operate in China, about half a century before the first Chinese modern bank was founded in 1897. From 1848 to 1872 a dozen foreign banks established branches in Shanghai, most of which later withdrew from the market. However, the two most important British banks in China were founded during this period: the Chartered Bank of India, Australia, and China; and the Hong Kong and Shanghai Banking Corporation. The latter was founded in Hong Kong in 1864 by merchants of many nationalities (British, German, American, Persian, and Chinese) and began to operate in Shanghai in 1865. Later it became an entirely British-owned company and grew to be the largest foreign bank in China. This concern, together with other British banks, had a virtual monopoly in financing China's foreign trade until 1889.

In that year the Deutsch-Asiatische Bank was founded in Shanghai by leading German banking interests. In 1892 a Japanese concern, the Yokohama Specie Bank, entered Shanghai and later Manchuria. In 1895 the Russo-Chinese Bank (later reorganized into the Russo-Asiatic Bank) was founded by Russian and French interests together with the Chinese government, with the immediate purpose of financing the Chinese Eastern Railway in Manchuria. A French concern, the Banque de l'Indochine, opened its branch in Shanghai in 1899. In the 1900's American, Belgian, and Dutch banks began to appear on the Chinese scene.[11]

During and immediately after the First World War, Japanese banks started an extensive drive to establish branches in China. Their influence, predominant in Manchuria, now extended to South and Central China. Other banks, particularly the American, made progress in these years. In addition, a number of small and short-lived Sino-foreign joint banks were founded. From 1916 to 1923 the Chinese government issued a large amount of government bonds, which could be used as reserve against issuing bank notes, and many banks were established to take advantage of this opportunity. After the start of the National government the Chinese modern banks began to gain strength and the foreign banks to decline. Very few foreign banks were established in China during this period.

The chief function of foreign banks in China was to finance foreign trade and to handle foreign exchange transactions. As late as the early 1930's over 90 percent of the total import and export business in Shanghai was still financed by foreign banks.[12] Not until after the Chinese currency reform in 1935 did Chinese modern banks begin to present real competition to foreign banks in handling external financial transactions.

Foreign banks were the natural places where foreign businessmen in China turned for loans. Not only short-term loans were provided but also long-term industrial loans. Many foreign industrial enterprises in Shanghai leaned heavily upon these banks. They also made loans to Chinese-owned enterprises. For instance, by 1900 the Kaiping mines owed the Deutsch-Asiatische Bank a total of 450,000 taels.[13] Between 1917 and 1922 several Chinese textile firms borrowed heavily from the British and Japanese banks in China.[14] Some mining enterprises, in particular the Hanyehp'ing Company, relied on loans, especially from the Japanese banks. On the whole, the number of Chinese firms that borrowed from foreign banks was small; but those that did, borrowed heavily. Foreign banks also made loans to the Chinese government or served as channels through which the Chinese government borrowed abroad.

Where did foreign banks in China obtain the financial resources to carry on their business? One source, of course, was their own capital. Since most banks had their head offices situated outside of China and since no separate statements were issued for the Chinese branches, it is difficult to estimate the total amount of capital that was used in China. Assuming that a certain percentage of the total paid-up capital was used in China, Wu arrived at the amount of Chin$134 million for the early 1930's.[15]

Another financial resource was deposits, which may be classified into two groups: official deposits and private deposits. Official deposits were those made by foreign and Chinese public authorities. Most of the foreign banks acted as treasury agents for their respective governments, which according to an estimate by E. Kahn spent some US$30 million in China during a normal pre-1937 year.[16] Funds of foreign municipalities and the agencies of foreign concessions in China also ran into substantial amounts and were administered by foreign banks.

Official deposits of the Chinese government consisted primarily of the customs and salt receipts that had been pledged as security against foreign loans, payments of the Boxer indemnity, installment payments on the interest or principal of foreign loans, and the revenue of various railroads that had been pledged as payment of foreign loans to the Chinese government. Of these, the customs and salt revenues constituted the main part. They amounted respectively to Chin$92 million, $208 million, and $422 million in 1913, 1925, and 1930.[17] The customs revenue was first deposited in foreign banks in 1911, and the salt revenue in 1913. After 1928 the custody of the main portion of the revenue of the Chinese government was transferred from foreign to Chinese banks.

Private deposits were made by both foreigners and the Chinese. Foreign firms and foreign religious, educational, and charitable institutions naturally placed their deposits in foreign banks. Deposits by Chinese firms were also important but declined in the 1930's when Chinese modern banks began to offer the same facilities on better terms. Savings of officials, politicians, and warlords represented the bulk of the fixed deposits that foreign banks held for private Chinese, who made their deposits in foreign banks not so much for high return as for safety.

Still another financial resource of foreign banks was the issue of bank notes. Taking advantage of extraterritoriality, a great number of foreign banks issued bank notes in China, although the Chinese government always maintained that no such right was ever granted to any foreign bank except the Sino-foreign joint banks. Table 14 gives a general picture of the period and areas of circulation of the bank note issues.

There is no doubt that foreign bank notes were widely circulated in China in the latter part of the nineteenth century. At the turn of the twentieth century some modern style banks were

Table 14. Areas of circulation of foreign bank notes in China before 1936.

Bank	Period	Principal area
British		
Chartered Bank of India, Australia, and China	1850–1936	Hong Kong, Shanghai, Tientsin, Kwangsi, Kwangtung, Hunan, Hupei.
Hong Kong & Shanghai Banking Corporation	1860–1936	Hong Kong, Shanghai, Tientsin, Kwangtung, Kwangsi, Hunan, Hupei Peiping
Mercantile Bank of China	1890–1936	Hong Kong, Shanghai, Kwangtung
American		
National City Bank of New York	1907–1934	Shanghai, Tientsin, Hunan, Hupei, Kwantung, Peiping
American Oriental Banking Corporation	1918–1935	Foochow, Amoy, Shanghai, Chungking
Asia Banking Corporation	1919–1923	Hankow, Hunan, Tientsin, Peiping
Japanese		
Yokohama Specie Bank	1903–1936	Shantung, Manchuria, Hankow, Tientsin, Peiping
Bank of Taiwan	1912–1936	Foochow, Amoy, Hankow
Bank of Korea	1916–1936	Manchuria
French		
Banque de L'Indo Chino	1899–1936	Kwangsi, Yunnan, Kweichow
German		
Deutsch-Asiatische Bank	1904–1936	Shantung
Belgian		
Banque Belge Pour L'Etranger	1910–1936	Shanghai, Hopei
Sino-foreign		
Russo-Asiatic Bank	1890–1926	Manchuria, Sinkiang
Banque Industrielle de Chine	1913–1921	Hankow, Mukden, Hopei, Shanghai
Commercial Guarantee Bank of China	1910–1935	Hopei
Chinese American Bank of Commerce	1919–1930	Shanghai, Hankow, Peiping
Exchange Bank of China	1917–1928	Shanghai, Hopei

Source: Hsien K'o. *Chin pai-nien lai ti-kuo chu-yi tsai-Hua yin-hang fa-hsing chih-pi kai-k'uang.*

founded by the Chinese government and granted the right to issue bank notes.[18] By 1912 a few more private banks had also been founded and granted the notes-issuing right. The amount of bank notes issued by these government and private modern banks was not large. However, a number of provincial banks, that had been founded toward the end of the Manchu Dynasty, issued a large amount of paper currency. The currency was often over-issued relative to cash reserve and was circulated at a large discount and with great fluctuation in value.[19] In addition, there was no such institution as a central bank that could function as the lender of last resort. It was common, in those days, to hear of bankruptcies or cessation of redemption. It was against this background that foreign bank notes found favor among the Chinese public.

In the first few years of the republic foreign bank notes increased their popularity. The provincial banks issued more notes to finance deficits of the provincial governments, but then the two government-controlled banks, the Bank of China and the Bank of Communications, were forced in 1916 to stop redeeming their notes because of civil war. This resulted in an increase in circulation of foreign bank notes. They continued to have wide acceptance during the 1920's, although there was a setback in 1919, when the anti-Japanese movement restricted Japanese bank notes, and in 1921, when the Paris office of the Banque Industrielle de Chine failed and its branch office in China was unable to redeem its bank notes. The relative importance of foreign bank notes did not really decline until the 1930's, when Chinese banks began to gain strength, the silver standard was abandoned, and in 1935, the *Fa-pei* (a kind of managed standard) was introduced. After 1935 the issuance of paper money became the monopoly of the four government banks.

The issuance of bank notes by foreign banks in China had the effect of strengthening their financial resources. It is true that the banks had to observe the laws of their own countries regarding the issue and had to put up gold or silver as reserve. But inasmuch as a 100 percent reserve was not required, the issuance of bank notes strengthened their lending and therefore their earning power. The bank notes, whether issued in or brought to China, were tantamount to an export of capital from China when they were issued to finance China's export trade and the proceeds were not used to finance imports. They were equivalent to an interest-free loan from the Chinese public to the foreign banks, as were the foreign bank notes issued in China for domestic circulation. When a foreign bank went bankrupt and could not redeem its bank notes, the effect was the same as when a debt to the Chinese public was not repaid.

It is difficult to state accurately the total circulation of foreign bank notes in China. Some of the banks circulated bank notes not only in China but also in other countries, but no separate reports were ever published by these banks for the Chinese portion. Therefore, any estimate regarding the total circulation of such bank notes in China is inevitably speculative. Perhaps this is why there is so much disagreement among the various estimates, as shown in Table 15. The volume of bank notes issued by Chinese banks is also presented in Table 15 for comparison.

Table 15. Volume of circulation of bank notes in China (Chin$ millions).

| Year | Foreign banks | | Chinese banks |
	Hsien's estimates	Other estimates[a]	
1910	35.4	100.0	—
1912	43.9	100.0	—
1916	65.3	—	—
1918	310.3	—	—
1919	197.5	—	—
1921	212.4	—	96.0
1922	—	—	115.0
1923	—	—	140.5
1924	128.6	—	151.5
1925	323.3	370.5	205.0
1926	—	—	229.0
1927	—	$\begin{cases} 945.0 \\ 482.1 \end{cases}$	262.2
1928	—	—	308.8
1929	—	—	350.2
1930	—	5.2	413.2
1931	—	4.0	393.4
1932	—	4.0	430.3
1933	299.3	3.2	494.1
1934	222.8	2.1	729.0
1935	322.0	3.0	832.0
1936	360.8	3.6	1269.0

Source: Hsien K'o, *passim.* With regard to the other estimates of foreign banks, for 1910, 1912, and 1930–1936, see "Paper Currency in China," p. 554. For 1925, see Chin Lu-chin, pp. 1–9. For the first estimate under 1927, see Yang Yin-p'u, pp. 80–81; for the second estimate, see Peng Hsüeh-p'ei, pp. 303–304. For Chinese banks, see *China Yearbook, 1936,* p. 196, and the *China Yearbook, 1940–1941,* pp. 501–502.

[a] It is not known whether the figures for 1930–1936 cover all of China or only Shanghai.

Shipping

British vessels began to navigate in Chinese waters along the coast in 1842, after the five ports were opened, although this was not legally permitted by the Chinese government. The legal right to navigate Chinese coastal routes was not granted to any foreign power until 1844, when a treaty between China and the United States was signed whereby the latter was accorded this privilege. Other treaty powers obtained the same right by virtue of the most-favored-nation clause.[20]

The right to navigate inland waterways was first granted to the British in 1858, when British vessels were permitted to trade upon the Yangtze River. In the same year the Amur, Sungari, and Ussuri rivers in Manchuria were opened for Russian trade and navigation. In 1869 the right to trade and navigate in nontreaty ports or places in the interior was first granted to British merchants, provided that they would use vessels of the Chinese type or propelled by sail or oar. Treaties in later years between China and foreign powers increased the number of treaty ports and hence the coastal and inland area open to foreign navigation. In addition to the Yangtze River, the Pei Ho (in Hopei), the Siang River (in Hunan), and the West River (in Kwangtung and Kwangsi) were all thrown open. The restrictions were entirely removed in 1898, when the Inland Steam Navigation Regulations were issued by the Chinese government as a result of British demand. China agreed to the demand partly because of the belief, as expressed by the Tsungli Yamen (foreign affairs office), that foreign shipping in Chinese waters would not be detrimental to Chinese shipping but would instead promote trade and increase likin revenue.[21] The regulations were given treaty status in 1902 by a treaty with Great Britain.

The first foreign shipping company in China was the Shanghai Steam Navigation Company. It was founded in Shanghai in 1862 by an American trading firm, Russell and Co., with the help of capital supplied by Chinese and foreign merchants in China.[22] The enterprise was very successful; from 1867 to 1872 it virtually monopolized steam traffic on the Yangtze River and enjoyed a very dominant position in some routes on the China coast. In

1877 the company withdrew from the Chinese scene by selling its entire fleet and properties to the newly established Chinese firm, the China Merchant's Steam Navigation Company.

A British trading firm, Butterfield and Swire, founded the China Navigation Company in Shanghai in 1872.[23] Another British trading firm, Jardine, Matheson & Co., with the capital of Chinese comprador-merchants and British merchants in China founded the Indo-China Steam Navigation Company in 1875. These two British companies together with the Chinese company became known as the Big Three and dominated Chinese steam shipping until 1907. In that year the Nishin Kisen Kaisha was founded as the result of consolidation of four Japanese shipping companies that had unsuccessfully competed with the Big Three. Subsidized heavily by the Japanese government in its initial years, this Japanese concern grew to be another giant in Chinese shipping.[24] These large firms, trying to avoid painful price wars, frequently organized conferences to set freight rates. The restrictive practices were not particularly successful because of the frequent entry of newcomers and the competition from the smaller shipping companies.[25]

In 1936 there were about thirty foreign shipping companies in China plus a number of other business concerns that owned vessels and participated in shipping as a sideline. There were 710 vessels in all, with a total tonnage of about 810,000 (British: 470,000; Japanese: 250,000).[26] This figure may be compared with the tonnage of steamers owned by the Chinese, which totaled 675,000 in 1935.[27] The relative share of various countries in Chinese shipping may be seen in Table 16, which shows the total tonnage of foreign ships engaged in China's foreign, coastal, and inland trade.

Railroads

The first attempt to introduce railroads in China was made by foreign merchants. In 1863 a group of British firms in Shanghai proposed to build a railroad between Shanghai and Soochow.[28] The proposal was rejected by Chinese authorities. In 1864 a British merchant constructed a toy railroad about one third of a mile long in Peking for the purpose of demonstrating the advantages

Table 16. Foreign shipping in China, 1868–1936.

Year	Tonnage (in millions)[a]	Percentage distribution[b]				
		Britain	Japan	United States	Germany	Others
1868	6.4	52.2	0.1	35.0	7.3	5.4
1872	8.5	46.8	0.1	41.1	7.2	4.9
1877	8.0	81.1	1.4	6.9	6.2	4.3
1882	12.6	85.7	1.5	1.3	7.0	4.4
1887	16.5	85.7	1.9	0.4	9.0	3.0
1892	22.9	84.4	2.8	0.3	6.4	6.1
1897	25.9	84.4	2.5	1.0	6.4	5.6
1902	44.6	60.4	16.5	1.1	16.2	5.9
1907	63.4	52.5	24.6	1.6	10.5	10.8
1913	73.4	51.9	31.9	1.2	8.6	6.4
1916	64.6	55.5	37.5	1.2	0.1	5.7
1920	76.6	52.6	36.8	6.2	0.0	4.4
1924	108.1	51.5	32.1	5.9	1.9	8.5
1928	116.1	48.3	33.6	5.5	3.2	9.4
1930	126.4	45.3	36.1	5.1	3.4	10.1
1934	99.3	59.3	20.3	5.4	2.4	12.6
1936	100.8	56.8	24.7	3.7	2.6	12.1

Source: Yen Chung-p'ing, ed., *T'ung-chi tzu-liao,* pp. 244–245.
[a] Including steamers and sailing vessels entered and cleared in foreign, coastal, and inland trade. Manchuria is not included for 1934 and 1936. (Steamers entered amounted to 9.1 million tons in 1936. Japan owned more than two thirds of the tonnage.) Hong Kong is not included. (Ships entered and cleared amounted to 20 million tons in 1936; Great Britain owned nearly 50 percent.)
[b] Percentages may not total 100 because of the rounding of numbers.

of railroads to the Chinese public. The reaction of the people was suspicious and hostile, and the line was finally destroyed by order of the local authorities.

In 1865, under the auspices of the British merchant Jardine, Matheson & Co., a company was formed to build a railroad from Shanghai to Woosung, a distance of twelve miles. Ignoring the Chinese opposition, the company decided to carry through their plan and purchased land under the pretense of constructing a carriage road. By February 1876, about one third of a mile of the track was completed and a small locomotive was put on for a trial run. Thoroughly alarmed, the Chinese authorities took steps to stop the work of construction. But the British consul maintained that the merchants, having lawfully acquired the land, had a right to make use of it in any way, and by June 1876, the line was completed as far as Kiangwan. This marked the formal opening of China's first railroad — about half a century after the opening of the world's first railroad, but four years before the opening of Japan's, between Yokohama and Tokyo.

Despite persistent opposition from Chinese authorities, the British continued to operate the line until August 1876, when a Chinese was run over and killed. This accident at once became an issue on which all the opposition elements could focus. Eventually it was agreed that the Chinese government should purchase the line. In 1877 the rails were torn up and shipped to Formosa, where a railroad was to be built. As the necessary funds were not available, the construction plan was dropped and the rails and rolling stock were left rusting on the beach.

The Chinese opposition to railroad construction, especially by foreigners, was not entirely groundless. It was argued that the construction and operation of railroads by foreigners would allow them to penetrate the interior, and cause unnecessary troubles; that the introduction of modern transportation would render the emperor more vulnerable to enemy attack; that this labor-saving device in the transportation field would take away the means of livelihood of coolie carriers; that the necessity of purchasing railroad materials from abroad would benefit the foreign producers and drain China of her wealth; and that the construction of railroads would provoke serious opposition from the people because of their religious beliefs.[29] The latter was particularly emphasized in the early years.[30]

The negative point of view toward the construction of railroads gradually gave way and changed into enthusiasm out of necessity. When Li Hung-chang, an advocate of railroad construction, petitioned the government in 1878 on behalf of the K'aip'ing Coal Mining Company (then entirely Chinese-owned) to build a railroad between the mine and Pei Tang, the petition was granted despite the opposition of the conservatives.[31] The Tangshan-Hsukochwang Railway was finished in 1880. It demonstrated the practical value of a railroad and marked a turning point in the attitudes of high court officials toward railroad construction in China. Railroad proposals were no longer turned down automatically; the views of the advocates were now heard and considered.[32] Real progress in railroad construction was not made until after 1895, however, when China, defeated by Japan, was trying feverishly to imitate Western arts and science — among them, the construction of railroads.

The Sino-Japanese War also revealed the weakness of China to the world and opened the chapter that has been called the scramble for railroad concessions in China from 1895 to 1903. The right of railroad construction came to be regarded as a prize of international profits, "a means to an end, an incident in a larger policy of colonialization." [33] The powers began to construct railroads in China on a large scale.

The earliest railroad concession was obtained by France in 1895. It was agreed in the Convention of 1895 that "railways, either those already in existence or those projected in Annan may, after mutual agreement and under conditions to be defined, be continued on Chinese territory." In the subsequent years 1896, 1898, and 1899 France continued to seek and obtain railroad concessions from China, practically all of which were on the borders between China and French Indo-China. The Yunnan Railway, beginning at Kunming and ending at Lao-Kai, was begun in 1904 and opened to traffic in 1910. This was the only line that the French constructed and owned completely in Chinese territory.

Russia obtained railroad concessions in Manchuria in 1896 as compensation for her part in forcing Japan to retrocede the Liaotung Peninsula to China. This peninsula had been occupied by Japan during the Sino-Japanese War. Russia was given permission to extend the Trans-Siberian Railway across Manchuria to Vladivostok in a straight line, instead of following the long northward curve through Russian territory along the Amur and Ussuri rivers. This line across Manchuria was known as the Chinese Eastern Railway. In 1898, Russia also obtained the right to build a railroad from Port Arthur and Dairen to the Chinese Eastern Railway, or a branch from the main line to a point on the coast of the Liaotung Peninsula between Newchwang and the Yalu River. This line later became the South Manchuria Railway. When Japan defeated Russia in 1905, the South Manchuria Railway was transferred to Japan and came under the management of the

South Manchuria Railway Company. The Chinese Eastern Railway was also sold to Japan in 1935, a few years after Japan occupied Manchuria.

Following the murder of two German Catholic missionaries in Shantung in 1897, Germany occupied Kiaochow and demanded as compensation the lease of that territory and the right to build a railroad from Kiaochow to Tsinan, as well as any other railroad starting from that city. The line became known as the Kiaochow-Tsinan Railway. During the First World War Japan drove out the Germans and took over control of Tsingtao and the Kiaochow-Tsinan Railway. In 1922 China purchased the line from Japan for 40 million yen.

Other countries, notably Great Britain, also obtained railroad concessions during the scramble. The British section of the Canton-Kowloon Railway was under construction in 1906 and opened to traffic in 1910.

The foreign-owned railroads in China were obviously constructed for political and military reasons. They were instruments for gaining spheres of influence in China, and also for transporting troops into China, if needed, in order to protect their respective interests and to maintain the balance of power. Commercial profit was of little concern, if at all. Before the construction of the Yunnan Railway and the Chinese Eastern Railway, for instance, French trade in Southern China was insignificant and the commercial intercourse between the Chinese and Russians took place chiefly in places outside Manchuria. After their construction, both railroads were operated at a loss.[34]

Not only were the foreign lines unrelated to China's most urgent economic needs at that time, but they influenced the later development of China's railroads, since existent lines had to be considered when new construction, aimed at an integrated system, was undertaken. It has often been suggested that from the viewpoint of China's development, the network of her railroad system, as shaped during the period of the foreign scramble, lacked planning and coordination.[35]

Furthermore, the Chinese government received no payment from the powers in exchange for their right to build railroads in China, and could collect no tax on the property or income from the foreign-owned lines. In the case of the Chinese Eastern Railway, the Chinese government had the right to purchase it thirty-six years from the date of its completion by paying in full all the capital and debts of the railroad; or they could obtain it free of charge after eighty years. In the case of the Yunnan Railway, the Chinese government could take back the line at the end of eighty years by paying in full the "costs of construction, industrial profits, interest paid, and the expenses of every sort attributable to the railway," if such costs had not been fully repaid by the revenue of the line.[36]

The mileage of the foreign-owned railroads was as follows:

Chinese Eastern Railway (Russia)	1073 miles
South Manchuria Railway (Japan)	709 miles
Yunnan Railway (France)	289 miles
Kiaochow-Tsinan Railway (Germany)	284 miles
Canton-Kowloon Railway, British section	22 miles
	2377 miles

This total accounted for 41 percent of all railroad mileage in China in 1911 and 18 percent in 1937.[37] In terms of amount of investment for the year 1930, Remer assigns US$319 million to the South Manchuria Railway, 211 million to the Chinese Eastern Railway, 32 million to the Yunnan Railway, and 8 million to the British section of the Canton-Kowloon Railway.[38]

In addition to the above-mentioned foreign-owned railroads, there were the 90-mile-long Tien-Tu Railway, built by a Sino-Japanese concern, and the 63-mile-long Tsin-fu Railway, almost entirely owned by the Japanese. Both lines were built in Manchuria in the 1920's. After occupying Manchuria in 1931, Japan began to undertake railroad construction there on a relatively large scale. From 1932 to 1937 thirteen lines were built in Manchuria by Japan with a total length of 2030 miles — almost the same as the total increase in railroad mileage in all the rest of China during the same period.[39]

Mining

With the opening of the treaty ports to foreign commerce in the 1840's, foreign merchants also began to be interested in the mining industry, especially coal mining. Steamers frequenting the coastal and river ports found that the native coal was too expensive (due to high duties) or poor in quality, and they had to rely upon imports of coal from abroad. In 1859, for instance, over 57,000 tons of coal were imported to Shanghai, principally from England and the United States.[40] Between 1871 and 1875 the average annual import was 119,000 tons. Under such conditions it was natural for foreign merchants to be interested in developing modern coal mines in China, to satisfy not only needs of the steamers but also the requirements of the treaty ports.

In 1850 the British requested the right to mine coal in Chilung, Taiwan, but were turned down by the Chinese government. It was feared that the native people would be opposed to the undertaking for religious reasons. According to their belief, the opening of a mine would disturb the spirits, destroy the *feng-shui* ("wind and water" or good luck in geomancy), and bring misfortune to the people. It was for this reason that mining in the region had long been prohibited.[41]

In 1866 another attempt was made by the British to mine coal in an island near the Pescadores, but they were again turned down on religious grounds. In negotiating the Treaties of Tientsin in 1868, the British brought up the matter of coal mining in China again, but obtained from the Chinese government no more than an agreement that certain coal mines could be opened up by the Chinese with the use of Western machines and engineers, and that the product would be made available both to Chinese and foreigners. China also agreed to lower the taxes levied on native coal to make it cheaper for foreign steamers.

Further attempts were frequently made by foreigners to mine coal, as well as gold and lead, but no tangible result was ever achieved prior to 1894. For instance, in the case of Chi-lung, Taiwan, a coal mine was finally opened with the help of modern technology and machines by the Chinese government in 1875 for the purpose of supplying coal to the Foochow shipyard and the Chinese navy. When the mine was damaged in 1884 during the Sino-French War, the Chinese government, now financially stricken, turned to private capital to continue operations of the mine. The private capital was later withdrawn because of the financial failure of the mine, and the Chinese government resumed full ownership in 1887.

Two years later, after the mine had suffered severe financial losses, a Chinese official (Liu Ming-ch'uan) suggested to the court that the mine be leased to a British firm that had already expressed interest. The main terms of the lease proposal were:[42] (1) the lease would be for twenty years and, during this period, the firm would be given a complete monopoly of modern coal-mining in Taiwan; (2) the Chinese local government in Taiwan would get, free of charge, 1000 tons of coal per month (at the time the daily output was 100 tons and was expected to increase to 500 tons); (3) on all coal mined for export there would be a tax of Chinese $0.10 per ton (the price of coal was Chinese $2.5 per ton in 1878);[43] (4) the Chinese government would have the right to send Chinese to the mine to learn the art of modern coal-mining; and (5) in case of war, the mine would revert to Chinese control. The proposal was quickly rejected by the Chinese government. It felt that a monopoly for twenty years would be against Chinese interests, that coal was important in national defense and should therefore not be controlled by foreign hands, and that the lease would set a precedent for other foreigners to request mining rights all over China. It is interesting to note that no judgment was passed by the court as to the amount of royalties or the economic consequences of the lease.[44]

If the foreigners were frustrated in their fruitless efforts to obtain mining rights in China before 1895, they had reason to congratulate themselves on their achievements from 1896 to 1913. In these years they founded scores of mines, either entirely on their own or in joint-ownership with Chinese, although the initial capital of the mines was not large.[45] The Germans, Russians, British, Japanese, French, Belgians, and Americans all participated, with coal mining being their main target. Other minerals such as iron, silver, copper, and mercury were also included. Virtually all the principal foreign and Sino-foreign mines in China were founded during this period.

By the very nature of mining, foreigners had to go to the Chinese interior, outside of the treaty ports, although they were permitted by treaty to trade and manufacture only in the ports. They worked mines in a number of provinces, including Manchuria, Sinkiang,

Mongolia, Hopei, Honan, Shantung, Anhuei, Hupeh, Szechwan, and Kueichow, but they were able to do so only by special negotiations and agreement with the Chinese government or by observing the Chinese mining regulations. It was to obtain these agreements that the battle of concessions was fought, especially from 1895 to 1906, not only between the Chinese government and the foreign powers but among the latter themselves in establishing their respective spheres of influence. While the Chinese mining regulations will be discussed later, the mining rights that the various foreigners obtained from the Chinese government by special negotiation or agreement are described below.

The Yunnan Syndicate. The first mining concession was obtained by France in 1895, when it was agreed that "China, for the exploitation of its mines in the provinces of Yün-nan, Kwang-si and Kwang-tung, may call upon, in the first instance, French manufacturers and engineers." [46] In 1898 the Yunnan Syndicate was founded by the French together with the British for the purpose of working mines in Yunnan. It obtained from the Chinese government a sixty-year concession covering almost half of the province and including all kinds of minerals. It was agreed that no other mining companies except those with exclusively Chinese capital were to be allowed within the area of the concession. The syndicate would pay 25 percent of its "net profit" to the imperial government and 10 percent to the provincial government. Net profit was defined as the difference between "profit" and the following three deductions: 8 percent of the capital as interest; 10 percent of the capital as amortization of plant, school construction, buildings, etc.; and 10 percent of the profit as a reserve fund. [47] In addition, the syndicate was to pay the Chinese government 5 percent in kind of all minerals extracted.

The syndicate never worked any mine, however. It made some attempts to prospect for various mineral deposits, but when it became interested in the tin ore at Kochiu for export, the syndicate aroused so strong a protest from the local tin merchants that the provincial government finally in 1911 bought back all the rights granted to it by paying, in installments, a total of 1.5 million taels. [48]

The Russian Concessions. Russia obtained her mining rights in China in 1896, when the statutes of the Chinese Eastern Railway

Company were signed. The company was empowered, "subject to the sanction of the Chinese government, to exploit, in connection with the railroad or independently of it, coal mines, as also to exploit in China other enterprises — mining, industrial, and commercial." Accordingly, agreements were concluded in 1901 and 1902 between the company and some provincial governments in Manchuria, whereby the railroad company obtained the right to mine coal in Kirin, Fengtien, and Heilungkiang. The railroad was to have the exclusive right to mine coal within ten miles of either side of the railroad line; and for the mines outside the ten-mile zone, the railroad was to be given priority over other foreign or Sino-foreign enterprises.[49]

When these agreements were brought to Peking for ratification, they were severely criticized as being too favorable to the Chinese Eastern Railway Company and were rejected. Finally in 1907 a revision was reached by which the Chinese would also be allowed the right to mine coal within the ten-mile limit, whereas outside the ten-mile zone the company would receive no more preferential treatment than that accorded to the Chinese or other foreigners.[50]

Prior to 1907, however, the company had already begun to work mines in Fushun and Fengtsin, Chalainor in Heilungkiang, and Taochiatun and Shihpeiling in Kirin (the latter two were also known as the Kuanchangtze coal field).[51] As a result of the Russo-Japanese War all these mines were transferred to the Japanese, with the exception of the Chalainor mine, which remained to be operated by the Chinese Eastern Railway.

The Fushun Colliery. The passing of the Fushun mine into Japanese hands was most tragic for China, inasmuch as it later became the largest coal mine in China. Originally it was jointly owned by the Chinese and Russians, and was occupied by the Japanese over the objection of the Chinese owners and the Chinese government. In 1909 and 1911 Japan was finally able to get government consent to its ownership by agreeing to the following terms.[52] (1) The South Manchuria Railway Company, which operated the mine, agreed to pay to the Chinese government a tax of 5 percent of the value of the coal produced. The value of the coal was fixed at one Haikwan tael per ton if the daily output was less than 3,000 English tons, and at one Japanese yen per ton if the daily output exceeded 3,000 tons.

(2) The company agreed to pay to the Chinese Maritime Customs an export duty of one tenth of a Haikwan tael per ton, while all other taxes and transit dues were exempted. In lieu of these taxes the company was to pay 50,000 taels annually to the Chinese government. (3) The concession was to last for a period of sixty years; and if the mine was not exhausted by the end of the period, the concession would be extended.

The mine became very successful, producing about one fourth of all the coal produced in China before 1937. When the Japanese first took over the mine, the daily output was about 300 tons. It jumped to 4,000 tons in 1911 and 27,000 tons in 1937.[53] In addition to mining, many by-products such as shale oil, gas, and coal bricks were developed.

The German Concessions. Following the murder of the two German missionaries in 1897, the Kiaochow Convention was signed in 1898, so that the Chinese could give "a special proof of their grateful appreciation of the friendship shown to them by Germany." By this convention Germany obtained the right to construct railroads in Shantung and to hold and develop mining property within ten miles on either side of these railroads.

Accordingly, the Shantung Bergban Gesellschaft was organized in 1898 with a capital of 12 million marks, to be subscribed only by Germans and Chinese. Although the company was given the exclusive right to work mines within the ten-mile limit of the railroad, the existing Chinese-owned mines were to be allowed to continue, provided that they did not injure the works of the company. Outside the ten-mile zone, no mine could be worked without special permission by the governor of Shantung. The company was bound to sell its coal to the imperial navy first, at a price 5 percent below the market price prevailing in Tsingtao. The company was to pay to the Chinese government a progressive tax based on the net income of the mining enterprises of the company, ranging from 5 to 50 percent of the net income after a 5 percent dividend had been paid on the paid-up capital used for the mines.[54]

When the company made demands to close down several Chinese mines that seemed objectionable to them, constant troubles began between the company and the local Chinese miners. Finally in 1911 the Chinese government bought back the mining concessions (except the Tsuchuan district, the Fangtzu coal field, and the Chinlingchen iron deposit) from the company for a total of Chin$210,000.

After the First World War broke out, Japan proceeded to take over control of the German railroad as well as the mines in Shantung. According to the Shantung Settlement reached at the Washington Conference, the three mines were transferred to Luta, a Sino-Japanese joint company, which grew to be one of the largest coal enterprises in China.

The Peking Syndicate. The two large mines in which the British had an interest were the Kaiping coal mine and the Peking Syndicate. The Peking Syndicate, organized in London in 1897, acquired in 1898 from the Chinese government the right to work coal and iron mines in Shansi for sixty years. None of the plans in Shansi was carried out because of opposition from local miners. Finally in 1908 the syndicate gave up all its mining rights in the province for a redemption payment of 2,750,000 taels.

At the time that it secured mining rights in Shansi, the syndicate also secured from the Chinese-owned Yu-Feng Company its mining rights in Honan, in return for an agreement to make loans to the company. The agreement was sanctioned by the governor of Honan in 1898. The following features may be noted. (1) Each mine was to have one foreign and one Chinese manager, the foreigner to control the works, the Chinese to attend to all matters between natives and foreigners. (2) A "producer's tax" was to be paid to the Chinese government, amounting to 5 percent of the total output valued at cost. (3) When profits were made, the first payment was to go to the stockholders, amounting to 6 percent of the capital employed in the mines. Another amount equal to 10 percent of the capital was to be set aside as a sinking fund for yearly repayment of capital until the invested capital was wholly repaid. From the remaining profit the Chinese government was to receive 25 percent. (4) The syndicate was to control the mines for sixty years, after which all the mines of the syndicate, together with all the property acquired by the capital of the mines, were to be handed over gratis to the Chinese government. (5) At first, foreigners were to be employed as mining engineers and foremen; but later, qualified Chinese were to be selected for such positions. (6) The syndicate was to establish a school of engineering and mining at the mines, and from twenty to thirty promising young Chinese were to be selected by local officials and the gentry to study there under foreign instructors. The expenses for the school were to be met by the syndicate. (7) The Chinese were allowed to buy shares of the company's stock.

Despite the above agreement, the syndicate became the sole source of management. The Yu-Feng Company never borrowed money from the syndicate, but was in fact reorganized into another company.[55] Although the syndicate began to work the mines in 1902 after the Boxer Uprising, it was not until 1907 that coal was first produced, due to technical difficulties. The output was small — about 900 tons a day from 1907 to 1911. During these years the syndicate suffered a loss on its mining operation.[56]

In 1912 three coal mines were operated by the Chinese in competition with the syndicate. Because of a dispute over mining boundaries, the syndicate refused to allow its railroad to transport the coal of one of the Chinese mines. This immediately became a political matter. The syndicate, realizing the potential trouble from the local miners, finally came to an agreement with them. The three Chinese companies were to form the Chung-Yuan Company, which in turn would join the syndicate to form the Fuchung Corporation. The Chung-Yuan Company and the syndicate would continue to work their mines separately but would sell their coal jointly under the Fuchung Corporation — a separate-mining, joint-selling scheme to eliminate competition.

In 1915 the Fuchung Corporation was founded with a capital of 1 million taels, supplied equally by the Chung-Yuan Company and the syndicate. The corporation was to be jointly administered by the two companies on an equal basis. Net profit of the corporation was to be distributed between the two companies in proportion to the amount of coal supplied by each. Under this new arrangement the Peking Syndicate mines became quite successful, reaching a daily output of 4,000 tons in 1923–1924 [57]

When the May 30th Incident occurred in Shanghai in 1925, the wave of patriotism reached the mining areas of the syndicate and a labor strike shut down the mine.[58] The ensuing civil wars in China further paralyzed the mine. Local opposition mounted to a new high with serious charges against the syndicate: it had been guilty of forcing out and then occupying without compensation some native mines; it had sold coal to the local people at a price higher than what was agreed upon when the Fuchung Corporation was formed; it had not met its obligation to assume the total expenses of the mining and engineering school that the syndicate had founded in 1909; it had failed to pay royalties on its profits to the Chinese government. Finally, the governor of Honan, Han Fu-chü, proposed in 1929 that all the property of the syndicate be confiscated in order to pay for the alleged losses.[59]

The central Chinese government did not take the same view, and a new settlement was reached, reopening the mines of the syndicate in 1933. The Fuchung Corporation was dissolved, and a Chung-Fu Joint Mining Administration was established. Chung-Yuan subscribed 51 percent and the syndicate subscribed 49 percent of the capital. The Chinese government played an important role in the reorganization and in appointing key personnel of the Joint Administration.

The K'ailan Mining Administration. The history of the K'ailan Mining Administration is a complicated one, but a brief description will reveal how the British obtained their interests in this enterprise.[60] In 1877 two Chinese officials, Li Hung-chang and Tang Ching-hsing, founded the Kaiping Mining Administration to work the coal mine in Kaiping, Hopei. It was a "government-supervised" private joint-stock enterprise with an initial capital of 800,000 taels. By repeated improvements and enlargements the output of the mine increased from a few hundred tons a year in the first few years to 39,000 tons in 1897 and 732,000 tons in 1898.

In 1900, when the Boxer Uprising led to the landing of foreign troops in Tientsin, the general director of Kaiping, Chang Yen-mao, feared that the property of the company might be confiscated by foreign troops and consulted Gustave Detring for advice. Detring had been a long-time, trusted adviser of Li Hung-chang, a director of the Kaiping Mining Administration since 1895, and he had played an important role in securing foreign funds for the company. Chang appointed Detring attorney and general manager for the company, in which capacity Detring entered into negotiations with Herbert C. Hoover, who represented the British firm of Bewick,

Moreing and Co. The Detring-Hoover discussions resulted in an agreement signed on July 30, 1900, by which the entire assets and liabilities of Kaiping were to be transferred to a corporation known as the Chinese Engineering and Mining Company, registered under British laws. The capital of the new company was to be £1 million, at £1 per share. The shareholders of Kaiping were to receive 375,000 shares, leaving 625,000 shares for new subscription.

On February 19, 1901, a memorandum was issued stating that there were to be equal rights between Chinese and foreign shareholders in shareholders' meetings; that there would be two boards, one in China and one in London, with the China board in charge of the property in China; that Chang Yen-mao was to be director general in charge of all affairs of the new company in China; and that Chang would appoint a Chinese general manager whose authority would be equal to that of the foreign general manager in China. According to this memorandum, the Chinese Engineering and Mining Company was to be a Sino-British enterprise, with the Chinese enjoying the greater control. However, the memorandum was not observed. The bylaws of the new company were so drafted that the actual power of control was all in British hands. Furthermore, by a complicated maneuver on the part of Moreing, the 625,000 shares reserved for new subscription were distributed only among Moreing and a few others; and no more than £15,000 were ever actually paid.[61]

As Chang Yen-mao had not obtained its approval, the imperial government remained ignorant of the transaction until 1903, when the whole matter was brought to the attention of Yuan Shih-k'ai, Governor-General of Chihli. He subsequently impeached Chang for having secretly sold the mine without authorization. In 1905 Chang was sent to London to take legal action to recover control of the Kaiping mines, but the efforts failed.

In 1907 Yuan Shih-k'ai organized the Lanchow Mining Company to work the mines in the close vicinity of the Kaiping mines for the purpose of competing with them. The total capital of Lanchow was 5 million taels, of which the provincial government of Chihli provided 600,000 taels, leaving the rest to be subscribed by private Chinese individuals. No shares were allowed to be transferred to foreign hands. In 1910 the company produced a total of 357,000 tons of coal, as compared with the 1,159,000 tons produced in the same year by the Kaiping mines.[62] The Lanchow coal was sold almost entirely in Northern China, which had previously been a market for Kaiping.

Between 1907 and 1910 the movement for the recovery of mining rights reached a new peak, and efforts were made to recover the Kaiping mines. As a consequence, the Kaiping company resumed its policy of underselling. Coal dust, which usually sold for Chin$6.40 per ton, suddenly dropped to Chin$3.00,[63] resulting in heavy losses on both sides. Lanchow, which was already in trouble financially, asked for a truce, and complicated negotiations led to the signing of an agreement on June 1, 1912. By this agreement an association called the K'ailan Mining Administration was founded. The two companies retained their separate identities but turned over to the new association the job of mining and selling. If the total net profit of the new administration was less than £300,000, the British-controlled Kaiping company was to receive 60 percent and Lanchow 40 percent. Profits in excess of £300,000 were to be divided equally between the two companies. In management the British enjoyed the greater control. After ten years the Lanchow Company was to have the right to buy out Kaiping. Finally, the K'ailan Mining Administration was to observe Chinese mining regulations, provided that those regulations were approved by foreign countries, including Great Britain.

The Lanchow Company never did buy out Kaiping, despite urgings by the Chinese government. Upon a settlement of taxes with the Chinese government, the two companies became legally amalgamated as the K'ailan Mining Administration in 1934. This Sino-British enterprise proved to be a profitable one; it employed over 30,000 workers in the pre-1937 era and was the largest coal-mining enterprise in China proper.

The Hanyehp'ing Company. Japan was the only foreign country to have an important interest in Chinese iron mines. She obtained her interests not only through direct investment but also through loans. The three largest iron mines and ironworks in China — the Hanyehp'ing, the Anshan, and the Miao-Er-Kou — were all connected with Japanese capital.

Construction on the first modern iron and steel plant, the Han-yang ironworks was begun in Hankow in 1890 and completed in 1893 under the leadership of Chang Chih-tung, who had planned to establish an ironworks in Canton in 1889 when he was governor-general of Kwangtung and Kwangsi.[64] When he was transferred to Hupei, he had brought with him the machinery and furnace material already ordered from England. Iron was produced in the new plant in 1894, when no other modern steel plant had yet been founded anywhere in the Far East. The iron ore was supplied by the nearby Tayeh iron mine, but the coal had to be supplied from Europe or the Kaiping coal mine in North China.

Although from 1890 to 1896 more than 5 million taels of government funds were spent, little iron or steel was produced or sold. The government was reluctant to provide more funds and decided to invite private capital — a policy quite consistent with Chang Chih-tung's original idea, for in his 1889 memorial he had advocated that after the foundation was laid, the plant should be transferred to private hands. In 1896 the Han-yang ironworks was changed from a government enterprise into one under the system of "official supervising and merchant undertaking." Private capital showed little interest, however, and only about 2 million taels were recruited. Meanwhile, a coal mine capable of producing good coke was found in Ping-hsiang which, together with the Han-yang ironworks and the Tayeh iron mine formed the Han-yehp'ing Company, in 1908.[65] More money was required and there was no alternative except to borrow. The principal source of loans was Japan. From 1902 to 1930 thirty-one loans were secured from Japanese sources, principally from the Yokohama Specie Bank, which supplied twenty-four of them.[66] By the end of 1930 Japanese investment in the company totaled 40 million yen.[67]

The terms of the loans from Japan often included a stipulation that a certain quantity of iron ore be sold to the lender, that a Japanese be appointed as chief engineer or accountant, and that priority be accorded to Japanese sources regarding further loans. For example, the loans of 1913, which amounted to 15 million yen, stipulated that the company sell the lender 17 million tons of first-grade iron ore and 8 million tons of pig iron within forty years.[68] This represented almost 70 percent of the total ore reserve of the mine.[69] The selling price was a subject of frequent dispute, with the

Hanyehp'ing often placed in an unfavorable position. For instance, it has been stated that the company obtained much less than the market price during the First World War, when the price increased sharply.[70]

Between 1912 and 1914 there was a great deal of dissatisfaction among Chinese officials and the public with the unsuccessful state of the company, and its nationalization was frequently suggested. This was not realized, however, partly because of the lack of government funds and partly because of the Japanese opposition. Nationalization of the company was finally forbidden by the Twenty-One Demands, which the Japanese government handed over to China in 1915.

Hanyehp'ing remained one of the largest iron mines and iron-works in China, exceeded only by the Anshan mine in Manchuria. It accounted for 37 percent of total iron ore production in China in 1918–1923 and about 17 percent in 1924–1937. With regard to pig iron, it accounted for 41 percent of total production in 1915–1918 and 27 percent in 1919–1925. Thereafter it ceased to be a source of pig iron production.[71]

The Anshan Foundry. The right to take in part of the Anshan iron mine was first secured by Japan in 1915 when China was forced to accept the Twenty-One Demands. Group two of the demands stipulated that "the Chinese Government grant to the Japanese subjects the right of mining in South Manchuria and Eastern Inner Mongolia," subject to the Chinese mining regulations in force. In 1916 the Chen-Hsing Corporation was organized to work the mine. It was a Sino-Japanese enterprise with a capital of Chin$140,000, half of which was subscribed by the Chinese and half by the Japanese. However, the corporation was financed chiefly by bor-rowing from the South Manchuria Railway Company on the condition that all iron ore be sold to the Anshan Foundry, estab-lished by the South Manchuria Railway Company in 1917. The Chinese share of the Anshan iron mine was finally bought by the Japanese in 1934, ending the Sino-Japanese status.

The Anshan mine accounted for 9 percent of the total iron ore production in China in 1918–1923, and the share grew to 20 per-cent in 1924–1927, 31 percent in 1928–1931, and 41 percent in 1935–1937. The same may be said of its production of pig iron, which accounted for 18 percent of the total production in China in 1919–1925, increased to 47 percent in 1926–1931, and 60 percent in 1935–1937.[72]

The Miao-Er-Kou Iron Mine. The Miao-Er-Kou iron mine, like the Anshan iron mine, was also made available for Japanese participation through diplomatic pressure exerted on China by the Japanese government. In 1905 a Japanese obtained permission from Japanese authorities to work the coal mine in Penhsihu, Liaoning, which was then occupied by Japanese forces on account of the Russo-Japanese War. In 1906 the Chinese government protested and demanded stoppage of the work but obtained no result. Further negotiations led to the agreement of 1910, by which the Penhsihu Coal Mining Company was formed as a Sino-Japanese joint enterprise with a capital of Chin$2 million to be equally divided between the Chinese and the Japanese. In 1911 the Japanese demanded and obtained from the Chinese government the right for the Penhsihu Coal Mining Company to work the Miao-Er-Kou iron mine. The company then changed its name to Penhsihu Coal and Iron Company. Its capital was to be raised by Chin$2 million, contributed equally by its Chinese and Japanese shareholders.

There were several important features of the 1910 agreement.[73] The profit of the company was to be distributed as follows: profit up to 8 percent was to be paid as interest on paid-up capital and 25 percent of the remaining profit (*i.e.*, after the 8 percent deduction) was to be paid to the Chinese government. (The 25 percent provision was abolished in 1918 upon the request of the company.)[74] There were to be two directors-in-chief — one Chinese and the other Japanese. The rest of the posts on the staff were to be equally divided between Chinese and Japanese. (This provision was not entirely observed, since the posts were occupied largely by the Japanese and the Japanese director-in-chief had much more power than his counterparts.)[75] For every long ton of coal produced, the company was to pay likin of 0.06 K'u-p'ing tael of sycee silver and a tax of 0.10 K'u-p'ing tael of sycee silver. The company was to pay 0.1 K'u-p'ing tael of silver as customs duty. (The production tax was equivalent to about 3 percent of the value of output in 1916 — almost twice as high as required by the Chinese Mining

Regulations of 1914. The company applied for a reduction of this tax in 1916 without success.)[76]

The Miao-Er-Kou iron mine was the third largest iron mine in China, accounting for 5–6 percent of total iron ore production in 1918–1931 and 10 percent in 1935–1937. Its production of pig iron was more important, accounting for 11–12 percent of total production in China in 1915–1925, 16 percent in 1926–1931, and 18 percent in 1935–1937.[77]

In the development of foreign interests in mining in China, it is clear that the British and Japanese were the most active and obtained the most substantial results. Their investments were put almost exclusively into coal and iron. Foreign investments in other minerals such as zinc, lead, mercury, antimony, or gold were small. While being virtually the only foreign investor in Chinese iron mines, Japan also led the others in coal mining, as shown in Tables 50 and 51.

Manufacturing

Foreigners did not obtain from China the legal right to establish manufacturing firms in Chinese territory until 1895, when the Treaty of Shimonoseiki was concluded with Japan. However, long before that year they had in fact founded a number of firms of the manufacturing type — probably more than a hundred, if public utilities are included.[78] If the printing shop of a missionary can be regarded as a business venture, a foreign manufacturing firm made its appearance in China as early as 1843 when W. H. Medhurst reached Shanghai and founded the London Missionary Society Press.[79]

Printing was not an important field of investment, however. Probably no more than ten foreign printing and publishing firms were established in China before 1894, and they were principally in Shanghai and Tientsin.[80] Ship repairing, shipbuilding, and processing for export constituted the major manufacturing activities of foreign enterprises in the early days. Two of the four largest foreign shipyards were built in the 1860's; the other two were built at the turn of the century. Processing for export, principally of tea and silk, was undertaken by foreign merchants in China as early as the 1850's and grew very rapidly before 1894. Other manufactures were not important before 1894, but they covered a wide range of products, including drugs, sodas, flour, beer, wine, bricks, lumber, soap, ice, and cigarettes.

The figures in Table 17, though incomplete, show the relative

Table 17. Foreign investments in manufacturing in China, 1894.

Manufacture	Capital (Chin$ thousands)	Assets (Chin$ thousands)	Number of employees
Ship repairing and building	4,943	8,112	9,000
Tea processing	4,000	5,600	7,000
Silk reeling	3,972	5,309	6,000
Processing for export[a]	1,493	1,938	6,000
Others	3,793	4,910	4,600
Total	18,210	25,869	32,600

Source: Sun Yu-tang, I, 247 and II, 1201. These estimates are based on incomplete data, for some foreign firms never published financial statements.
[a] Excluding tea and silk.

importance of various fields of manufacturing that attracted foreign investment in 1894. The foreign manufactures, though employing a total of some 32,600 workers, were important as compared with their Chinese counterparts. In the same year all of the Chinese government manufacturing enterprises (modern type) employed between 14,600 and 16,810 workers, while the private Chinese manufacturing firms of the modern type employed 27,250.[81]

Foreign investment in manufacturing in China increased after 1895 and reached US$111 million by 1914, as estimated by Remer. Investment in shipyards and processing for export continued to grow, although the emphasis was apparently shifted to the production of consumer goods that were primarily for the Chinese domestic market. Textiles, food, drink, and tobacco were the main fields for foreign enterprises to exploit.[82]

The First World War curtailed China's imports and created an opportunity for both Chinese and foreign enterprises to invest in China. The revisions of Chinese tariffs in 1918 and 1922, though modest, also seemed to have a stimulating effect on investment in manufactures. Foreign investment in manufacturing in China amounted to US$372.4 million in 1931 and US$526.6 million in 1936.[83] It was primarily in fields for domestic consumption; very little was employed in industries for export. The distribution of foreign investment in manufacturing in 1936, both by field and by country, is given in Table 18.[84]

Table 18. Foreign investments in manufacturing in China by country, 1936
(US$ millions; percent in parentheses).[a]

Manufacture	Britain	United States	Germany	France	Japan	Total	
Textiles	64.6	1.2	3.9	0.0	112.4	182.1	(54.7)
Metal, machinery, equipment	20.8	3.6	0.1	0.5	4.1	29.1	(8.8)
Chemicals[b]	63.0	1.7	2.0	1.0	6.8	74.5	(22.4)
Lumber, woodworking	4.0	0.5	0.0	0.0	0.9	5.4	(1.6)
Printing, bookbinding	0.3	0.3	0.1	0.0	0.8	1.5	(0.5)
Food, drink, tobacco	23.3	1.1	0.9	0.5	5.8	31.6	(9.5)
Others	3.7	1.1	0.1	0.0	3.3	8.2	(2.5)
Total	179.7	9.5	7.1	2.0	134.1	332.4	
	(54.1)	(2.9)	(2.1)	(0.6)	(40.3)		(100.0)

Source: Tōa kenkyūjo, Rekkoku tai-Shi tōshi to Shina kokusai shūshi, pp. 7–8, 99, 102–104; Tōa kenkyūjo, Nihon no tai-Shi tōshi, pp. 278, 282, 284, 289, 305.
[a] Hong Kong is included; Manchuria is not.
[b] US$150 million is deducted from British investment in chemicals, as explained in Table 1.

Shipyards and Machine Works. Ship repairing and shipbuilding received the earliest attention of the foreigner. In the 1830's the number of foreign ships entering Canton yearly was already in the hundreds. After 1842 the number entering Chinese ports increased rapidly as more ports were opened to foreign trade. In 1865, for instance, more than sixteen thousand foreign vessels were going through the treaty ports. Prior to 1842 ship repairs were done by the local Chinese docks, whose main business it was to build and repair sailing vessels. The foreign shipping companies never had much confidence in the workmanship of the Chinese and usually sent someone to supervise the docking and repair. It is no surprise that the first foreign dock, known as the Couper Dock, was built sometime between 1845 and 1856 by a person who was sent by a foreign shipping company to look after its vessels in Chinese docks in Huang-pu, Canton.[85]

Foreign docks and shipyards began to increase in China after the 1850's.[86] In Hong Kong the first large shipyard — the Hong Kong and Whampoa Dock Company — was founded in 1863 by the head of the Jardine, Matheson & Co. and two others associated with shipping. With the exception of a few years in the 1870's, when it was under severe competition from some other companies that it later absorbed, the Hong Kong and Whampoa Dock Company remained the only large firm of its kind in Hong Kong until 1900, when the Taikoo Dockyard and Engineering Company was established by another leading British trading firm in China — Butterfield and Swire.

In Shanghai, as in Hong Kong, the British dominated the ship-repairing and shipbuilding industry. In the 1850's several small British shipyards were founded in Shanghai, together with a few small American shipyards. The first large British shipyard appeared in 1862 with the formation of Boyd and Co.; three years later another British company, S. C. Farnham & Co., was founded. These two companies competed with each other until 1901 when they were merged into S. C. Farnham, Boyd & Co., with a total capital of £750,000. In 1906 the company changed its name to the Shanghai Dock and Engineering Co. At about the same time another British company, the New Shipbuilding and Engineering Works, Ltd., was opened. This firm, after absorbing the Vulcan Ironworks, was a strong competitor of the Shanghai Dock and Engineering Co. until 1936, when the two were amalgamated into the Shanghai Dockyard, Ltd.[87] In 1929 there were thirteen ship-building concerns in Shanghai, most of which were foreign owned.[88] In addition, the British founded some shipyards in Amoy and Foochow, but these were rather small in scale. After the Russo-Japanese War in 1905 the Japanese also founded a few small ship-yards in Manchuria.

Foreign docks and shipyards did not serve foreign vessels only. In 1885 Li Hung-chang, the governor of Chihli, complained that the Chinese government had to send its larger ships all the way to the Hong Kong and Whampoa Company for repair. It was the only place along the Chinese coast where large vessels could be accommodated and repaired. Foreign shipyards also built various vessels, including gunboats, for the Chinese government, the Chinese Customs, and Chinese shipping companies.[89]

Aside from shipyards, a number of foreign machine works were founded in China (more than a hundred by 1936, excluding Manchuria).[90] Founded principally by the British and the Japanese in the 1920's and 1930's, they covered a wide range of fields: electric products, bicycles, pipes, motors, machines, and equipment for various other purposes.

Processing for Exports. The cheapness of Chinese labor and the high freight rates offered inducements to foreign merchants to do the first rough processing of raw materials for export in China. The Russian merchants were the first to set up factories in China processing tea for export, principally to Russia. S. W. Litvinoff & Co. was founded in 1863 and Tokmakoff, Molotkoff & Co. in 1866 by Russian tea merchants in Hankow. In 1868 a few Russian tea factories were located more than a hundred miles in the interior from Hankow[91] — at the time when foreigners were not even permitted to establish manufactures in the treaty ports. Late in the 1870's Russian merchants founded tea factories in Foochow and Kiukiang and contributed greatly to the increase of tea exports from those two ports. During the 1890's Russian tea factories in China employed probably seven thousand Chinese workers.[92]

The first modern silk filature, the Silk Reeling Establishment, was founded in Shanghai in 1861 by a leading foreign trading firm Jardine, Matheson & Co., for the purpose of improving Chinese silk. It did not last long, however, partly because of technical difficulties and partly because of the opposition of native handicraftsmen, who created difficulties in the supply of cocoons to their modern competitor. Not until the late 1870's did another foreign silk filature appear in Shanghai. This time it was founded by an American trading firm, Russell & Co., and was called the Kee Chong Silk Filature. Jardine, Matheson & Co. made a comeback and founded the Ewo Silk Filature in 1882 in Shanghai. Thereafter others followed suit, and more foreign silk filatures were founded in China, not only in Shanghai but also in other parts of the country such as Shantung and Manchuria. In the case of a Japanese firm founded in Shantung in 1917, it was labor rather than Chinese raw material that attracted the enterprise, for the silk cocoons were reared in Japan. On the whole, foreign capital in the silk industry of China was small as compared with Chinese capital.

Manufactures for export included a number of other products, such as wool, leather, cotton, eggs, tungoil, sugar, vegetable oils, bean products. Jardine, Matheson & Co. founded a sugar refinery in Hong Kong in 1876 and one in Swatow in 1878. Butterfield & Swire founded an even larger one in Hong Kong in 1882. The sugar refineries in Hong Kong finally forced the Swatow refinery to close in 1886. Attempts were also made by British and American merchants to set up sugar refineries in Taiwan and Quemoy in the 1880's but were not realized because of local opposition. A large Russian sugar refinery was established in 1908 in Harbin in Manchuria, not for export purposes so much as for local consumption. It had severe difficulties, however, in competing with imported sugar.

The German merchants were the first to manufacture egg products for export, including such articles as dried albumen, frozen albumen, dried yolk, moist and frozen yolk, and machine-made dried egg products. In 1872 a small but short-lived plant was founded in Yent'ai, Shantung, by German merchants. Later, similar plants were founded in Hankow and a number of other treaty ports. The International Export Company, a British concern, was the most important, having several plants in Hankow, Tientsin, and Nanking as well as more than 150 purchasing offices in various cities.[93]

Foreign capital was invested in the bean oil and bean cake industry in Manchuria, the world production center of soybeans. In 1865 a British firm in Newchwang ordered some machinery from Great Britain for processing bean oil and cake by steam power and began operations in 1868. The result was disappointing, for although the quality of the products was better, the cost was much too high to compete with the native methods. The plant was finally closed down after two years of operation. Foreign bean oil mills did not appear on any large scale until the late 1900's when some Japanese mills were founded in Manchuria.[94] In 1929 there was a total of three hundred oil mills in Manchuria, including the old-fashioned mills. Of the sixty in Dairen only two were foreign mills

(Japanese), and of the fifty in Harbin, only two were foreign (Russian).[95]

Export of hides from China began to increase after the 1870's, largely as a result of technical innovations such as press packing and scientific methods of curing.[96] In 1876 a British firm in Hankow began to use machines to press hides, thereby cutting down the freight charges for export to Europe. In 1881 the Shanghai Tannery Company, a British concern, was founded to tan hides in China instead of exporting the skins. During the same period some cotton-cleaning, fluffing, ginning, and packing factories were also founded, chiefly by the Japanese because the export of cotton to Japan was increasing, as well as several wool cleaning and packing plants.

Manufacturing for Chinese Consumption. A host of articles were manufactured for domestic consumption. Some were primarily for the residents, both foreign and Chinese, of the treaty ports, and these products were manufactured by foreign concerns in China earlier than the products that were primarily for the Chinese masses. Western drugs were among the first products to be manufactured in China. A British firm, J. Llewellyn & Co., was founded in Shanghai in 1853 to manufacture Western drugs as well as various cosmetics and sodas. A foreign bakery was opened in Shanghai in 1855, making Western bread, candies, and sodas. The Shanghai Steam Flour Mill was opened in 1863, and in the next year Caldbeck, Macgregor & Co., a British concern, was founded in Shanghai to brew and distribute liquors. The making of ice by modern methods attracted British attention, and they set up the Cooperative Ice Company in Shanghai in 1880. To meet the demand for materials for construction, the Shanghai Brick & Saw Mill Co. was established in the 1860's, the Shanghai Glass Works in 1882, and the Shanghai Concrete Company around 1891. A furniture-manufacturing concern was also begun in 1885.

Foreign manufactures for Chinese mass consumption did not appear until after the market had been reasonably well established by imports. A modern match-making company, the Major Brothers, was opened by the British in Shanghai in 1880. The Swedish were also pioneers in match-making and, along with the Japanese, dominated the industry.[97] Foreign firms began to manufacture paper in China in the 1880's, at about the same time that they started making soap. The most important industries for the mass market, however, were cotton textiles and cigarettes.

Cotton goods were long among the leading items in the list of Chinese imports. As early as the 1860's there were attempts by British and American merchants to open textile factories in Shanghai and Tientsin. None of the attempts succeeded because of opposition from the Chinese government and the handicraft textile industry. In 1894 Jardine, Matheson & Co. proposed to import machines and establish a textile concern in Shanghai. While negotiations with the Chinese government were still in process, the Treaty of Shimonoseki was concluded with Japan, giving foreign nationals the right to establish manufactures in the treaty or open ports. The Ewo Cotton Spinning and Weaving Co. was founded by Jardine, Matheson & Co. in Shanghai in 1897, a few years after its Chinese counterpart had begun operations in Shanghai in 1890.[98] In the same year the Laou Kungmow Cotton Spinning & Weaving Co. (British), the International Cotton Manufacturing Co. (American), and the Soychee Spinning Co. (German) were founded in Shanghai. These four foreign firms had a total of 160,548 spindles. With the exception of the German firm, a substantial portion of their capital stock was held by the Chinese, and their boards had Chinese directors.[99]

The achievements of the foreign cotton mills in China were disappointing. They never made much profit and for a few years after 1899 were unable to declare any dividends. This probably accounted for the scarcity of new entries by British or American firms in later years. The Japanese, who in 1895 had thought it unprofitable to operate cotton mills in China, made their appearance in the field in 1902 by acquiring a Chinese cotton mill. By 1913 there were eight foreign cotton mills in China, with about 339,000 spindles and 2,000 looms.[100] They were owned by the British, Americans, Germans, and Japanese, with the British and Japanese leading.

After the First World War broke out, the British and Japanese became the only foreign investors in the industry, as the German mill was sold to the British and the American mill to the Japanese. Although the war presented a good opportunity for investment in the industry because imports declined and profits rose, little foreign investment took place. Great Britain was busy with the war; Japan was enjoying a prosperity at home and, at any rate, could not have gotten necessary machines from Great Britain or the United States. In 1918 the Chinese tariff was revised so that differences between coarse and fine cotton yarns were recognized, as were differences between coarse and fine cotton piece goods. The higher duty imposed upon the finer yarns, which Japan had been exporting to China, served as an inducement to open mills in China. In 1922 there was another upward tariff revision. Japanese investment in textiles in China took a sharp increase in 1921–22 as a result of these tariff revisions, the depressed situation of the textile industry in Japan, and the prosperity of the textile industry in China. From 1925 to 1931 no new Japanese cotton mills were founded, but the existent ones continued to grow and expand. After 1931 renewed efforts were made by the Japanese to establish cotton mills, especially in Tsingtao and Tientsin in North China. Japan was overwhelmingly predominant among foreign textile mills in China after World War I, as Table 19 shows.

As with other products, the manufacture of cigarettes in China by foreign concerns came after the market had been opened up by imports, although in this case the time lag was exceedingly short. The American Tobacco Company's agent, Mustard & Co., began to import cigarettes in 1890, and, discovering their wide acceptance by the Chinese, it imported machines and started their manufacture in China the next year.[101] Large-scale production of cigarettes took place in 1902, when the British-American Tobacco Company entered the Chinese scene, having just been formed in London by American and British interests. It proceeded to acquire or gain control of the existing foreign enterprises and became the largest concern both in the import and production of cigarettes in China.

The company had a number of factories in China, first in Shanghai, Hankow, Mukden, and Harbin and later in Tientsin and Tsingtao. At first it had to import tobacco for its plants because the Chinese tobacco was not suitable for cigarettes. Within ten years, however, it was able to cure the Manchuria leaf in Mukden to be used in mixture with American tobacco in its Hankow plant. After the First World War the company continued its efforts to substitute Chinese leaf for imported leaf. After some experiments it

Table 19. Foreign cotton textile mills in China, 1897–1936.[a]

Year	Yarn spindles (in thousands)			Looms		
	British	Japanese	Total[b]	British	Japanese	Total[b]
1897	80.5	0.0	160.5	0	0	0
1913	138.0	111.9	339.0	800	886	1,986
1919	244.1	332.9	577.0	2,353	1,486	3,839
1922	257.9	621.8	879.7	2,800	2,986	5,786
1924	250.5	932.7	1,183.2	2,863	3,929	6,792
1925	205.3	1,268.2	1,473.5	2,348	7,205	9,553
1927	205.3	1,292.0	1,497.3	2,348	9,625	11,973
1928	153.3	1,397.3	1,550.6	1,900	10,801	12,701
1929	153.3	1,462.2	1,615.5	1,900	11,467	13,367
1930	169.2	1,587.8	1,757.0	2,480	13,554	16,034
1931	170.6	1,715.8	1,886.4	2,691	15,983	18,674
1932	183.2	1,790.7	1,973.9	2,891	17,592	20,483
1933	184.9	1,803.5	1,988.4	2,891	19,017	21,908
1934	184.9	1,946.5	2,131.4	2,891	21,606	24,497
1935	227.1	1,944.5	2,171.6	4,021	23,127	27,148
1936	221.3	2,135.1	2,356.4	4,021	28,915	32,936

Source: Yen Chung-p'ing, Mien-fang-chih, pp. 149 and 369; Yen Chung-p'ing, ed., T'ung-chi tzu-liao, pp. 134–135.
[a] Manchuria not included after 1932. It is estimated that in 1936 Japanese cotton mills in Manchuria had a total of 211,600 spindles. See Min-yeh yüeh-k'an (Cotton industry monthly), 1.4:626 (Apr. 1937).
[b] Includes other foreign cotton mills in China.

introduced American tobacco to the farmers in Shantung, Hupeh, Anhuei, and Honan. At first the Chinese farmers were reluctant to accept the new crop, but by the 1930's home-produced leaf was of such a quality as to satisfy most of the domestic demand and replace the imported. It is estimated that in 1934 there were about 300,000 Chinese families engaged in growing American tobacco.[102]

Inasmuch as the products were for Chinese domestic consumption, the company had a very comprehensive marketing system. Its selling agents were primarily Chinese and could be found all over the country.[103] In many areas, especially the interior, cigarette smoking was introduced by these agents. It is estimated that cigarette consumption in China increased from 300 million in 1900 to 88,500 million in 1933.[104] The increase was taken care of primarily by domestic production because imports declined sharply during the First World War and the 1920's, and became insignificant in the 1930's.

The British and American Tobacco Company, though undoubtedly the largest in the industry, was not unchallenged by others. Apart from the Chinese firms, to be discussed later, the company had to compete with some Russian and Japanese companies in Manchuria. Two Russian cigarette-making firms, founded in Harbin a few years before it had entered the Chinese scene, were its strong competitors before 1914. During the first decade of the twentieth century, some Japanese firms were opened in Manchuria and Greek firms in Shanghai and Tientsin.[105] After the 1920's the company's main competition was from Chinese and Japanese firms.

Public Utilities. Foreign-owned public utilities, such as gas, electricity, water, etc., were established primarily to satisfy the demands of foreign residents and concessions in China.[106] A gas company was organized by British merchants in 1864 to supply the needs of the British concession in Shanghai. This company, which later took the name of the Shanghai Gas Co., was responsible for the use of gas to light some streets in Shanghai in 1865. After the Shanghai Gas Co. turned down a request to light streets in the French concession, on grounds of an inadequate supply, the French founded their own gas company in 1865.

British merchants also founded the Shanghai Waterworks Co. in 1881 and the Shanghai Electric Co. in 1882, both located in the British concession in Shanghai.[107] At the turn of the century electricity plants began to be introduced by foreigners in other cities, such as Tientsin, Hankow, Peking, and a few cities in Manchuria. The French, the Germans, and the Belgians participated along with the British, and the Japanese were particularly active in Manchuria. In addition to electricity, gas, and waterworks, foreign tramways and omnibus companies were also founded in China. In public utilities it was quite common for the Chinese to be shareholders.

During the 1870's a Danish and a British firm introduced telegraphy to China on a commercial basis. In 1881 a British telephone company was founded in Shanghai. However, foreign investment in the telephone and telegraph never grew large due to opposition by the Chinese government. The government insisted that China never grant foreigners the right to install wires and poles across the countryside, lest such installations arouse opposition from the people from fear that they would destroy the *feng-shui*. Telegraph became an entirely nationalized industry after the turn of the century, and in the telephone field the government was dominant at both central and local levels. Foreign participation was therefore unimportant.

Chapter 4

Framework of Analysis
of the Effects of Foreign Investment

In the previous chapters a general factual picture of foreign investment in China has been presented. The task now is to examine the impact of foreign investment on the Chinese economy. This is, of course, an enormous task and no attempt will be made in this study to examine all the possible effects on the economy — if, indeed, such an attempt is at all possible. At the beginning it will be helpful to outline the approach that will be used to analyze the problem.

One determinant of the impact of foreign investment on the Chinese economy is the quantity of investment. Given a marginal capital-output ratio, income growth is obviously related to the size of investment. However, foreign investment may not or should not be expected to carry the whole load in the development of an economy. It should play a catalytic role, overcoming initial difficulties of development and setting up an environment conducive to domestic capital formation. Even in this limited role a certain crucial size of foreign capital may still be necessary to clear away the obstacles to economic progress, especially if an accelerated or speedy development is desired.

The amount of foreign investment in China in various years has been shown. Was it large enough to play the catalytic role? Was it large as compared with foreign investment in other underdeveloped countries? While detailed answers to these questions will appear in the following chapters, it may be anticipated that both the amount and inflow of capital were small in the Chinese case. Why? A clue to the answer will be found by examining the fields in which foreign capital was employed, for they should reflect the underlying determining forces. A large part of foreign investment was employed in fields related to China's foreign trade, and the trading firms figured importantly in foreign direct investment in China. Why investment in trade could not grow large will be made clear.

A striking feature of foreign investment in China was that it was relatively unimportant in primary production, that is, in mining and agriculture. The explanation is found in the institutional arrangements under which such investments took place. The restrictive nature of Chinese mining regulations and the barriers to foreign investment in agriculture will be critically examined.

The small amount of foreign investment in manufacturing cannot easily be explained in an institutional or legal setting, for it was made in the treaty ports under the full protection of extraterritorial and other rights. It was small largely because of economic factors — profitability in particular. Profit rates on investments in China and in the investing countries will be presented and analyzed. The reasons that profit rates were not higher in China will also be suggested.

Catalytic Effect

Was the Chinese economy stagnant before 1937, as is commonly assumed? Evidence will be presented to show that it had undergone changes toward modernization and that the modern sector, although small compared with the entire economy, had experienced a continuous growth. Were there any beneficial links between foreign investment and economic modernization? An attempt will be made to answer this question by examining the following: the share of foreign capital in the economy; the Chinese response to foreign economic intrusion (that is, whether the Chinese government and public made adjustments so as to develop and modernize the economy); the extent to which foreign enterprises helped the Chinese in the training of personnel, transmission of technological knowledge, and entrepreneurship; and the extent to which the various "linkage effects" of foreign investment took place.

The fact that the Chinese economy remained an underdeveloped one suggests that the positive effects of foreign investment were limited. To put the role of foreign investment into perspective with the whole complexity of forces underlying the Chinese economy, and to explain why China remained economically underdeveloped, a broad hypothesis will be suggested.

Oppressing Effect

A persistent and widely accepted theme has been that the establishment of foreign enterprises in China retarded or "oppressed" the development of Chinese-owned modern enterprises. It has been suggested that foreign enterprises could easily outcompete their Chinese counterparts because of stronger financial background, better technological and managerial knowledge, and immunity from Chinese taxation and official exactions or abuses. An examination of this assertion will be made.

Data will be presented to show the long-term relative shares of foreign and Chinese enterprises in various industries so that a comparison may be made as to whether the foreign enterprises outgrew the Chinese ones. Efforts will be made to examine the various forces that made it possible for the Chinese-owned enterprises to coexist with the foreign firms.

Destructive Effect

The increase of imported products from abroad and the development of the modern sector at home has often been suggested as having had a destructive effect on the traditional or indigenous sector of the Chinese economy. An examination of this assertion will be made. Data will be presented to show whether the traditional sector (or segments of this sector) actually declined. It will be argued that the development of the modern sector tends to have both positive and negative effects on the traditional sector. The conditions under which the traditional sector could compete with the modern sector will also be discussed.

Drain Effect

According to many Chinese in the closing decades of the nineteenth century, any profit made by foreign traders and investors was made at the expense of the Chinese and meant a drain of wealth from China. A more recent version of this thesis (advanced by Singer, Prebisch, and Myrdal) includes not only the remittance of income made by foreign investors but also the gains accrued to the investing countries through a favorable movement of the commodity terms of trade. The data on reinvestment ratios of foreign enterprises in China will be presented and analyzed, as will the total outpayment on account of foreign investments (remittance of profits on direct investments and amortization and interest payments on loans). An analysis of the movements and effect of the Chinese commodity terms of trade will also be made.

Instability Effect

A major objection to what is called the colonial type of foreign investment is that it results in a lopsided export development and the accompanying evil of excessive external instability. Was there a lopsided export development in China? How stable or unstable were China's exports? Did China suffer serious balance of payments difficulties because of foreign investment? All these questions will be handled.

Unanswered Questions

In order to form a final judgment on the effects of foreign investment on China not only the economic consequences have to be studied but also the psychological, social, and political consequences should be examined. These forces are mutually determining and reinforcing, especially for a country that embarks on a new road of modernization and has to make all the necessary adjustments. Although space will not allow such an exhaustive study here, the existence of foreign concessions and settlements in the treaty ports where foreign direct investments were situated had many profound effects on China.

For instance, they affected the consumption habits of the people. The wealthy Chinese classes imitated the Western way of life as well as the Western way of production. Though subject to further verification, it may be hypothesized that the very existence of foreign concessions in China greatly raised the consumption function of many wealthy Chinese and thereby limited their capacity for investment. Many of them, in fact, lived right in the foreign concessions. Although factors such as personal safety contributed to this phenomenon, there is little doubt that the "demonstration effect" emphasized by Nurkse also played its role. It would be interesting to compare changes in the consumption pattern of the wealthy class of Japan in her early stages of development with the changes undergone by the wealthy Chinese. It is often said that the Japanese retained their traditional way of living. However, it may also be noted that foreign loans rather than direct investments were dominant in the early days of Japanese development.

Investigation should also be made into the pattern of consumption of foreign businessmen in the treaty ports. Many of them lived their entire lives in China yet did not become Chinese in terms of their mode of living. While they remained Westerners, they were not subject to the kind of competition or discipline that prevailed in their own countries. They belonged to a special class of citizens of the world. It would be inviting to study their income and standard of living (relative to productivity) as compared with that of their counterparts in their homelands. It would also be interesting to investigate how much they retained of the capitalist, Calvinist, growth-promoting economic mentality. The drain argument mentioned above may not take the simple form of remittance of profit or interest payments, but may also include the element of consumption by the foreigners who made their living in China.

Because of the extraterritorial rights enjoyed by foreign nationals, foreign concessions in fact constituted a foreign state established inside of China. The Chinese government not only had no control over foreign nationals but also found it difficult to exercise control over its own citizens when the latter took refuge in foreign concessions. It is therefore easy to understand why the government from the Manchu dynasty to the Nationalist regime was always suspicious of, and hostile to, foreign investment in China. Whatever Chinese legislation was enacted, consideration always had to be given to problems that might arise due to the presence of foreign concessions.

It may be argued that, given the state of political degeneration in China, the Chinese government could not have contributed much to the process of social adjustment, and that the presence of foreign concessions rendered a real protective service to whatever forces contributed to China's modernization. However, the question remains as to whether foreign investment furthered Chinese political instability. For instance, did the political loans, especially during the Peking government period, prolong political instability in the sense that they contributed to the financial strength of the Peking government? Or, did foreign concessions offer a real protection to the opponents and critics of the government and hence foster democratic tendencies?

Foreign investment in China did not take place in a vacuum. It cannot be separated from the whole environment in which it took place: extraterritorial rights, leased areas, treaty ports, spheres of interest, railroad zones, stationing of foreign troops, the treaty tariff and other unequal treaties, not to mention the repeated military intrusions which the Chinese have always regarded as a national humiliation of the first order. How did all of these elements affect the political system, the social structure and conflicts (the newly created "compradore class," for instance), social psychology, the traditional values and institutions, and the processes of social change? Such questions remain to be investigated. It might also be asked: what would have happened to the Chinese society if there had not been such external intrusions which may conveniently be called the treaty port system? For instance, would the Chinese government have been stronger and therefore better able to undertake or promote development programs if there had been no external wars, no indemnity payments to foreign powers, and no restrictions imposed upon China by the treaty port system? It seems that in an evaluation of the effect of foreign investment on China, one should not only examine what actually happened but also consider what the treaty port system might have prevented from happening. The concept of opportunity cost is applicable here. It is clearly beyond the competence of an economist, however, to speculate on such matters.

Chapter 5

Determinants of Foreign Investment in China

Amount and Inflow

Any attempt to make an international comparison of the amounts of foreign investment is subject to the danger that the comparison will be made on things that are not comparable. The definitions and methods of measurement of foreign investment may differ significantly from country to country, and the population figures that are necessary for such a comparison may not be reliable. However, even after allowance is made for a large margin of statistical discrepancy, the figures given in Table 20 can hardly fail to convey the impression that foreign investment in China was, on a per capita basis, very small as compared with that in other underdeveloped economies in 1938. Based on the 1936 figure of US$3483 million and an estimated total population of 450 million, per capita foreign investment in China was still less than United States $8.

No comprehensive data are available to show the share of foreign capital in the total capital stock of China. There is no doubt, however, that foreign capital was predominant in many fields of the modern sector of the Chinese economy. In view of the fact that the modern sector, in which foreign investment was made almost exclusively, could contribute no more than 13 percent of the national income in 1933, the amount of foreign investment in China cannot be regarded as large. It is true, of course, that historically foreign investments have never constituted a sizable proportion of capital formation or national income in a large country, but in the Chinese case even the absolute amount of foreign investment was not large.

Table 20. Foreign capital in underdeveloped countries, 1938.

Country	Total foreign capital (US$ millions)	Total population (millions)	Per capita foreign capital (US$)
Asia	*10,653*	*946.0*	*11.3*
China (including Manchuria)	2,557	452.4	5.7
India, Burma, Ceylon	3,113	325.6	9.6
Indochina, New Caledonia	477	23.0	20.7
Iran	197	16.2	12.2
Iraq, Palestine, Syria	137	9.2	14.9
Malaya	696	4.1	169.8
Netherlands East Indies	2,378	67.4	35.3
Philippine Islands	306	15.4	19.9
Portuguese Asia	2	1.4	1.4
Siam	200	14.5	13.8
Turkey	590	16.8	35.1
Latin America	*11,151*	*123.2*	*90.5*
British Indies	210	2.5	84.0
Costa Rica	64	0.6	106.7
Cuba	807	4.4	183.4
Dominican Republic	49	1.6	30.6
Guatemala	152	2.7	56.2
Haiti	20	3.5	5.7
Honduras, British Honduras	59	1.0	59.0
Nicaragua	11	0.9	12.2
Panama	52	0.6	57.8
Salvador	21	1.6	13.1
Mexico	1,778	18.7	95.1
Argentina	3,193	14.0	228.1
Bolivia	145	3.2	45.3
Brazil	1,964	38.7	50.7
Chile	1,288	4.8	268.3
Columbia	322	8.5	37.9
Ecuador	28	2.8	10.0
Paraguay	58	0.9	64.4
Peru	326	6.7	48.7
Uruguay	248	2.1	118.1
Venezuela	356	3.4	104.7
Africa	*3,805*	*118.9*	*32.0*
Belgian Congo	428	10.2	42.0
British Africa	1,914	41.8	45.8
Egypt, Suez	513	16.0	32.1
French Africa	754	39.7	19.0
Liberia	12	1.5	8.0
Portuguese Africa	184	9.7	19.0
Europe	*2,656*	*87.4*	*30.4*
Bulgaria	110	6.2	17.7
Greece	486	7.0	69.4
Hungary	369	9.1	40.5
Poland	730	34.4	21.2
Romania	650	15.5	41.9
Yugoslavia	311	15.2	20.5
Grand Total	*28,265*	*1,275.5*	*22.2*

Source: For investment figures, see C. Lewis, pp. 292–297. For population figures, primarily for 1937, see United Nations, *Demographic Yearbook 1949–1950*, pp. 71–83. Some countries not regarded as underdeveloped are included for comparison.

A part of the increase in foreign direct investment in China was due to the rise of price levels and a part was due to the plowing back of profits. Some foreign loans of the Chinese government were provided by foreign banks and merchants residing in China, and some were used to pay interest on previous loans borrowed abroad. Capital inflow, therefore, was smaller than the increase of total foreign investments might suggest. Remer estimates that remittances to China represented only 50 percent of the increase in the value of direct investments during 1902–1913, and 45 percent during 1914–1931.[1]

Available data do not permit a calculation of year-to-year capital inflow figures. According to Remer, the average annual inpayments in gross terms, with regard to government loans and direct investment, were about US$52 million for the entire period from 1902 to 1930 (Table 21). Prior to 1902, most of the foreign loans to the Chinese government were contracted to pay an indemnity imposed upon China by Japan, and hence did not involve much capital inflow. However, there should have been

Table 21. Annual inpayments and outpayments on foreign investments in China, 1894–1936 (Chin$ millions).[a]

Period	Inpayments			Outpayments			Balance (net outpayments)
	Govt. loans	Direct investment	Total	Govt. loans	Direct investment	Total	
1894–1901	21.3	—	—	20.9	—	—	—
1902–1913	61.0	52.8	113.8	89.2	69.3	158.5	44.7
1914–1930	23.8	73.6	97.4	70.9	138.8	209.7	114.3
1928	4.0	96.0	100.0	63.0	179.0	242.0	142.0
1929	0.0	170.0	170.0	79.1	198.5	277.6	107.6
1930	0.0	202.0	202.0	111.4	198.0	309.4	107.4
1931	—	—	43.6	135.2	87.2	222.4	178.8
1932	—	—	60.0	90.0	56.0	146.0	86.0
1933	—	—	30.0	93.0	24.0	117.0	87.0
1934	—	—	80.0	112.6	15.0	127.6	47.6
1935	—	—	140.0	107.4	55.0	162.4	22.4
1936	—	—	60.0	127.8	70.0	197.8	137.8

Source: For 1894–1930, see Remer, Foreign Investments, pp. 160, 220–222. For 1931, see W. Y. Lin, p. 26. The estimate is K. Tsuchiya's. For 1932, see T. F. Koh, "Silver at Work," in Finance and Commerce (1935), quoted by W. Y. Lin, p. 26. For 1933–1936, see Bank of China, Annual Reports, as cited in Yen Chung-p'ing, ed., T'ung-chi tzu-liao, pp. 86–88. The estimate on outpayment on direct investment for 1934 is from W. Y. Lin, p. 26. [a] Manchuria is not included after 1931.

some inflow of capital with regard to foreign direct investments, which, still insignificant in 1895, reached US$503 million in 1902. If it can be assumed that foreign direct investment was close to US$100 million in 1895 and half of the increase in foreign direct investment during 1895–1902 was from new investment from abroad, the annual inflow of capital with regard to direct investment was approximately US$30 million (or Chin$60 million) during the period.

If allowance is made for remittance of interest and profits on foreign investment, Remer estimates that there was not only no net inflow of capital but a considerable net outflow throughout the period from 1902 to 1930. The inflow-outflow ratio for the period was 57 percent. Remer's estimates, as well as some estimates for later years, are presented in Table 21 and Table 22.

Table 22. Inpayment-outpayment ratio of foreign investments in China, 1902–1934 (percent).

Period	Government loans	Direct investments	Total
1902–1913	68.39	76.19	71.80
1914–1930	33.57	53.03	46.45
1902–1930	52.97	60.74	57.36
1928	6.35	53.63	41.32
1929	0.00	85.64	61.24
1930	0.00	101.76	65.29
1931	—	—	19.60
1932	—	—	41.10
1933	—	—	26.55
1934	—	—	54.86

Source: See Table 21.

It may be of interest to compare China with Japan with regard to the amount and inflow of foreign capital. Japan began to modernize herself after the Meiji Restoration of 1868. In the twenty-seven years from 1868 to 1895 remarkable progress was made with respect to the transformation of economic institutions and attitudes, and with little help from foreign capital. The progress was largely the result of expansion and improvements in agriculture as well as exploratory ventures in industrialization.[2] Large-scale industrialization and the manufacture of arms took place in Japan from 1896 to 1914, and her national income per capita may have increased about 4 percent per year.[3] Since her total capital requirements seemed to outrun her domestic savings and the sources of foreign exchange, she resorted to foreign borrowing. At the end of 1913 the outstanding foreign debt of both the Japanese government (central and local levels) and private corporations (chiefly semigovernment corporations) stood at ¥1970 million.[4]

Another category of foreign funds available to Japan was the indemnity payments of China. The indemnity following the Sino-Japanese War yielded Y360 million in sterling during 1896–1898, and the one following the Boxer Rebellion yielded ¥24 million from 1902 through 1913.[5] To this inflow of loans and indemnity payments should also be added the relatively small amount of foreign direct investment in Japan, totaling perhaps ¥100 million during 1896–1913. After allowing for additions to Japanese specie holdings and investments abroad, the total net capital inflow may have been about ¥1500 during 1896–1913.[6]

This inflow of foreign capital was quite substantial relative to the Japanese economy at the time. The net inflow during 1904–1913 (¥1083 million) was equivalent to excess imports of goods and services amounting to one sixth of the total imports. The total foreign borrowing by the national government during this period provided about one sixth of its revenues from all sources.

In real terms, after allowance is made for net remittance of interest and profits on foreign investment, the net contribution of foreign capital in this period (1896–1913) constituted 12 percent of the entire net real-capital formation in Japan or 20 percent of the net real capital formation of the "productive" type. Similarly, the net real foreign contribution was about 2.3 percent of the average national income, while the whole net capital inflow (gross of foreign investment service) came close to 3 percent of the average national income.[7]

Although Japan became a creditor nation after World War I, foreign investments in Japan continued to grow, especially in the 1920's when foreign direct investments assumed importance for the first time. Foreign loans to the Japanese government and private corporations amounted to ¥2466 million (US$1233 million) in 1930, while foreign direct investments totaled some ¥245 million (US$122.5 million) in 1929.[8] Thus, in absolute terms foreign investment in Japan was nearly 42 percent of that of China in 1930. On a per capita basis, foreign investment in Japan was almost three times as high as that in China in 1930.[9]

Reinvestment Ratio

The reinvestment ratio is defined as the ratio of undistributed profit to profit of business concerns. The undistributed profit is the difference between profit and dividends and is assumed to have been plowed back into business. Using this definition, the reinvestment ratios of foreign enterprises in China are calculated and shown in Table 23.

Table 23. Frequency distribution of foreign direct investments in China, 1872–1936, by reinvestment ratio (percent).

Reinvestment ratio[a] (percent)	Foreign trade	Insurance	Banking	Shipping	Public utilities	Manufacturing	Unclassified	Total investment
0– 9.99	12.9	3.8	14.5	20.0	7.9	10.9	9.6	10.2
10–19.99	19.4	6.4	18.2	12.7	13.9	14.3	12.0	13.0
20–29.99	6.5	7.0	14.5	5.5	20.8	13.9	7.2	11.9
30–39.99	6.5	12.7	7.3	16.4	8.9	13.9	15.7	12.1
40–49.99	6.5	6.4	12.7	7.3	13.9	11.3	12.0	10.5
50–59.99	6.5	5.1	7.3	9.1	5.9	7.6	7.2	6.8
60–69.99	6.5	16.6	6.4	9.1	7.9	5.0	2.4	8.0
70–79.99	0.0	22.9	4.5	3.6	1.0	2.9	3.6	7.0
80–89.99	9.7	12.1	3.6	1.8	2.0	1.7	3.6	4.6
90–100	9.7	3.8	3.6	5.5	4.0	13.9	13.3	8.3
$D > P$	16.1	3.2	7.3	9.1	13.9	4.6	13.3	7.6
Total	100.0	100.0	100.0	100.0	100.0	100.0	100.0	100.0
30–100	45.4	82.8	45.4	52.8	43.6	56.3	57.8	57.3
40–100	38.9	70.1	38.1	36.4	34.7	42.4	42.1	45.2
50–100	32.4	63.7	25.4	29.1	20.8	31.1	30.1	34.7
No. of ratios	31	157	110	55	101	238	83	775

Source: Financial statements of foreign firms in China during 1872–1936, published in the *North China Herald*, various years (1893 and 1897–1899 are not covered).
[a] The reinvestment ratio is defined as $100(P - D)/P$, where P denotes profit and D dividends. Insofar as possible, profits are recomputed by modern accounting methods (see Table 24).

The dividend and profit figures are taken from the financial statements of foreign firms published in the *North China Herald*. While the adjustments that it was necessary to make for the profit figures will be explained later, it may be noted here that the ratios given in Table 23 are no more than preliminary approximations. For the entire period 1872–1936 (except 1893 and 1897–1899) no more than 775 financial statements can be found for our purposes. Yet, the total number of foreign firms in China, according to Chinese Customs reports, reached 636 in 1897 and 7055 in 1917.[10] It is true that the financial statements used here are in large part those published by British firms, but the number of British firms was 374 in 1897, 655 in 1917, and 1027 in 1930.[11] Furthermore, the number of firms whose financial statements can be found for successive years is not large, with the result that there is a shifting character to the sample. Therefore, the extent to which the ratios given in Table 23 are really representative of the entire population is a question that remains to be answered. They are presented here not as conclusive evidence for any firm statement but as an addition to whatever data further research may supply.

According to the information given in Table 23, nearly 57 percent of the foreign firms reinvested 30 percent or more of their profits, while 45 percent of the foreign firms reinvested 40 percent or more of their profits. Insurance companies had the highest reinvestment ratio, while public utilities had the lowest. As will be shown, insurance companies also had the highest profit rate.

It should be noted, however, that the distributed profits may not have been remitted to foreign countries but may have been invested in China instead. Remer estimates that the remittance by China with respect to direct investments was at the rate of 4 percent of the value of such investments for the period from 1902 to 1930.[12] If one assumes that profits constituted 10 percent of the value of such investments, it follows that 60 percent of the profits were reinvested in China.[13]

Unequal Treaties

Among the factors most favorable to foreign investment in China, especially direct investments, were the unequal treaties concluded between China and the powers. They have been labeled as unequal because the privileges accorded to foreign nationals by China were not reciprocally accorded to the Chinese. It is beyond the scope of this study to examine all the characteristics of these treaties or the motives of the powers in imposing such treaties, but it is safe to say that important economic implications or consequences can be traced to them.

Extraterritoriality. Extraterritorial jurisdiction may be regarded either as the extension of the jurisdiction of the governments of foreign states over their citizens in China, or as the removal of those citizens from the jurisdiction of the Chinese government. The system of extraterritoriality in China was first brought into existence as a result of the Opium War, which was terminated by the Treaty of Nanking in 1842. Extraterritorial rights were not, however, explicitly granted in the treaty. Instead the General Resolutions, issued in 1843 in pursuance of the treaty, expressed the understanding of the treaty negotiators that extraterritorial rights should be enjoyed by British traders residing in China.[14] Other countries followed Great Britain in obtaining extraterritorial rights through a series of treaties, most of which were signed in the period from 1848 to 1919.[15]

Extraterritorial rights in China applied not only to foreign subjects but also to the property and all personal or proprietary rights and liabilities of foreign subjects.[16] Consequently, foreign firms were free from any control by the Chinese government with reference to their organization, and they were free from any other Chinese rules and regulations concerning the operation of business. Geographically, the rights applied not only in the treaty ports but throughout all China — to missionaries stationed in the interior as well as to foreigners traveling there on business or pleasure.

A most controversial issue in connection with extraterritoriality in China was the matter of taxes. The general situation may be summarized in a statement made by Dr. Wang Chung-hui, speaking in behalf of the Chinese Delegation at the Peking Tariff Conference of 1925–1926: "As far as China is concerned, ever since she entered into trade relations with foreign countries, in no treaty of any sort is there to be found any provisions which concede to foreigners living in or outside settlements in China an exemption from taxation. But in recent years, when China commenced to enforce her revenue laws, foreigners declined to perform their obligations on the pretext that they reside in the settlement or that they had not received instructions from their governments."[17] While further research remains to be done regarding the extent to which foreign firms obeyed or disobeyed Chinese tax laws, there is little doubt that China met serious difficulties in collecting new taxes such as the sales tax, stamp duties, or wine and tobacco taxes. For instance, the sales tax law was promulgated and put into effect in June 1930, but Shanghai authorities were unable to collect the sales tax from foreign firms, who insisted that it violated their extraterritorial rights.[18] A number of provinces introduced the tobacco tax around 1916 but failed to collect it from foreign firms, which were the most important tobacco manufacturers in China. Not until 1921 was China able to collect tobacco taxes from foreign firms, and then only on terms that the latter agreed upon.[19] The matter of taxation was not as serious as it appeared, however, for taxes on modern-type business firms and factory products were introduced in China very late and on a modest scale. Apart from the sales and tobacco tax, taxes on cotton products, matches, and cement were not introduced until 1931, and the income tax only in 1936.

Leased Areas. Leased areas were those places that were "leased" by China to various countries primarily for the purpose of maintaining the balance of power among the other countries. Examples include the Japanese-leased area on the Liaotung Peninsula in Southern Manchuria, the French-leased area at Kuangchowwan, the British-leased area at Kowloon, and the German-leased area at Kiaochow. The leased area was completely under the control of the foreign power during the term of the lease, which was usually ninety-nine years. Consequently, foreign businesses were free to engage in any kind of business in accordance with the laws of their own countries. In these areas the extraterritorial jurisdiction of other foreign powers was held not to apply.

Open Ports. Open ports were simply those places where foreign businessmen were permitted to reside, to acquire land, and to carry on business in trading (since 1842) and manufacturing (since 1895). An open port was established either by treaty with a foreign power (in which case the term "treaty port" is more appropriate) or by decree of the Chinese government (either voluntarily or under pressure by foreign powers). Open ports were generally located on the coast or on rivers navigable by ocean-going steamers, although some were located far into the interior of China. From 1842 to 1930 no less than 105 open ports were established, of which 73 were opened by treaties and conventions and 32 were opened voluntarily by the Chinese government.[20]

Foreign "concessions" or "settlements" were usually established in open ports by Chinese authorities as residential areas for foreigners. In most concessions the right to set up and maintain local administrative agencies for police purposes, sanitation, road construction, building regulation, etc., was given to the foreign government concerned. The administrative organs created for these purposes levied taxes, the proceeds of which were to be used exclusively for local administrative purposes. The concessions were often the center of foreign direct investment in China.

Spheres of Interest. Outside of open ports and leased areas foreigners were allowed to undertake direct investments in China only by special permission of the Chinese government.[21] While the negotiations for railroad and mining rights have been discussed before, an explanation of the "sphere of interest" may be made here. A sphere of interest refers to an area within which the foreign power concerned claimed the primary right of economic exploitation. In substance, the powers laying claim to the spheres sought to establish the following privileges: a guarantee on the part of China that the area in question would not be alienated to any foreign power; and the understanding that the power or nationals claiming the sphere should have preferential, or in some matters practically exclusive, rights with regard to the making of loans, the construction of railroads, the opening and operating of mines, and the carrying out of public enterprises such as conservation, etc. In some cases the powers also sought Chinese acceptance of a provision that in the employment of "advisers" or other scientific experts, nationals of the power in question should be preferred.[22]

The formal or conventional grounds upon which the spheres rested were either specific treaty engagements or other agreements on the part of China, or understandings or agreements between the claiming powers themselves. For instance, by a treaty signed at Peking in 1895 between China and France, the latter obtained her sphere of interest in the south along the borders of French Indo-China. By an agreement in 1898 Great Britain obtained from the Chinese government a nonalienation promise with regard to the Yangtze Valley.[23] By agreements of 1896 and 1899 Russia obtained her sphere in Manchuria. After the Portsmouth Treaty of 1905, which concluded the Russo-Japanese War, Russia transferred to Japan her interest in South Manchuria, and her sphere of interest was then confined to the northern part of Manchuria. This transfer from Russia to Japan received Chinese consent in the agreement of 1905 between China and Japan.[24] In addition to South Manchuria, Japan succeeded in extending her sphere of interest to the province of Shantung. It had been granted to Germany as her sphere of interest at the time of the 1898 lease of the Kiaochow area. In 1914 Japan took over the German rights in the province, and the formal transfer was provided for in the Treaty of Versailles of 1919.

Treaty Tariff, 1842–1928. As mentioned before, foreign investments in China were closely related to foreign trade. The volume of trade, and hence investments, depended among other things upon tariff rates. Prior to 1842 China had enjoyed fully the right to fix her customs duties. The Treaty of Nanking of 1842 for the first time imposed limitations upon China's freedom to fix her customs dues according to her own fiscal needs or economic policy. The tariff rates fixed at the time of the treaty were approximately 5 percent ad valorem for all imported and exported articles.[25] These rates were retained in the Tientsin Treaties of 1858, although schedules of specific duties replaced the ad valorem system.

The next tariff revision did not take place until 1902 (effective in 1903). According to this revision the specific duties on imports were based upon prices prevailing in 1897–1899, while the 5 percent ad valorem ratio was still retained. This rate soon became nominal for China because of the continued rise of prices. For many years the effective rate was never more than 4 percent.[26]

In 1918 an attempt was made to estimate the market values of commodities for the purpose of attaining the 5 percent ad valorem ratio, and it was agreed that the average prices prevailing at

Shanghai during the years from 1912 to 1916 inclusive should be accepted. In 1922 another revision was made. However, none of the revisions had any significant effect on the general effective rate.[26]

The indiscriminate tariff rate as applied to different commodities and the inflexibility of the system with regard to change of rates finally came to an end in 1929, when after a long struggle China succeeded in regaining her tariff autonomy. The effective tariff rate on imports (the ratio of actual import duty revenue to total import value) rose from 8.5 percent in 1929 to 29.7 percent in 1936.[27]

In connection with the conventional tariff, transit taxes must be mentioned. When the Treaty of Nanking was signed, it was the intention of the foreign powers that once tariff duties had been levied upon goods, they would be exempt from all other taxes. This, however, was not the understanding of the Chinese authorities, who sought to impose various taxes on goods for export on their way to the open ports and on imported goods after entering China. The difference in interpretation became a serious matter in 1853 when China introduced the likin for the purpose of increasing revenue to suppress the Taiping rebels. The likin was a tax imposed on goods in transit by land or by water from one province to another or from one district to another within the same province.[28]

Foreign traders attempted and finally succeeded in avoiding likin by means of treaties. The Treaty of Tientsin of 1858 provided that, in addition to the maritime duty, a fixed sum (one half of the export or import duty) would be levied on native products intended for export as well as on foreign commodities imported and carried to the interior. After this fixed payment there would be no other transit dues on these goods.[29]

To sum up, foreign direct investment took place under very favorable conditions.[30] A foreigner who wished to trade with the Chinese or establish business firms in the open ports in China had no reason to fear Chinese laws or other Chinese control. If foreign direct investments in the open ports of China were small, there must have been other than legal obstacles. In certain ways the open ports in China were not much different from the colonies of foreign powers, except that a colony usually served only one master whereas China had to serve them all.[31]

Mining Regulations

While foreign investors enjoyed full freedom in the treaty or open ports in China, their activities were very much restricted outside of these ports. The establishment of spheres of interest, though significant in preventing competition among the powers themselves, did not necessarily provide a situation conducive to investing in mining, railroads, or plantations outside of the treaty ports. To invest in these fields, special permission had to be obtained from the Chinese government. The struggle to obtain mining rights in China and the way in which some of the large mines were passed over to foreign hands have already been discussed. The Chinese attitude toward foreign mining in China is better understood, however, by a study of the Chinese mining regulations, which undoubtedly had a significant bearing on the amount of foreign direct investment in this field. These regulations not only provided the basis on which the general Sino-foreign joint mining enterprises were founded but also reflected the terms of settlement of the special cases. It is of interest to note that some of the conditions or terms that the present underdeveloped countries have insisted upon since 1945 regarding the use of foreign capital in mining were already included in the mining regulations of China in 1898.

After they had been promulgated by the Chinese government in 1898, the mining regulations underwent a number of revisions (in 1899, 1902, 1904, 1908, 1914 and 1930).[32] Yet, the crucial points with regard to foreign mining remained the same. Except for the 1902 regulations, the Chinese government insisted that foreign mining be undertaken in cooperation with Chinese capital. The minimum Chinese capital was set at 30 percent in 1898 and raised to 50 percent in 1899, 1904, 1908, and 1914. In the 1930 regulations the minimum was 51 percent.[33] There was also a provision in the 1898 and 1904 regulations to the effect that if the mining companies had to resort to foreign loans, approval from the Chinese government was required and such loans were to be a liability of the mining companies alone, not to be involved with either the Chinese or foreign governments. The 1904 regulations placed a ceiling on the amount of such loans, not to exceed 30 percent of the original estimated capital.

The Chinese government also insisted that the Chinese share in the administrative power of the joint mining companies. The 1898 regulations stated that all the mining companies had to be under Chinese control, regardless of the share of foreign capital. The 1914 regulations stipulated that for each important post of the Sino-foreign joint mining companies, a Chinese and a foreigner were to be appointed. According to the 1930 regulations, the chairman of the board, the manager, and more than half of the board of directors had to be Chinese.

To make sure that native Chinese would learn the skills of mining and to minimize the presence of foreign nationals in the interior, the 1902 regulations included a provision that, except in jobs in engineering and accounting, the Chinese should be employed as much as possible. This provision was given more force in the 1904 and 1914 regulations, which stipulated that the workers of the Sino-foreign mines must be Chinese.

In the 1898 and 1902 regulations it was required that the mining companies establish, at their own expense, training schools for the Chinese in the field of mining. This requirement was dropped in later regulations, except in the 1930 ones, which made it a duty of mining companies to accept Chinese graduates of mining schools for purposes of internship.

Mining taxes were of three types: a nominal fee on the mining area, a tax on output, and a tax on net profit. Prior to 1908 the output tax ranged from 3 to 25 percent of the market price at the place of production, depending on the type of minerals involved.[34] (For coal and iron it was 5 percent.)[35] The tax rate on output was lowered considerably in 1914, becoming 1.5 percent for virtually all minerals, including coal, iron, gold, silver, antimony, and diamonds. A universal 2 percent tax was adopted in the 1930 regulations. A tax on net profit was levied in the 1898, 1902, and 1908 regulations. In the main the rate was 25 percent of net profit, which was the difference between profit and an amount for interest and amortization on capital.

For fear that foreigners would not observe the mining regulations because of extraterritorial rights, the Chinese government made it clear in the regulations that Chinese law had to be observed by foreigners in mining and related matters. Disputes between Chinese and foreign partners were to be resolved by arbitration and were to be no concern of foreign governments. In the Chinese view, foreign participation in mining was a privilege to be sought from the Chinese government and not a right stipulated by any treaty. In granting such a privilege, the Chinese government had the right to set the conditions.

It may be suggested that the terms and tax rates outlined above were modest by present-day standards. Nevertheless, they were deemed very severe by foreigners at the time. The latter constantly demanded modifications so that, as stated in the Sino-British treaty of September 5, 1902, and the Sino-American treaty of October 8, 1903, "foreign capitalists would not be at a greater disadvantage than they would be under generally accepted foreign regulations." [36] The powers also objected to the regulations on the ground that they violated the Chinese commitment on extraterritorial rights.

Despite foreign protests, the Chinese government maintained its position and included the crucial provisions in virtually all revisions of the mining regulations. To what extent the regulations were actually observed by foreigners cannot be easily assessed. Except for the special cases discussed before, foreign direct investments in mining were, on the surface at least, limited to Sino-foreign joint ownership. When the matter of taxes came to a dispute, the Chinese government never failed to seek a solution, as evidenced by the experiences of the Peking Syndicate and the Kailan mines. In some cases, such as the Sino-Japanese Luta and the Penghsi mines, all taxes were paid according to the original agreements.

There were instances when the Chinese government was not able to enforce the mining regulations rigidly and exceptions were made. For instance, when the government entered into negotiations with a foreign firm concerning the exploitation of petroleum in Shansi, the most difficult problem proved to be the matter of control. The Chinese government finally agreed to depart from the mining regulations in this case and to permit foreign participation up to 55 percent of the total capital.[37]

Rate of Return

Although foreign governments were intimately involved with foreign investments in China, the investments were primarily made by private individuals, except in Manchuria. For private investors the expected rate of return obviously played a crucial role in determining the magnitude and direction of investment. There is little doubt that foreign businessmen had high hopes in exploiting what they believed to be an almost unlimited market in China. For instance, immediately after the Opium War it was believed among British business circles that the Chinese market for textiles would exceed the entire European market.[38] The question now is, was it as profitable to invest in China as expected?

From the viewpoint of a private investor, the best measurement of return on investment is perhaps the ratio of net profit (net of all expenses and taxes) to net worth (difference between total assets and total liabilities). Such information is usually given in the published financial statements (income and position statements) of a business firm. However, certain difficulties exist when a comparison is made between firms or within a given firm at different times. For instance, there is a difference between the cash basis and the accrual basis in calculating income and expenses; and if the accrual basis is uniformly used, there are still different methods of evaluating assets, especially inventories, or depreciation — all of which affect expense. The matter of depreciation is more difficult because it is generally computed on the basis of original cost. A substantial difference may exist between the replacement value and the book value of a fixed asset if there is a change in general price level. Thus, in a period of rising price levels the profit-net worth ratio of an established firm of long history tends to exaggerate its real earning power, because the income figures are in current prices while some costs, especially depreciation, are based on original cost. (This will be reflected in the book value of assets and hence in the net worth.)

There are other troublesome questions, but perhaps enough has been said to indicate the inherent difficulties of arriving at an accurate measurement of the rate of return on investment of a business firm. The profit-net worth ratios given in Table 24 are subject to all the limitations noted here, in addition to the fact that their

Table 24. Frequency distribution of foreign firms in China, 1872–1932, by profit-net worth ratio (percent).

Profit-net worth ratio[a] (percent)	Foreign trade	Insur- ance	Bank- ing	Ship- ping	Public util- ities	Manu- facturing	Unclas- sified	Total invest- ment
Net loss	5.0	0.8	1.7	7.3	3.2	10.4	6.8	5.0
0– 4.99	10.0	3.3	6.8	9.1	4.8	18.3	22.7	10.3
5– 9.99	45.0	10.6	37.3	40.0	32.3	20.0	34.1	25.9
10–14.99	20.0	16.3	32.2	23.6	32.3	21.7	15.9	22.6
15–19.99	15.0	17.9	13.6	18.2	14.5	12.2	6.8	14.4
20–24.99	0.0	20.3	1.7	0.0	9.7	7.0	6.8	9.0
25–29.99	0.0	13.0	1.7	0.0	3.2	4.3	2.3	5.2
30 and over	5.0	17.9	5.1	1.8	0.0	6.1	4.5	7.5
Total	100.0	100.0	100.0	100.0	100.0	100.0	100.0	100.0
0–10	60.0	14.7	45.8	56.4	40.3	48.7	63.6	41.2
0–15	80.0	31.0	78.0	80.0	72.6	70.4	79.5	63.8
No. of ratios	20	123	59	55	62	115	44	478

Source: Financial statements published in the North China Herald (1893 and 1897–1899 are not covered).

[a] Profits are recomputed according to modern accounting methods. Depreciation and bad debts, for instance, are regarded as expenses. Net worth includes not only paid-up capital but all surpluses. The recomputation is necessary because the published profit figures do not exclude depreciation, and capital includes only paid-up capital. For instance, using the published profit and capital figures, Sun reports that the rate of profit of the Shanghai Gas Company for 1879 was 23.4 percent (Sun Yu-tang, I, 181); according to the adjusted figures here, the rate was only 14 percent. (For the data, see North China Herald, April 1, 1880, p. 290. Depreciation and bad debts are deducted from the published profit figure and "depreciation fund" is added to capital stock to get net worth. Depreciation fund is regarded as earned surplus appropriated for expansion.)

representativeness is seriously limited by the small size of the sample (see section on reinvestment ratio above). Despite all these difficulties, it is believed that the published financial statements must have had some effect on foreign direct investment in China. In reaching a decision as to whether new investment should be made, the prospective investor must have made calculations with regard to expected rate of return, and the experiences of other firms as shown in their published financial statements must have exerted some influence in such calculations.

In terms of the data in Table 24, the profit-net worth ratios of

Table 25. Profit rates of Japanese firms in Manchuria, 1907–1937 (percent).

Year	Railroads of the SMR[a]	Entire SMR[b]	Principal manufacturing firms[c]	Average dividends[d]
1907	40.3	10.1	1.5	—
1908	23.3	—	1.4	—
1909	23.1	—	4.9	—
1910	16.9	—	7.3	—
1911	16.1	—	9.7	—
1912	17.2	—	16.7	—
1913	19.9	—	12.8	—
1914	20.3	—	20.5	—
1915	20.7	—	15.5	—
1916	25.5	—	26.9	—
1917	30.0	—	44.6	—
1918	26.3	—	57.1	15.6
1919	27.7	—	21.8	16.7
1920	29.2	34.2	14.6	11.0
1921	25.2	—	5.6	8.1
1922	28.3	—	7.0	8.2
1923	28.5	—	5.2	6.5
1924	26.5	—	2.3	5.2
1925	26.5	—	9.0	5.1
1926	27.5	—	4.4	5.0
1927	28.4	10.2	—	—
1928	29.8	—	—	—
1929	28.6	11.8	—	—
1930	21.7	—	—	—
1931	17.7	—	—	—
1932	23.8	15.8	—	—
1933	27.6	8.4	—	—
1934	25.3	8.5	—	—
1935	27.5	8.5	—	—
1936	26.7	8.1	—	—
1937	28.3	10.9	—	—
Weighted mean	25.5	10.4	9.0	—
Simple mean	25.3	12.7	14.4	9.0
Median	25.4	10.2	9.4	8.2

Source: For railroads of the SMR, see Reports on Progress in Manchuria prepared by the South Manchuria Railway Company, various issues. For the entire SMR, see Report on Progress in Manchuria, various years, and Japan Manchoukuo Yearbook, various years. For principal manufacturing firms, see W. H. Wang, p. 1107. For average dividends, see Manchuria Yearbook, 1931, p. 278.

[a] Percentage of profit on capital investment of the railroads of the South Manchuria Railway Company.

[b] Net profit as a percentage of paid-up capital of the South Manchuria Railway Company. In addition to railroads, the company operated coal mines, railroad workshops, harbors and wharves, warehouses, and hotels. It administered the railroad zone and conducted schools, hospitals, and various hygienic institutions. It controlled

foreign firms in China were mostly between 5 and 20 percent.[39] About 41 percent of the firms had a profit-net worth ratio of less than 10 percent, and about 64 percent of the firms had a profit-net worth ratio of less than 15 percent. Fabulous profits were made on occasion, as 13 percent of the firms had a profit-net worth ratio of 25 percent or higher. It may be specially noted that the manufacturing firms were among the lowest in profit rates; nearly half of them made a profit of less than 10 percent of their net worth.

The profit rates in Table 24 may be compared with other estimates. Remer is of the opinion that in years of ordinary prosperity American direct investment in China produced a return 10 percent to 20 percent and that there must have been a profit expectation above 10 percent to bring about such investments.[40] An expected return of 10 percent was also required to bring about British investments, and higher returns were both expected and received up to about 1910.[41]

Table 25 shows some estimates of the profit rates of Japanese investments in Manchuria, not covered in Table 24. The South Manchuria Railway Company evidently made very handsome profits on its railroads, averaging nearly 26 percent of total capital investment in the railroads for 1907 to 1937.[42] However, the profit rate on all the activities of the company together was considerably lower than that on its railroads, as shown in Table 25. The actual earning rate (profit-net worth ratio) of the company should be even lower than what is shown in Table 25, for net worth is usually larger than paid-up capital by the amount of earned or paid-in

---

Table 25 (continued)

a number of joint-stock companies, electric and gas works, shipping and dockyard companies, and several industrial concerns and factories. It also carried on a chemical research laboratory, a geological research institute, an economic research committee, and several experimental agricultural stations and farms. According to the *Fifth Report on Progress in Manchuria*, p. 70, the "capital outlays" of the company during 1907–1936 were distributed in various activities as follows: railroads, 38 percent; hotels, 0.7 percent; harbors, 12.5 percent; collieries, 14.9 percent; shale oil plant, 1.3 percent; local public works, 24 percent; others, 8.6 percent.

[c] Profit as a percentage of the paid-up capital of 77 Japanese manufacturers in Manchuria, excluding the South Manchuria Railway Company, shipping companies, and very small concerns.

[d] The average dividend (presumably as a percentage of paid-up capital) of the companies in Manchuria formed under the Japanese Commercial Code.

Table 26. Profit rates in Japan, the United States, and Great Britain (percent).

| Year | Great Britain[a] | | United States[b] | Japan[c] |
	All capital	Ordinary capital	Manufacturing	Dividend rates
1900	—	—	8.34	—
1901	—	—	7.72	—
1902	—	—	8.25	—
1903	—	—	7.57	—
1904	—	—	6.45	—
1905	—	—	7.09	—
1906	—	—	8.34	—
1907	—	—	7.90	—
1908	6.83	8.38	6.07	—
1909	7.74	9.40	6.89	—
1910	9.35	11.97	7.26	—
1911	9.95	12.82	7.10	—
1912	10.88	14.47	6.20	—
1913	11.53	16.08	6.16	—
1914	10.37	13.72	5.60	—
1915	12.39	17.46	—	—
1916	12.93	17.86	—	—
1917	12.88	17.43	—	—
1918	13.67	18.62	—	23.35
1919	14.60	19.92	18.3	20.50
1920	13.24	17.58	12.3	22.55
1921	6.81	7.75	2.9	14.50
1922	9.05	11.18	10.2	13.75
1923	9.94	12.67	11.2	12.40
1924	10.68	13.77	10.0	11.95
1925	11.37	14.91	12.1	11.20
1926	10.81	14.06	12.4	11.35
1927	10.84	14.07	9.5	—
1928	10.74	13.77	11.0	—
1929	10.56	13.44	—	—
1930	8.68	10.55	—	—
1931	5.73	6.18	—	—
1932	5.72	6.41	—	—
1933	6.69	7.92	—	—
1934	8.04	9.80	—	—
1935	9.05	11.51	—	—
1936	10.62	13.66	—	—
1937	12.10	15.83	—	—

Source: For Great Britain, see Hargreaves Parkinson, "British Industrial Profits," pp. 597–603. For the United States, 1900–1914, see Epstein and Gordon, pp. 122–128. For the United States, 1919–1928, see Ralph C. Epstein, p. 56. For Japan, see *Manchuria Yearbook, 1931*, p. 278.

[a] Profits (after debenture interests) as percentage of paid-up capital of British joint-stock companies. The figures include the results of all industries except banks, some home or foreign railroads, and gold or base-metal mining enterprises. The companies

surplus.[43] The same may be said of the profit rates (profit as a percentage of paid-up capital) of the 77 Japanese companies in Manchuria, excluding the South Manchuria Railway Company, as shown in Table 25.

Profit rates on foreign investment in China alone would not determine the inflow of capital to China. The rates of return on investment in the foreign investing countries were equally important. However, one faces an almost impossible task in selecting the relevant profit rates in the investing countries to compare with those in China. There was, as always, a certain degree of immobility and imperfection in the financial market; there was only a small group of people or business firms that had an interest in or would consider investing in China. There is also the question as to how much higher the profit rates had to be in China in order to induce investment. In spite of all these difficulties, the figures in Table 26 should provide enough grounds to question the often-held assertion that foreign enterprises in China reaped fabulous profits as compared with those in the investing countries. As is shown in Table 26, the rate of earnings on ordinary capital (common shares) of the British joint-stock companies in 1908–1937 ranged from 6.4 percent to 19.9 percent, with the mode being 13 percent. In the United States the profit rates of the manufacturing firms for 1919–1928 ranged from 3 to 18 percent, with an average of 11 percent.[44] Though not the same as profit rates, the dividend rates of the Japanese companies that averaged 16 percent in 1918–1926 should in the long run reflect their earning power and the expectations of the investors. Accordingly, the profit rates of foreign firms in China

---

Table 26 (continued)

covered were engaged mainly in domestic business. All capital includes both preferred and ordinary (common) stock.

[b] For 1900–1914 the figures refer to ratios of profits to net worth of 24 "industrial companies," makers of durable or nondurable goods. The figures represent the simple arithmetic averages (unweighted) of the profit ratios of the companies. The General Electric Company scored the highest ratio of 23.7 percent in 1902.

For 1919–1928 the figures refer to the ratios of income (before federal income tax) to capitalization of 2046 manufacturing corporations. The income-to-capitalization ratios are only slightly higher than the profit-to-total-capital ratios (before federal income tax) for 1924–1928, when the latter are available.

[c] Dividend rates (presumably dividends as percentage of paid-in capital) of the companies in Japan proper.

did not appear exceedingly high on the basis of what evidence is available.[45] This seems particularly true in the field of manufacturing.[46]

Role of the Merchant

An examination of the occupational distribution of foreign capital in China will reveal that a large portion of it was employed in fields related to foreign trade. In 1931, 27.8 percent of total foreign investment was used in the import-export business (14.9 percent), banking and finance (6.6 percent), and shipping (6.3 percent). An additional 4 percent was put into communications and public utilities, chiefly to serve foreign merchants and others residing in China. To all this may be added the investment in mining (4 percent) and manufacturing for export (1 percent).[47] Thus, nearly 37 percent of total foreign investment in China in 1931 was associated with Chinese external trade. In terms of direct investment, the fields related to trade became even more important. Investment in shipping, banking and finance, trading, and mining accounted for no less than 40 percent of total direct investment in 1931. Moreover, investment in real estate and public utilities (accounting for 18 percent of total direct investment) may have been made in part by foreign merchants. Investment in railroads — clearly politically motivated — accounted for about 16 percent of total direct investment; and only about 15 percent of total direct investment was employed in manufacturing, mainly import replacing.[48]

As described before, the foreign merchant was active in investment in almost all fields associated with trade. To carry on his main business, external trade, he had to see that the related fields were also being developed. He was also active in other fields. This was particularly true of the British trading firms that had been firmly established on the Chinese scene for decades, such as Arnhold & Co., Jardine, Matheson & Co., and Butterfield and Swire. Jardine, Matheson & Co. was perhaps most illustrative. It had investments in such divergent industries as silk reeling, packing, cold storage, engineering, shipping, shipyards, insurance, cotton textiles, and breweries, not to mention the loans it made to the Chinese government. While it cannot be ascertained how much of the total British direct investment in China was made by the trading firms, there is little doubt that the latter figured significantly. There were, of course, large British industrial firms that founded subsidiaries in China, such as the British-American Tobacco Company and the Lever Brothers, but these cases were few.

In the case of Japanese investment in China, the Japanese government was prominent for its control of the South Manchuria Railway Company. Private investments were made largely in fields related to trade and the manufacture of cotton textiles. Although the textile manufacturers in Japan were active in establishing cotton textile factories in China, the Japanese merchants who handled China's external trade in cotton and cotton textiles also figured significantly in Japanese investment in the Chinese textile industry.[49]

If foreign direct investments were primarily associated with China's external trade and if the trading firms figured importantly in such investments, it is not difficult to see why such investments could not be large. Investments of this type are obviously a function of external trade. The volume of external trade, as shown by the experiences of many countries, is a function of national income. When an economy remains underdeveloped, as the Chinese economy was, national income and external trade are small. Therefore investment is small. This is not to say that more trade cannot lead to more investment or more investment to more national income; but in order to increase national income, investments have to be made not in fields that simply facilitate trade but in fields that enlarge the capacity to produce for either home consumption or export. Foreign investments in both fields were small in China.[50]

Furthermore, the foreign merchant in China's external trade was not often the one who went to China with large capital. Instead, he made his fortune in China and by the device of reinvestment enlarged his business. This seems especially true of the British merchants. Jardine, Matheson & Co., founded as a small trading firm in the 1830's, became the largest trading company in China. Archibald Little, who came to China in 1859 as a tea taster for a German firm, later became an outstanding pioneer in trade (wool and bristles in particular), insurance, mining, and steam shipping.[51] Some American firms developed in the same manner. As Remer puts it, some of them "started on a shoe string" or were "built up from nothing." [52] Moreover, the merchant, though tireless to exploit opportunities for profit wherever available, was not unmindful of his main business — trade — and was always careful when diverting capital from trade into other investment. For example, when Edward Cunningham of Russell and Company, a leading trading firm in China, saw a profitable opportunity in shipping along the Yangtze River and the eastern coast, he could not convince his company to undertake the new venture; finally he had to seek capital from the Chinese and other foreign merchants residing in China to establish the Shanghai Steam Navigation Company in 1862. [53]

International Capital Movement

It may be of use at this point to describe briefly some aspects of international investment in general. International capital movement, though traceable to the Middle Ages, did not assume importance until after the beginning of the seventeenth century. [54] During the seventeenth and eighteenth centuries the Dutch, English, Spanish, and Portuguese were the important investors, with investments made largely in Europe. Merchants were the first foreign investors, and their investment was made mainly in connection with foreign trade, although, in some cases, government and private borrowings were also prominent.

By the beginning of the nineteenth century the British had become predominant in foreign investment and London was the financial center of the world. In the early years of the century, Europe and the United States received the greatest share of British capital, and government loans and railroad construction were the main fields in which British capital was employed. After 1850 France made rapid strides in the domain of finance, to be followed somewhat later by Germany. By the end of the nineteenth century the United States had also begun to show a capacity to export capital on a large scale.

From 1874 to 1914 the long-term foreign investments of the United Kingdom, France, and Germany increased from US$6 billion to US$33 billion — a rate of increase never surpassed in the history of international investment. During the fifty years before

1914 Great Britain invested abroad about 4 percent of her national income. From 1905 to 1913 the proportion was 7 percent. At its peak in 1913 foreign investment took over half the total of British savings.[55] At the outbreak of the First World War the approximate value of long-term foreign investments by the principal creditor countries was about US$44 billion; of this total, the United Kingdom held 41 percent; France, 20 percent; Germany, 13 percent; and the others (notably the United States, Belgium, the Netherlands, and Switzerland) 26 percent.[56]

What accounted for this "golden age" of international investment in the few decades before 1914? Undoubtedly the relative political stability and the widespread adoption of the gold standard, assuring exchange stability, had their share in contributing to the boom.[57] However, a closer look at the capital-receiving countries will reveal that this period was a rather exceptional one in economic history. Roughly two thirds of British capital exported before 1914 went to the so-called "regions of recent settlement": the spacious, fertile, and virtually empty plains of Canada, the United States, Argentina, Australia, and other new countries in the world's temperate latitudes.[58] A unique feature was the fact that the export of capital to these places was accompanied by a migration of about sixty million people, including many trained and enterprising persons from Europe.[59] Only about a quarter of British export capital went to what are known today as the low-income, often densely populated, truly underdeveloped economies.[60]

Of the total British overseas investments in publicly issued securities at the end of 1913, which amounted to some £3763 million, 30 percent was in the form of government and municipal loans, 41 percent in railroads, 5 percent in other public utilities, 10 percent in raw materials, 6 percent in commerce and industry, and 8 percent in banks and finance.[61] The government and municipal loans were used primarily in railroad construction, public utilities, and road and harbor works.

The British capital that went to the "regions of recent settlement" was mainly in the form of securities with a fixed rate of return and was used primarily in the development of public utilities, especially railroads. Very little was employed in primary production, although it may be said that the investment in public utilities was induced by the raw material needs of the industrial centers — especially by the British demand for wheat, wool, meat, and dairy products.[62] In the underdeveloped economies foreign capital was used to develop not only railroads and other public utilities but also the extractive industries — mines, plantations, oil wells — for export, mainly to the industrial centers. It is this type of investment that is known as "colonial" foreign investment.[63]

International capital movement resumed its normal course during the 1920's after the disruption of the First World War. The capital importers were principally the developed or semideveloped countries, such as Germany, Czechoslovakia, Italy, Argentina, and Australia, while the underdeveloped countries received much less, either absolutely or relative to their population.[64] In the 1930's international capital movement was virtually brought to a standstill.

The Crucial Factors

With the above background in mind, it is impossible to link together the various elements that explain why the amount of foreign investment in China was small. China obviously did not have the characteristics possessed by the "recent regions of settlement." In the cultivable areas she was already densely populated; and above all, she had developed a civilization that was sophisticated and integrated enough to make it difficult for any alien culture to penetrate. There was no appreciable immigration to China.

China's fate was therefore different from many other underdeveloped economies. Though a target of exploitation by the Western powers, China never became a colony. Thanks to the international power struggle, she managed to maintain her sovereignty, even though infringed upon in certain respects. While the powers were free to pursue whatever economic activities they chose in their respective colonies, in China they were confined mainly to the treaty ports. For economic activities outside of these ports, such as construction of railroads, mining, plantations, they had to negotiate with the Chinese government. Despite setbacks, China was mainly successful in stopping foreign economic penetration in the interior. The restrictive mining regulations were not repealed or substantively modified, despite foreign demands. With the exception of missionaries, foreign nationals were not permitted to own or lease land outside the treaty ports.[65]

Whether a substantial amount of foreign capital would have gone to mining or agriculture in the absence of such restrictions is of course a matter of speculation. Mineral reserves, especially coal, were not lacking, but transportation lines would have had to be built. Agricultural products such as tea, cotton, sericulture, or tobacco could have been developed on a large scale, but it would have been a formidable task to organize the Chinese farmers and refashion their practices. The fact remains that the Chinese resistance was an important obstacle to foreign attempts to invest in primary production in China.

It is true that in some cases there was foreign penetration in Chinese agriculture. For instance, the South Manchuria Railway Company introduced and cultivated rice along its railroad lines in Manchuria. Certain Japanese cotton merchants had some success, at times, in improving cotton by distributing American cotton seeds to the Chinese farmers in North China. The British-American Tobacco Company tried in Hupeh, Shantung, Anhwei, and Honan to improve the quality of the Chinese tobacco leaf by distributing American seed and teaching the farmers improved methods.[66] However, these efforts were limited in scope and had little effect on Chinese agriculture in general.

Why was the amount of foreign investment no larger in the treaty ports, where foreigners were protected by extraterritorial rights? Investments directly in connection with China's external trade could not be large because the volume of trade was small, a concomitance of the low level of national income. No substantial amount of foreign investment was made in manufacturing because it was not as profitable as expected. For the products that the Chinese masses could afford to buy, the traditional handicrafts proved to be a stubborn and effective competitor of modern technology. (This point will be discussed in Chapter 7.) For the products that were beyond the reach of traditional technology, the market was limited because of the lack of adequate transportation and the poverty and low purchasing power of the masses. China was no exception to the general rule that foreign capital tended to shy away from manufacturing for native consumption in the underdeveloped economies. As emphasized by Nurkse, the lack of purchasing power of the native masses offered no inducement to such investment.[67]

Chapter 6

Foreign Investment and Economic Modernization

Indicators of Economic Modernization

Before 1937 China was an economically underdeveloped or low-income country, as it still is today.[1] This is not to say that there was economic stagnation in the sense of a lack of any change in economic organization or structure. A closer look at the components of the economy shows unquestionably that there was a significant trend toward "economic modernization" before 1937. For instance, China had almost no railroads before 1866, but possessed about 13,000 miles of them in 1937. Chinese-owned steamers totaled only 20,000 to 30,000 tons in the 1880's, but had increased to 675,000 in 1935. There was only one Chinese-owned modern bank in 1896, while by 1937 there were 164, with 1,627 branches. In 1918 capital invested in native banks formed more than 80 percent of the total capital investment in Chinese banks,[2] whereas in 1934 it formed no more than 30 percent. Modern mines, which were nonexistent before the 1870's, produced 77 percent of the country's coal in 1933 and 82 percent of its iron ore in 1935–1937. In 1933 more than a million workers were employed in factories, with about 3 million in the modern sector of the economy.[3] According to the annual reports of the Ministry of Agriculture and Commerce, there were 977 Chinese-owned business concerns organized in corporate form in 1912, with a total capital investment of about Chin$111 million; by the end of 1937 the number of such firms was 2,900, with a total paid-up capital of Chin$870 million.[4] The cumulative value of imported machines has been estimated at £6 million in 1912, £106.7 million in 1932, and £130.6 million in 1938.[5]

The rates of growth of some key modern industries in China are given in Table 27. Contrary to common belief, the modern sector of the economy grew continuously, not sporadically. All the indi-

Table 27. Rates of growth of the modern sector of the Chinese economy before 1937.[a]

Indicator	Period	Annual rates in percent (compound)[b]
Physical quantity of imports	1867–1932	2.5
Physical quantity of exports	1867–1932	2.4
Railroad mileage[c]	1894–1911	22.1
	1911–1935	2.2
	1894–1937	10.3
Tonnage of Chinese-owned foreign steamers[d]	1882–1910	5.1
	1910–1924	11.2
	1928–1935	12.8
Pig iron production of modern mines	1900–1937	9.8
Coal production of modern mines	1912–1936	8.2
Cotton yarn spindles	1890–1936	11.6
Loans of Chinese modern banks	1921–1936	12.3

Source: For imports and exports, see Nankai Social and Economic Quarterly (July 1937); for railroads (1894–1935), see Chang Chia-nau, Pt. 1; the 1937 railroad figure is from Yen Chung-p'ing, ed., T'ung-chi tzu-liao, p. 190; for steamers, iron and coal mines, and cotton mills, see ibid., pp. 227–229, 102–103, 134–135; for banks, see Bank of China, An Analysis of the Accounts of the Principal Chinese Banks, 1921–1931, and Bank of China, Ch'üan-kuo yin-hang nien-chien, 1936.

[a] Manchuria included, except for cotton yarn spindles after 1931.

[b] All trends are fitted by the freehand method except imports and exports, which are fitted by the method of least squares. All trends appear obvious when plotted in a semilogarithmic scale.

[c] For railroads, there were apparently two trends: 1894–1911 and 1911–1935. Although no single trend can be easily fitted for the entire period 1894–1937, the growth rate based on the mileage in the first and last years is reasonably indicative of the general development. Railroad mileage for various years was assumed to be as follows:

Year	Miles
1894	195
1903	2,708
1911	5,796
1914	6,052
1920	6,856
1926	7,683
1935	9,773
1937	13,042

[d] Three trends are calculated for steamers because no single series is available.

cators (except railroads) in Table 27 display a linear trend when plotted in a semilogarithmic scale, showing a constant rate of growth in the long run. This was achieved despite drastic changes on the political scene: the Manchu government (up to 1911), the Peking government (1912–1926), and the National government

(1927–1937). It does not seem entirely baseless, therefore, to assume that in the modern sector of the Chinese economy there were fundamental forces at work, pointing to a cumulative development. What brought about the development of the modern sector of the Chinese economy? It is my contention that important links may be found between this development and the penetration of foreign economic forces as represented by trade, investment, and related activities.

Share of Foreign Capital

The most obvious link between foreign investment and China's economic modernization was that the former not only performed the pioneering entrepreneurial function of introducing modern technology into a number of fields but actually financed a large share of the modern sector of the economy. For instance, railroads were in the main either foreign-owned or built with foreign loans. According to one calculation, railroads under foreign control (foreign ownership or control through loans) accounted for as much as 78, 93, and 98 percent of all railroads in China (Manchuria included) in 1894, 1911, and 1927 respectively. The percentage went down to 74 in 1931, but went up again to 91 in 1937 after Japan had built more railroads in Manchuria.[6]

In water transportation, too, foreign capital remained predominant, as shown in Table 28. The figures in Table 28 refer to steamers only; Chinese junks and foreign sailing vessels are not included. However, the situation would not change materially by the latter's inclusion.[7] As expected, the Chinese share in domestic shipping (between Chinese ports) was higher than its share in foreign shipping (between a foreign and a Chinese port). If junks and sailing vessels are included, the Chinese share in domestic shipping increases from 23 percent in 1909–1913 to 28 percent in 1925–1929, 30 percent in 1930–1934, and about 36 percent in 1935–36.[8]

Foreign capital also dominated iron and coal mining. It was present in virtually all modern iron mines and works through either Sino-foreign joint ownership or loans. Almost 100 percent of the pig iron and 95–100 percent of the iron ore that was produced by modern iron mines in China before 1937 came from mines that were financed wholly or in part by foreign capital. Modern mines

Table 28. Foreign share in the modern sector of the Chinese economy (percent).

Year[a]	Total shipping[b]	Yangtze shipping[c]	Cotton yarn spindles[d]	Coal[e]	Iron ore[f]	Pig iron[g]
1897	77	—	41	—	—	—
1902	83	—	37	—	—	100
1903	—	73	37	—	—	100
1907	84	—	34	—	—	100
1914	—	77	46	90	100	100
1916	78	—	—	80	100	100
1918	77	79	43	77	100	100
1920	76	—	42	77	100	100
1922	76	—	37	78	100	100
1924	79	76	40	76	100	100
1926	80	—	—	78	99	95
1928	78	77	43	78	99	96
1930	83	78	43	76	99	99
1934	—	77	43	80	99	96
1936	—	82	46	66	99	97

Source: Yen Chung-p'ing, ed., T'ung-chi tzu-liao, pp. 123–124, 127–129, 134–135, 221–222, 248.

[a] For the sake of space a number of years are omitted, which might affect the trends slightly.

[b] Tonnage of steamers entered and cleared through maritime customs (sailing vessels not included).

[c] Including the China Merchant's Steam Navigation Company and the three largest foreign shipping companies in China: Butterfield, Swire & Co., Jardine, Matheson & Co., and Nishin Kisen Kaisha.

[d] Fifty percent of the Sino-foreign jointly owned mills are included. Only spindles in operation are included. Manchuria not included after 1932. Handicrafts not included.

[e] Modern (machine-using) mines only. Includes mines that were completely foreign-owned and that were Sino-foreign jointly owned or controlled through loans. Completely foreign-owned mines accounted for 20–25 percent (1912–1925) and 28–40 percent (1926–1937) of total mine production, including "native" or small mines; or 43–31 percent (1912–1925) and 41–50 percent (1926–1937) of the production of modern mines. Manchuria included.

[f] Modern mines only. Includes mines that were Sino-foreign jointly owned or that had a large amount of foreign loans. Mines with foreign loans accounted for 100 percent in 1912–1914, 91.4 percent in 1915, 80 percent in 1925, 43 percent in 1935, and 22 percent in 1937. Manchuria included.

[g] Modern mines only. Includes mines that were Sino-foreign jointly owned or that had a large amount of foreign loans. Mines with heavy foreign loans accounted for 100 percent of the foreign share in 1900–1914, 82 percent in 1915, 52 percent in 1920, 28 percent in 1925, and became insignificant after 1925. Manchuria included.

accounted for 82 percent and 77 percent, respectively, of total pig iron and iron ore production in 1933.[9]

More than one half of the total output of coal from 1912 to 1937 was produced by mines that were either completely foreign-owned or controlled by means of co-ownership or large loans. If only the coal that was mined with the use of modern machines is included, the proportion is even larger, ranging from 92 percent in 1912 to 66 percent in 1936.

In each of a number of manufacturing industries of the factory type — such as sawmills; shipbuilding; water, gas, and electric works; tanneries; and makers of cigarettes, soda water, and egg products — foreign-owned firms accounted for more than 50 percent of the total output in 1933; although the ratio was only 35 percent for the manufacturing industries as a whole (Table 29).[10]

Table 29. Gross products of factory industries in China, 1933.[a]

Industry	Chinese		Foreign		Total	
	No. of factories	Value of product (Chin$ millions)[b]	No. of factories	Value of product (Chin$ millions)[b]	No. of factories	Value of product (Chin$ millions)
Woodworking	18	3.8 (20)	48	14.7 (80)	66	18.5
Machine works	222	20.1 (61)	40	12.7 (39)	262	32.7
Metal	82	61.0 (92)	17	5.4 (8)	99	66.4
Electrical instruments	5	11.3 (57)	19	8.4 (43)	74	19.7
Transportation	29	5.2 (43)	16	7.1 (57)	45	12.3
Bricks, earthenware, etc.	105	15.4 (51)	64	14.7 (49)	169	30.1
Water, gas, electricity	603	117.5 (47)	65	133.3 (53)	668	250.8
Chemicals	159	77.5 (68)	78	36.2 (32)	237	113.7
Textile	808	592.5 (67)	72	294.1 (33)	880	886.5
Cotton fluffing and ginning	*26*	*11.4*	*5*	*2.0*	*31*	*13.4*
Cotton spinning	*87*	*384.2*	*44*	*280.7*	*131*	*664.9*
Cotton weaving	*317*	*85.5*	*7*	*0.7*	*324*	*86.2*
Silk reeling	*136*	*47.3*	*5*	*1.0*	*141*	*48.2*
Silk weaving	*204*	*41.8*	*0*	*0.0*	*204*	*41.8*
Wool spinning and weaving	*38*	*22.3*	*8*	*6.6*	*46*	*28.9*
Linen weaving	*0*	*0.0*	*3*	*3.1*	*3*	*3.1*
Clothing	165	37.5 (88)	15	5.2 (12)	180	42.7
Leather, rubber	85	38.2 (76)	28	11.9 (24)	113	50.2
Food, drink, tobacco	493	377.5 (65)	136	208.2 (35)	629	585.7
Paper, printing	37	47.6 (74)	50	17.0 (26)	287	64.6
Scientific and musical instruments	74	5.6 (90)	6	0.6 (10)	80	6.2
Miscellaneous	32	4.8 (82)	20	1.0 (18)	52	5.8
Total	3167	1415.5 (65)	674	770.7 (35)	3841	2186.2

Source: Ou Pao-san, "So-te hsiu-cheng," pp. 130–133.

[a] Manchuria included, but not Hong Kong. A factory is defined as a manufacturing firm with more than thirty employees and using power.

[b] Percent of the total value of the product is in parentheses.

In cotton textiles, the most important light industry in China before 1937, foreign mills accounted for more than 40 percent of total yarn spindles and nearly 70 percent of all looms during the 1930's (handicrafts not included).

Finally, as noted before, the largest part (perhaps as high as 90 percent as late as 1930) of China's import-export trade and other international transactions was handled by foreign banks and import-export firms in China. There is no doubt, therefore, that foreign capital was dominant in the modern sector of the Chinese economy. While it may be charged that the economy (at least its modern sector) was too much controlled by foreigners and that its destiny was in the hands of the powers with conflicting interests,[11] the fact remains that foreign capital was largely responsible for the development of whatever economic modernization took place in China before 1937.[12] Foreign capital was responsible for the initial appearance of most modern industries; and there were practically no modern industries in which foreign capital was not to be found.

The Chinese Response: Retaliation Effect

The growth of the modern sector of the Chinese economy was not the product of foreign capital alone, however dominant the latter may have been. Chinese capital and entrepreneurship also contributed to this growth, as the Chinese shares in various industries testify. The crucial questions are: what brought about the Chinese efforts toward economic modernization in China? Did foreign economic penetration retard or promote these efforts?

One of the most important effects of economic intercourse with the West was the change of attitude of the Chinese government toward economic affairs. It is true that the Chinese government had always been concerned with the national economy, although the degree and extent of government intervention is still a subject for further research, but conscientious efforts to modernize the economy so as to make the country militarily strong and to catch up with the Western industrial economies did not seem to begin until the latter part of the nineteenth century, after China had been greatly humiliated by the foreign powers. The extraterritorial rights, the leased areas, the treaty ports, the spheres of interest, the foreign troops, the treaty tariff, and other features of unequal treaties all served to strengthen Chinese antiforeign sentiment. The fact that foreign powers always demanded economic privileges after each military victory could only lead the Chinese to regard the presence of foreign businessmen on Chinese soil as a symbol of invasion. Their fear of foreign domination was aggravated by the mercantilist belief that whatever profit foreign traders and investors made was at the expense of the Chinese.[13] They further feared that foreign economic penetration would cause many Chinese to lose their livelihood and would upset the Chinese economy. Because of these fears, the Chinese government began to adopt measures to modernize the economy in order to counterbalance foreign economic influence.

First, the government tried to develop the manufacture of ammunition and weapons in the hope that China would become militarily strong enough to defend herself against foreign invasion or to drive out the foreigners from Chinese soil. In the 1860's, some ten arsenals and dockyards were constructed by the government. Then it was realized that the way to counterbalance foreign economic penetration was to adopt economic countermeasures. For instance, the declared purpose of the establishment in 1873 of the China Merchant's Steam Navigation Company was to compete with foreign shipping in China. In addition to establishing state enterprises, the government now adopted the formula of "official supervising and merchant undertaking" (Kuan-tu shang-pan).[14] According to this formula, the government was to exercise initiative and supervision while the private businessman supplied capital and business skill. The result was not impressive, for between 1870 and 1900 only a dozen or so enterprises were formed under this arrangement in the fields of mining, textiles, communications, and banking.[15]

The total expenditure of official funds for all the enterprises, either government-owned or merely receiving government loans, was probably a few million taels a year in the 1860's and 1870's and close to 10 million in the 1890's.[16] Such sums were very small indeed in terms of the total population or total national income, but they were by no means small as compared with the total revenue of the Chinese government (at the central level), which has been estimated to be as low as 60 to 70 million taels in the

1860's and 1870's, and 80 to 90 million in the 1890's.[17] As a result of the indemnities imposed on China in 1895 and 1900, the financial condition of the Chinese government became even worse; a budgetary deficit was a constant phenomenon in the closing years of the Manchu regime. This financial background should be borne in mind in evaluating the performance of the Imperial government. It should be noted that the Meiji government, which has been credited so much for its important role in Japan's economic development, allocated no more than 5.5 percent of its ordinary revenue for industrial investment from 1868 to 1881.[18]

It is true that in the case of China only a small proportion of the total expenditure on modern enterprises was drawn from the central Imperial government; the largest part was provided by the provincial governments. Although their combined revenue was perhaps nearly twice as much as that of the imperial treasury, the provincial governments were equally tight financially. After 1895 they frequently had to resort to printing paper money in order to meet the increased demand from the central government.

Whether the Chinese government could have introduced drastic financial, fiscal, or other reforms to raise its revenue and undertake economic projects on a larger scale is, of course, a matter of speculation or opinion. As it was, there is little doubt that the shortage of funds was a factor of primary importance in limiting the economic activities of the state. It can even be argued that the shortage of funds was mainly responsible for the slow growth of the established enterprises, as indicated by the constant complaints of financial difficulties by the officials who were connected with government-controlled enterprises. The fact that the enterprises often had to rely upon funds borrowed at high interest rates (probably 8 or 9 percent a year) and that they sometimes received demands for funds from the official bureaucracy (Feuerwerker calls these "official exactions") was testimony to the fiscal inability of the government to develop them.[19]

In its efforts to strengthen itself the government did not limit itself to establishing industrial enterprises. In addition to founding language and technical schools and sending students abroad,[20] the government made adjustment in laws and regulations to offset foreign economic influence. At the suggestion of Li Hung-chang in

1882, factory-produced cotton goods were exempted from the burdensome inland transit tax, and later this exemption was extended to all machine-produced articles. Monopoly rights in a certain area and for a certain period were granted to those who introduced Western-type manufactures. In 1898 a regulation was issued by which inventors were assured of patents and founders of modern educational undertakings such as schools, libraries, or museums were to be rewarded with official ranks or titles.[21]

In 1903 the Ministry of Commerce was finally set up for the purpose of promoting domestic commerce and industry. According to the regulations of 1903, 1906, and 1907 promoters and founders of modern corporations or enterprises were to be rewarded with official ranks. Efforts were also made to encourage the consumption of commodities produced by Chinese factories.[22] In 1914 the government went so far as to guarantee dividends at about 5 or 6 percent of paid-up capital to stockholders of certain industrial corporations.[23] Measures to examine and improve the quality of goods were also attempted. For instance, the improvement of hats by a firm in Szechwan and of ink by a firm in Hopei were undertaken under the guidance of the government.

The extent to which all of these measures was effective remains a question. No definite answer can be given in terms of our existing knowledge of the processes of change within the Chinese economy during the modern era. For instance, a great deal more research must be done on the operation and development of the enterprises that the imperial government helped to establish.[24] However, in view of the limited financial resources that the government could mobilize for development purposes, it is probable that their efforts had no important direct impact on the economy.

On the other hand, during the 1860's and 1870's when some far-sighted officials realized the need to modernize the country if its political integrity was to be maintained, there was still enormous opposition both in and out of the government.[25] The fact that the officials were able to obtain the approval of the court to adopt their programs was itself a great triumph over the "conservatives." If their policies did not result in the establishment of an industrial base, they surely awakened the country to the need for economic change and weakened the forces hostile to such change. The measures that were adopted upon their insistence also undoubtedly helped to create an atmosphere that encouraged private individuals to undertake economic modernization. Therefore, while the government took the initiative in founding new industries before the 1890's, private enterprises became predominant in later periods, as shown in Table 30. In terms of the capital of the modern industries established each year, it was not until 1894 that the completely privately owned enterprises began to outrun the government-owned or supervised ones.

The conditions under which this change took place were complicated, but there seems to be no doubt that the Movement of Recovering Economic Interests, a symptom of the growing nationalism, was a contributing factor. During the few years from 1903 to 1908 when the movement was at its peak, no less than 265 corporations were formed by private individuals, with a total capital of Chin$126 million.[26] The bylaws of many corporations explicitly stated that the purpose of their establishment was to resist foreign economic influence in China, and that no foreign capital was to be permitted to participate in the firms.

In short, the Chinese had long had a sense of superiority concerning their own culture and opposed any foreign penetration. The manner in which foreign powers promoted their economic interests in China could only sharpen the Chinese opposition. To a large extent, the desire to counterbalance or retaliate against foreign economic influence prompted the Chinese government and people to attempt to modernize the country. An industrialist was no longer despised, even in theory, but rather was regarded as a patriot. Foreign investment — a symbol of foreign invasion — supplied the fuel for nationalism, and the nationalistic spirit provided the will to develop modern industries. In this paradoxical manner foreign investment, though feared as an evil, actually contributed to China's economic modernization.

Imitation Effect

Foreign investment encouraged economic modernization in ways other than the negative ones described above. First, it helped establish an environment in which one could expect profits from industrial undertakings. Foreign factories were the precursors of

Table 30. Total capital of new Chinese and Sino-foreign joint enterprises in mining and manufacturing, 1872–1911 (Chin$ thousands).[a]

Year	Private	Government and govern-ment-private joint enter-prises[b]	Sino-foreign joint enter-prises	Total No. of new firms	Capital
1872	36.0	—	—	1	36.0
1876	—	661.9	—	3	661.9
1877	139.9	—	—	1	139.9
1878	—	2,055.9	—	1	2,055.9
1880	—	28.0	—	1	28.0
1881	159.9	—	629.4	3	789.2
1882	32.0	939.9	—	3	971.9
1883	136.0	—	—	2	136.0
1884	385.7	—	—	3	385.7
1885	30.0	419.6	—	2	449.6
1886	66.0	—	—	2	66.0
1887	129.9	811.2	—	4	941.1
1888	140.0	—	—	5	140.0
1889	185.9	7,272.7	—	7	7,458.7
1890	449.7	755.2	—	7	1,204.9
1891	329.8	741.3	—	7	1,071.0
1892	206.9	1,342.7	—	6	1,549.6
1893	363.8	—	—	8	363.8
1894	2,013.0	1,174.8	—	8 .	3,187.8
1895	3,729.9	489.5	—	17	4,219.4
1896	1,322.9	1,516.7	699.3	13	3,539.0
1897	4,730.4	1,188.9	—	16	5,919.2
1898	2,088.1	1,200.0	699.3	15	3,987.4
1899	1,536.7	—	6,403.4	11	7,940.2
1900	3,014.1	—	83.9	10	3,098.0
1901	100.0	—	279.7	5	379.7
1902	1,191.6	3,182.0	902.3	15	5,275.9
1903	432.8	57.3	109.1	9	599.3
1904	4,793.0	429.9	—	23	5,223.0
1905	7,810.3	424.1	6,579.0	54	14,813.4
1906	12,987.8	5,414.7	2,875.9	64	21,278.4
1907	8,259.4	3,672.9	2,640.7	50	14,573.0
1908	15,352.5	3,292.0	3,882.8	52	22,527.3
1909	3,972.3	5,883.8	91.2	29	9,947.3
1910	4,289.8	569.9	85.0	25	4,944.7
1911	1,238.8	251.8	800.0	14	2,290.5
Unknown	6,897.6	—	564.6	25	7,462.2

Source: Yen Chung-p'ing, ed., T'ung-chi tzu-liao, p. 93. As Yen admits, this is only a preliminary estimate.

[a] Including modern manufacturing firms with a capital over Chin$10,000 and all modern mines.

[b] Including kuan-tu shang-pan enterprises.

many industries and performed an important entrepreneurial function. As time went on, the Chinese began to follow suit and started the same manufactures, as in silk reeling, flour milling, printing, and the making of cigarettes, machines, and enamelware.[27] Second, when foreign factories were started in China, the operators employed were Chinese, who thus acquired the necessary techniques. The Chinese were then able to open factories and employ operatives who had gained training and knowledge in foreign factories.[28] Third, owing to the existence of foreign factories, progress was made in the technique of Chinese manufacturing. Silk reeling and spinning are cases in point.[29]

Special mention should be made here of the compradores who served as representatives of foreign firms in conducting business with the Chinese.[30] They not only acquired knowledge about Western enterprises but also earned a very handsome income from the foreign firms in China. This was the group that was first called upon to operate the government-sponsored modern enterprises and that figured prominently in the establishment of Western-type enterprises.

The compradores were not alone in imitating foreign firms and opening up modern enterprises. Bureaucrats, merchants, and to a lesser degree landlords also began to invest in varying degrees in Western-type enterprises.[31] The Schumpeterian innovator (the foreign firm in this case) was indeed followed by a "cluster" of Chinese imitators. Furthermore, the occasional visits by leading Chinese officials to foreign firms in China must also have had an important impact on their thinking on modernization.

The change in their use of savings by bureaucrats and landlords was important. Traditionally the chief fields in which they had used their savings were land and usury. However, the purchase of land was unproductive and undesirable from the social point of view, for in the final analysis the sellers of land were usually the poor and the small farmers, who did not sell from a profit motive but rather because they needed money to finance such events as marriage, illness, funerals, or other emergencies, or to pay debts that had usually been incurred for these purposes. Therefore, the purchase of land by the rich simply represented a transfer of ownership; no real investment resulted.

Linkage Effects

An important aspect of economic development is the process of one thing leading to another. For instance, when a railroad is built, it stimulates the development of those industries that supply materials to railroads. This may be called the backward linkage effect. The development of the railroad will also reduce transportation costs and make it possible for many industries to grow because of access to a larger market. This may be called the forward linkage effect.[32] From the viewpoint of economic development these induced or linkage effects are more important than the profits made by the railroad directly.

Foreign investment in China undoubtedly originated in China's foreign trade. As late as 1931 no less than one third of total foreign investment was made for the purpose of promoting external trade, and for earlier years the percentage was undoubtedly higher. However, the effects of foreign investment were certainly not confined to the trade sector; they were spread into other sectors by means of the linkages.

The first economic contact between foreigners and Chinese was through trade, and it did not take long before shipyards were built to repair the trading ships. Banks were opened to finance the trade, export and import processing was developed, and public utilities were founded.

Mines were worked to supply the coal for steamers as well as for export; but to transport the minerals, railroads had to be developed. Their development in turn reduced the cost of transportation, increased the extent of the market for both imported and domestic products, and made more products available for export. The increase of imports established a market for many articles, which were then produced in China in order to take advantage of cheap local labor and raw materials. The opening up of a market was perhaps the most important function of trade in economic modernization. This was especially so in the case of textiles, the most important manufacture in China before 1937.

The cumulative nature of development resulting from the linkages was certainly not confined to foreign enterprise; Chinese-owned enterprises were also affected. The establishment of foreign enterprises in the open ports provided many external economies from which the Chinese-owned enterprises could also benefit. The development of transportation (shipping and railroads), in which foreign capital figured so importantly, undoubtedly created profitable opportunities for Chinese-owned firms. The presence of foreign firms and nationals must also have created demands for a variety of goods or services that the Chinese could supply.

In addition, foreign as well as Chinese investment in the modern sector created employment opportunities for many who either had been employed in less productive fields or were simply unemployed. Their purchasing power was thus increased, enlarging the market for a variety of modern enterprises. By increasing the volume of China's foreign trade, foreign investment also created bright profit opportunity for Chinese merchants, who conducted trade on an intra- and interprovincial level.[33] Like the compradores, the merchants also took part in the establishment of modern industries in China, especially after the First World War.

Coexistence of Chinese and Foreign Enterprises

While the dominant position of foreign capital in the Chinese economy has been made clear, the same data should reveal another equally important phenomenon — namely, that the Chinese share remained remarkably stable in the long run. For the most part there was a persistent coexistence between Chinese and foreign enterprises in the modern sector of the economy during the years before 1937.

For example, in the construction of railroads, although an accurate measurement is unavailable, it seems certain that relatively more Chinese capital was used as time went by.[34] The Chinese share in total shipping — including steamers, sailing vessels, and junks, traveling between a Chinese and foreign port or between Chinese ports — suffered a decline from 30.4 percent in 1880 to 19.3 percent in 1900. Thereafter, the Chinese share gradually went up until it reached 30.5 percent in 1936 (Manchuria not included for 1936). For shipping between Chinese ports, the Chinese share increased from 23.2 percent in 1909–1913 to 36.9 percent in 1936 (Manchuria not included for 1936). For steamers alone (between a Chinese and foreign port or between Chinese ports), after an initial decline from 1877 to 1892 the Chinese trend appeared to be stabilized at about 23 percent. For shipping in the Yangtze, the position of the China Merchant's Steam Navigation Company vis-à-vis its three largest foreign competitors also appeared stable from 1910 to 1936.

In mining, although foreign-controlled mines remained overwhelmingly predominant in the production of iron ore and pig iron, the entirely Chinese-owned modern mines made modest progress in the production of coal. After a low start at 8 percent in 1912, their share of the total production fluctuated between 20 and 34.3 percent, entering a modest rising trend from 1916 to 1937.

In terms of cotton yarn spindles, Chinese-owned mills accounted for 60 to 70 percent of the total in 1897–1912, and then their share was stabilized between 53 and 60 percent for 1913–1936 — except 1921 and 1922, when their share was 66 and 63 percent respectively. In cotton yarn production the Chinese share, after an apparent decline for the few years immediately after the First World War, rose from 58 percent in 1927 to 71 percent in 1936.[35] In cotton looms the trend of the Chinese share appeared stable after foreign participation in 1913, but experienced a slightly downward development in the 1930's. In thread spindles the Chinese share, having been 100 percent in 1920–1924, dropped to 41 percent in 1925 and then settled in the neighborhood of 32 percent in the 1930's.

No data are available to indicate the trend of the Chinese share for manufacturing as a whole. The fact that the foreign share, in terms of gross products, was held to 35 percent in 1933 would seem to suggest that Chinese-owned enterprises had made long-term progress. As noted before, it was the foreign firms that had pioneered in many of the manufacturing industries. In the field of financing, though late in starting, Chinese-owned modern banks scored important gains in the 1930's. The same, perhaps, may be said of trading firms.

The fact of coexistence between foreign and Chinese enterprises implies that the latter were able to grow as fast as the former over the long run. Since the mortality rates of Chinese firms (of foreign firms too, for that matter) are not known in general, it is difficult to ascertain the extent to which the apparent ability of the Chinese

Table 31. Growth records of several Chinese-owned enterprises.

Year	Jung Ts'ung-Ching Textile Mills (thousands of spindles)[a]	Ta-sheng Textile Mill (thousands of spindles)	Nanyang Brothers Tobacco Co. (thousands of cigarette chests)[b]
1899	—	20.4	—
1900	—	20.4	—
1901	—	20.4	—
1902	—	20.4	—
1903	—	20.4	—
1904	—	40.7	—
1905	—	40.7	—
1906	—	40.7	—
1907	—	66.7	—
1908	—	66.7	—
1909	—	66.7	—
1910	—	66.7	—
1911	—	66.7	—
1912	—	66.7	4.8
1913	—	66.7	7.0
1914	—	—	10.5
1915	—	—	18.6
1916	13.0	—	26.2
1917	30.0	—	33.8
1918	30.0	—	37.0
1919	39.0	—	—
1920	64.0	—	—
1921	74.7	—	—
1922	134.7	—	—
1923	134.7	—	—
1924	139.7	—	—
1925	173.4	—	—
1926	173.4	—	106.9
1927	180.5	—	121.0
1928	190.8	—	85.0
1929	307.3	—	—
1930	397.4	—	—
1931	526.8	—	—
1932	536.8	—	98.7
1933	529.8	—	116.5
1934	556.3	—	113.1
1935	555.0	—	109.9
1936	567.2	—	97.8

Source: For Jung Ts'ung-Ching Textile Mills, see Yen Chung-p'ing, ed., *T'ung-chi tzu-liao*, p. 164. For Ta-Sheng Textile Mill, see Wang Ching-yü, II, 1075. For Nanyang Brothers Tobacco Co., see *Nanyang hsiung-ti yen-ts'ao kung-ssu shih-liao*, pp. 25, 52, 171, 220–221.

[a] Includes spindles bought or leased from other mills, so that the growth of this firm was not a net gain to the industry. Spindles bought or leased from other mills accounted

firms to grow side by side with the foreign ones was a matter of group efforts (another appeared after one was downed by foreign competition), or was a matter of real staying power on the part of the established firms. In cotton textiles and coal mining, however, the mortality rate does not appear high, because the leading firms had long records of establishment.[36] The growth records of some of the large Chinese firms are impressive, as shown in Table 31, and to a certain degree may be indicative of the strength of Chinese firms in the face of foreign competition.

How was it possible that Chinese-owned enterprises as a group were able to grow as fast as their foreign counterparts in China, despite the various advantages that the latter are often said to have enjoyed? Is it true, as has been suggested, that the foreign firms were stronger financially, either because of their large paid-up capital or because of their ability to borrow from foreign sources at lower costs; that they had better technological and managerial knowledge than their Chinese counterparts; that by interpreting favorably their extraterritorial rights, they were exempted from Chinese taxes and levies; and that they were immune from Chinese official exactions or abuses? To answer these questions fully would require a number of careful case studies of native and foreign enterprises in China. What will be presented below, therefore, can be regarded only as tentative hypotheses that may facilitate further studies.

Financial Resources, Management, and Earning Power

A common argument in support of the supposed superiority of the foreign firms in China as compared with their Chinese counterparts is that they had greater financial resources, better management and technology, and therefore greater ability to earn a profit.

Table 31 (continued)

for 57 percent of the total in 1917–1918; 12–27 percent in 1920–1924; 30–36 percent in 1925–1929; and 42–45 percent in 1930–1936.

[b] One chest contained 50,000 cigarettes. Figures for 1912–1918 are for the Hong Kong plants; figures for 1926–1936 are for the Shanghai plants. The latter began operations in 1917. The Hong Kong plants continued to grow in sales until 1925, when they still accounted for nearly 45 percent of total sales of the company. By 1936 the Shanghai plants had become predominant.

It is maintained that their paid-up capital was larger to begin with, and that in time of financial need they could always borrow at a low cost from foreign banks in China. Their management is supposed to have been better, if only because their Chinese counterparts were so poor in comparison. Chinese firms were controlled in the early days principally by Chinese officials (either active or retired), and later by merchants. These officials and merchants, it is argued, did not have the industrial outlook or mentality required by modern enterprise. For example, an industrial concern should emphasize long-run plans rather than short-run speculation for a quick profit in inventory or other assets. Chinese traditions such as nepotism are also frequently mentioned as contributing to the inefficiency of management of the Chinese firms.

These charges remain to be substantiated. It is probably true that the capital of foreign concerns in almost every field was usually larger than that of their Chinese counterparts. How much larger? is the question. In the cotton textile industry in 1930, the capital in Japanese firms may have been, on an average, twice as large as in Chinese ones.[37] The differential may have been greater in mining, shipbuilding, and the manufacture of cigarettes and soap. However, the fact remains that foreign concerns never had the large concentration of economic power in China that they did in many economically advanced countries. It would be difficult to find any foreign firm in China that could account for a substantial portion (say 20 percent) of the total production of the industry.

More important than a comparison of capital is the question of whether larger capital was equivalent to greater efficiency.[38] Although it was generally true that capital per worker in foreign concerns was larger than in Chinese concerns, this did not necessarily mean lower cost or higher profit per unit of output if labor was relatively cheap. Where the problem of capital indivisibility was not severe and the degree of substitutability of labor for capital was quite high, China primarily developed light industries without great loss to internal economies. The average size, as well as capital-labor ratio, of British cotton mills in China was greater than that of the Japanese firms, but there is no evidence to suggest that the former exceeded the latter in efficiency, profit rate, or growth rate.

Statistics on unit cost of production and profit rates for both foreign and Chinese enterprises are extremely scarce. For one thing, few firms were willing to make their detailed financial statements available to the public. Moreover, in cases where statements are available, there is still the question of comparability. The accounting practices of most of the Chinese concerns were so much at variance with those of the foreign enterprises that a simple comparison of the published results would be extremely misleading, if not entirely useless.

Frequently cited evidence regarding the relative efficiency of foreign and Chinese manufacturing enterprises has to do with the cost of production of cotton yarns. As shown in Table 32, the reported data reveal that the unit cost of production of the Chinese

Table 32. Production cost per bale of cotton yarn (20 counts) in Chinese and Japanese cotton mills in China (Chin$).[a]

Costs	Chinese mills	Japanese mills
Manufacturing Costs:		
Wages	10.50	5.80
Power	5.50	4.80
Repairs (machine)	1.80	0.60
Maintenance	0.40	.40
Other Materials	1.70	.50
Packing	1.50	1.20
Salaries	1.20	0.60
Sundry	1.50	.50
Insurance (employees)	0.20	.50
Total	24.30	14.90
Operating Costs:		
Transportation	0.20	0.20
Operation	2.50	2.00
Taxes and Interest	15.00	2.70
Insurance	0.20	0.10
Sundry	1.50	.50
Total	19.40	5.50
Grand total	43.70	20.40

Source: Ku Cheng-k'ang, in *Fang-chih chou-kan* (Textiles weekly), Vol. 5, No. 15, as cited in Chin Kuo-pao, pp. 74–75; also in Yen Chung-p'ing, *Mien-fang-chih*, p. 217.
[a] No date is given; presumably the data refer to the early 1930's.

mills was as high as 214 percent of that of their Japanese competitors. However, the evidence given is far from conclusive. First of all, it is not known how many firms were covered or whether they were representative. Second, the costs included are not complete, and the two most important items are not included — cost of raw materials and depreciation. The cost of raw materials of both the Japanese and Chinese firms is not known, but the depreciation cost in the Japanese firms must have been substantially higher because of their high capital-worker ratio. (The higher labor cost in the Chinese firms apparently reflects the more intensive use of labor per unit of output.) Third, it is not correct to include interest charges in cost of production when comparing efficiency. According to modern accounting theory, interest charges are a reward to creditors of the firm just as profit is a reward to the owners. They are a device to allocate income rather than a cost of production.

Therefore, if allowances are made for the cost of raw materials (which usually figured as much as 70 or 80 percent of the total cost of production), the cost of depreciation, and the interest charges (which undoubtedly account for the largest part of the taxes and interest category in Table 32), one wonders whether there was any significant difference in total cost per unit between the Japanese and Chinese cotton mills.

On the matter of interest charges, it remains to be studied whether or not Chinese firms were unable to borrow because of their low credit standing. It is well known that a number of Chinese mines borrowed heavily from Japanese sources — so heavily as to pass the power of control to the creditors. Some Chinese cotton mills also borrowed a great deal from foreign banks in China, especially the Japanese. In addition to foreign sources, Chinese concerns had access to Chinese sources, especially the native banks in the early days and modern banks in the 1930's. The extent to which Chinese enterprises relied upon borrowed funds is still a matter for research. It is estimated that in the 1930's borrowed funds perhaps equaled or even exceeded capital for many of the Chinese cotton mills.[39]

The cost of borrowing for Chinese firms appeared to be high, perhaps 8 to 12 percent a year in most cases.[40] The question is to what extent and at what interest rates the foreign enterprises borrowed? As with Chinese firms, no comprehensive picture can be given for foreign firms as a whole. Although it has been suggested that Japanese cotton firms could borrow at an interest rate as low as 3 percent a year in the 1930's, this was probably not generally true, for it is also known that some foreign firms had to pay as high as 8 to 12 percent a year. To assess fully the relative burden of borrowing assumed by both foreign and Chinese firms, a comparative study of a number of such firms is required. In order to be comparable, the period covered, the purpose of borrowing, and the credit standing of the firm have to be considered. In the absence of such a study it is dangerous to conclude that Chinese firms were always in a very unfavorable position with regard to the ability to borrow and the terms at which they borrowed.

As to efficiency and production costs, not all factors were in favor of foreign firms. The fact that for a long period they had to rely extensively upon the expensive compradore system suggests how important and useful local knowledge and connections were to the success of a business. Foreign firms not only had to pay a high salary to attract foreigners to work and stay in China but even had to pay a higher salary and wage scale to Chinese employees. The high scale could not be entirely justified on the grounds of high productivity. A certain differential appeared necessary to overcome the nationalistic and racial feelings among the Chinese employees — a point that will be discussed later.

Furthermore, because of legal restrictions, the available living accommodations, and banking facilities, foreign firms (except mines and railroads) were confined to the treaty ports; they could not move to other locations. Yet the success of the Ta Tung Cotton Mill in Nantung was believed to be the result of its proximity to raw materials and the market for its final products. Moreover, in the period 1932–1936 when business conditions were unfavorable, Chinese cotton mills tended to move away from coastal textile centers such as Shanghai, Tientsin, and Tsingtao and to go to the interior cities.[41] It is questionable whether the over-all unit cost was lower in the interior than in the coastal centers, but the movement itself indicated a certain degree of freedom in location available to the Chinese firms.

Reinvestment Policy

Another reason that is frequently mentioned for the supposed failure of the Chinese firms in their struggle against foreign "oppressors" is that the Chinese firms emphasized immediate dividends with few profits reinvested for the purpose of growth, whereas the foreign-owned enterprises plowed much of their profits back into their businesses. There appears to be little doubt that the foreign firms in general had a high rate of reinvestment, and undoubtedly reinvestment contributed much to their growth. However, a high reinvestment ratio is not necessarily incompatible with large dividends. As a matter of fact, the available evidence, though scattered and limited, seems to suggest that the dividend rates (dividends as a percentage of paid-up capital) ran quite high, perhaps 10 to 12 percent in most cases.[42]

It is doubtful that the dividend rates of the Chinese firms were much higher than those of the foreign concerns, if at all, insofar as available evidence indicates. As for the reinvestment ratio of the Chinese firms, little is known. One can cite cases where the reinvestment ratio was zero, just as one can cite cases where the ratio was extremely high, as in the Ta-Sheng Textile Mill (1899–1913), the Nanyang Brothers Tobacco Company (1911–1926), or the Shen-Hsin Cotton Mill (1915–1936).

ʹA frequently condemned practice of the Chinese firms is that of giving a certain amount of dividend to the stockholders in the name of interest on capital, regardless of whether any profit was made, or even of whether there was any balance in what a modern accountant calls the earned surplus account.[43] Doubtless such a practice was unhealthy from the viewpoint of reinvestment or growth of the individual firms. Taking the industrial sector of the country as a whole, however, such a practice may not have been entirely harmful. One has to remember that in the early stages of economic development it is always difficult to change people's habits in the disposition of savings. Traditionally they employed their savings in such fields as land ownership, usury, and commerce, where they could usually reap a food return. When new opportunities were available to them in the industrial sector, it was only natural that they were skeptical about the new ventures and demanded a guaranty against minimum returns. There were even cases where wealthy Chinese returned to their traditional fields of investment after some not-too-successful years in industry. Therefore, the interest-on-capital arrangement (called kuan-hsi) seemed to be a matter of necessity — a device to attract capital that otherwise would not have gone into industry.

Taxes, Levies, and Official Exactions

The contention that Chinese-owned enterprises were burdened with more taxes, local levies, and official exactions than their foreign competitors is a familiar one. Here again the question is, how severe was the burden? Consider the matter of taxes. By the Treaty of Shimonoseiki of 1895, all articles manufactured in China by the Japanese (and nationals of all treaty powers by virtue of the most-favored-nation clause) were to be regarded for tax purposes as imports, which could be sold anywhere in China after the payment of a 5 percent import duty (ad valorem) and another 2.5 percent for transit dues. They would not be burdened with all the internal levies, especially the likin, which was a very burdensome and troublesome tax. In 1896 Japan further secured from the Chinese government the national treatment of taxes for her nationals in China.

As noted before, likin was a tax imposed on goods in transit by land or by water from one province to another or from one district to another within the same province. There were likin stations in all the large towns and along the main land and water routes, sometimes at intervals of twenty miles or less. Although the amount collected varied from place to place and from time to time, generally it was 3 percent at the departure station and 2 percent at each inspection station. The amount collected within a province was usually arranged so as not to exceed 10 percent, but when goods were transported through several provinces it could reach from 15 to 20 percent.[44]

In an effort to encourage Chinese-owned modern enterprises, Li Hung-chang proposed in 1882 that all cotton goods produced by Chinese factories be exempt from likin.[45] The exemption was later extended to virtually all other factory-made articles. Therefore, insofar as the likin burden on the final product was concerned, there did not seem to be any preferential treatment accorded to foreign-owned enterprises. It is misleading, of course, to compare the level of taxes on the final products only. Inasmuch as there was no exemption of likin for raw materials or articles that were not factory-produced, the Chinese firms were placed in a disadvantageous position, because they used more native raw materials while the foreign enterprises used more imported material. The cotton textile industry is a case in point.

The situation in mining was indeed complicated, but available evidence strongly suggests that there was somewhat equal taxation of both foreign and Chinese concerns, at least insofar as formal taxes were concerned. The tax rates were required of all mining firms whether they were entirely Chinese-owned or jointly owned. Even for the Sino-foreign mines that were founded through special negotiation with the Chinese government and conformed with none of the mining regulations, the terms with respect to taxes were on the whole similar to those provided in the mining regulations.

In the 1930's the problem of taxes became less of a source of conflict between foreign firms and the Chinese government. However, new complications arose when a number of commodity taxes were introduced by the government to replace the likin, which had been formally abolished in 1930. It has been argued that these new taxes were very favorable to foreign firms. For instance, in the case of cotton yarns it has been calculated that the tax rate (tax as a percentage of market price) was 6 percent on yarns of ten counts, 5.1 percent on yarns of 16 counts, 4.9 percent on yarns of 20 counts, 5.4 percent on yarns of 32 counts, and 4.5 percent on yarns of 42 counts.[46] These rates have been considered unfavorable to the Chinese firms because the latter primarily produced coarse yarns (below 20 counts).

The same may be said of the tax on cigarettes. It is estimated that from 1934 to 1937 the tax rate on high-quality cigarettes was 16 percent, while it was 40 percent on middle-grade cigarettes and 58 percent on cigarettes of the lowest grade.[47] While the calculations of these rates might be questioned because of the difference in methods of selecting market price, clearly the tax rates were higher on the lower-quality cigarettes. Inasmuch as the Chinese firms were engaged primarily in the production of the low-grade cigarettes, it has been held that they were put in a disadvantageous position.

The Chinese firms disliked those differential rates, as their complaints and protests revealed. However, whether these differential rates were proportional to the actual burden assumed by the cigarette producers is quite a different matter. It is, of course, a matter of price elasticity of supply and demand. If the elasticity of demand for cigarettes was low, the producers would have been able to shift a large proportion of the tax to the consumer in the form of a higher price. Or if the supply of the inputs had a low elasticity, the producers would have found it possible to shift some of the tax to the factors of production. In the absence of any accurate information on these elasticities, it does not seem possible to ascertain the portion of the tax burden that had to be assumed by the Chinese producers.

This sketch suggests that up to the 1930's there did not seem to be a discrepancy in taxes on Chinese and foreign enterprises. Even if there had been, the consequences could not have been very great. It must be remembered that the taxes on factory-type products were very few and the tax rates were very modest. Only in the 1930's were a number of new taxes introduced with high tax rates.

Formal taxes were only a part of the story, however. Undoubtedly what really handicapped the Chinese enterprises was not the formal taxes but the surtaxes or other levies collected by the local governments or warlords. Above all, the exactions and abuses by Chinese officials were a constant burden to business concerns. It is believed, although rarely documented, that the local levies and official exactions ran to gigantic proportions, especially when there was internal disorder or civil war, which was frequent in the modern history of China. Foreign firms were immune from this heavy burden.

While this speculation seems to be true, it should not be exaggerated. In the first place, most of the Chinese-owned modern enterprises were situated in treaty ports, where the influence of local officials and warlords was at a minimum. Second, the large Chinese firms were usually either owned or backed by influential Chinese officials. It is difficult to believe that they were subjected easily to severe official abuses or exactions. Finally, the extent to which the dishonest officials invested their funds in modern enterprises would have to be considered, no matter how illegally and immorally their funds may have been secured.

Boycotts and the "Buy-Chinese" Appeal

Economic contact between China and the West in the modern era was imposed upon her by the West. The Chinese regarded it as intolerably humiliating. All the unequal treaties were regarded as schemes to control or exploit China. For a people that had possessed for centuries a feeling of cultural superiority, it was only natural to do everything possible to counteract foreign penetration — be it military, economic, or otherwise. While the measures the Chinese government adopted to industrialize the country have been described, it should be added that in some cases, although infrequently, a special subsidy was given to Chinese firms. The China Merchant's Steam Navigation Company was subsidized; for a number of years it shipped rice for the Chinese government at a freight rate twice as high as the market rate. In later years government subsidy was also given to other Chinese shipping concerns.[48]

In such an antiforeign atmosphere the government and the public naturally tried to encourage the consumption of articles and commodities produced by Chinese firms. It is difficult to assess the extent of public response to the "buy-Chinese" appeal. Judging from the widespread antiforeign sentiment among the public (as witnessed by the furious and exciting "recovering economic interests" movement after 1898), it must have achieved some results.

After the turn of the century the "buy-Chinese" sentiment intensified as the technique of boycott came into more frequent use. The first large-scale Chinese boycott was directed against the United States in 1905, in connection with a dispute with the United States over the American immigration policy and abuse of the Chinese. Thereafter, a number of boycotts were carried out against Japan and Great Britain, with Japan being the main target. Japan was boycotted in 1908, 1909, 1915, 1919–21, 1923, 1925–26, 1927, 1928–29, and 1931–32. Great Britain was boycotted in 1909, 1925–26, and 1927. Practically every one of these boycotts was provoked by an incident, an event, or a clash, and they were generally initiated spontaneously by Chinese merchants or students. The Kuomintang or the Chinese government did not begin to take an active part in boycotts until after 1925–26.

A very careful study of the economic effects of the boycotts has been made by C. F. Remer. He concludes that "a Chinese boycott initiated after some outstanding incident and carried on by familiar methods will, if it persists through a year and reaches all parts of China, reduce imports from the boycotted country into Northern China by about 10 percent and into Central and Southern China by from 25 to 40 percent." [49] The decrease of imports from the boycotted country did not mean a corresponding increase of demand for Chinese products; imports from other countries usually went up.

Boycotts were directed not only against imports but also against goods produced in China by nationals of the boycotted country. Remer reports that Japanese cotton mills in China had a large amount of unsold or undeliverable goods at the end of 1931, and they even had to close for some months in 1932 when a boycott against Japan was at its peak. Japanese shipping in Chinese waters was also affected by the boycotts. According to Remer, Japanese shipping companies in China operated at a loss during the entire 1931 boycott.[50]

A recent case study of the Nanyang Brothers Tobacco Company illustrates how this firm took advantage of the "buy-Chinese" sentiment in its struggle against the powerful British-American Tobacco Company.[51] In fact; it was during the boycott wave against the United States in 1905 that Nanyang Brothers, among others, was established in Hong Kong. The 1912 revolution aroused so much enthusiasm for the "New China" among the overseas Chinese in Southeast Asia that the company made tremendous progress in expanding its market there. In 1915 it was formally registered with the Chinese government for the avowed purpose of resisting foreign products in order to minimize the drain of wealth into foreign hands. This undertaking proved very successful. Sales in Kwangchou, Tientsin, Hankow, and Shanghai soared high in 1915 and 1916 in the prevailing antiforeign, especially anti-Japanese, atmosphere.

The nationalistic appeal of the Nanyang products must have

troubled its chief competitor, the British-American Tobacco Company. In 1919 when a Chinese boycott was directed against Japan, the British-American Tobacco Company launched a vigorous campaign accusing the Nanyang Brothers of associating with Japanese interests. Nanyang emerged from the battle even stronger than before, however, reaffirming its announced role of recovering China's economic interests from foreign exploitation. In later years whenever a foreign country was boycotted, the company always exploited "buy-Chinese" sentiment. Not only did sales rise on these occasions, but more branch factories were built to meet the increased demand.

Nanyang was not alone in exploiting the "buy-Chinese" movement. Whenever there was a series boycott, new companies were founded by the Chinese in the cigarette industry. From 1925 to 1931, when boycotts were repeatedly directed against Japan and Great Britain, no less than 145 cigarette firms were newly established by the Chinese.[52]

Chinese firms benefited from nationalism not only in the sale of their products but in labor-management relations as well. It is estimated that foreign firms, especially the Japanese and British, had far more frequent labor disputes than the Chinese. Undoubtedly nationalism accounted largely for the difference. From 1918 to 1933 there were no less than 45 labor disputes to be resolved by the Japanese textile firm in Shanghai, the Naigai-Wato Kaisha, which topped all other firms in the frequency of labor disputes. For the Chinese Electricity Company, which was also in Shanghai and had the most labor disputes among Chinese firms, the number of disputes from 1918 to 1933 was only 12. It is estimated that among the 19 large enterprises in Shanghai, both foreign and Chinese, that most frequently disputed with labor, more than 75 percent of the disputes during the 1918–1933 period occurred in foreign enterprises, with Japanese firms leading the list.[53]

Specialization and Division of the Market

There is still another factor that made it possible for the Chinese-owned modern enterprises to coexist with their foreign counterparts in China. Could it be that Chinese firms were actually not in any severe competition with foreign enterprises in China? Consider the cotton industry, for instance. There is little doubt that Chinese and foreign cotton mills in China had a fair degree of division of labor, with the Chinese being mainly occupied with the production of coarse yarns or cloth. Table 33 clearly shows that the percentage

Table 33. Percentage share of the Chinese cotton mills in total sales of cotton yarns in China, 1935–1936.

Count	Percent
Less than 10	97
10–12	95
13–16	77
17–22	62
23–34	39
35–41	21
42 and more	13

Source: Yen Chung-p'ing, *Mien-fang chih*, p. 216.

share of Chinese firms declined as the yarns got finer. The same is true with regard to cloth; that is, Chinese mills had a greater share in the sale of coarse cloth than of fine cloth. Mention has already been made of the cigarette industry, where Chinese firms were engaged primarily in the production of cheaper products. It may be assumed that this was also true of a number of other manufactures.

The reason that Chinese firms were primarily engaged in the production of articles of lower quality awaits further exploration. The important fact is that consumers of the coarse products were primarily those residing in the rural sector, while consumers of the finer products were basically the well-to-do urban residents. Their tastes were at great variance. Consequently the two products were not close substitutes and had separate markets. It may be true that Chinese firms could nót compete effectively with their foreign counterparts in the field of fine products for lack of technical knowledge or for other reasons, but apparently they had either an absolute or a comparative advantage in exploiting the market for the rural population and the urban poor. The low cross-elasticity of demand for the coarse and the fine products certainly eliminated a great deal of competition between Chinese and foreign enterprises. An examination of other industries leads to a similar conclusion. In the field of mining, the Chinese and foreign mines were often not in the same localities, and because of the high transportation cost, a great deal of competition was eliminated. In shipping it is known that the largest Chinese shipping concern, the China Merchant's Steam Navigation Company, had an agreement for years with its principal foreign competitors in China on freight rates, thereby eliminating much price competition.[54] The foreign banks in China primarily financed international transactions, while the Chinese banks dealt with domestic business. In the handling of external trade, Chinese trading firms confined themselves primarily to trade between China and Southeast Asia where the overseas Chinese were economically predominant. Therefore, in many areas competition between foreign and Chinese enterprises was quite limited. It would seem that this factor alone should account to a large degree for the apparent coexistence between the Chinese and foreign concerns in China.

Oppression Argument

In view of the above analysis, how much validity is there to the recurrent theme that Chinese enterprises were oppressed by their foreign counterparts in China? Unfortunately, no clear answer to this question is possible because the term "oppressed" has never been precisely defined. If, as was argued by Chang Chih-tung in protest against the Treaty of Shimonoseiki, it is taken to mean that the Chinese enterprises simply could not grow, or could not grow as fast as the foreign ones, because of the pressure of the latter, the oppression argument certainly lacks factual support. If it is taken to mean that foreign firms had certain advantages over their Chinese counterparts in areas such as capital availability and intensity, technical know-how, and immunity from official interference, the oppression argument undoubtedly has a great deal of force. By the same token, however, it can also be said that foreign enterprises were oppressed by their Chinese counterparts, inasmuch as the latter also enjoyed certain advantages, such as local knowledge, nationalism, and mobility.

Would the Chinese firms have grown faster if there had been no foreign pressure? The pioneering role of foreign enterprises in China's economic development has already been noted. Whether in the twentieth century a withdrawal or slowing down of foreign firms would have resulted in a greater rate of growth of Chinese enterprises is still a matter of speculation. Apart from the various favorable effects of foreign firms on the Chinese economy, there is still the question whether more Chinese savings would have been available for modern industry.

Obstacles to Development: Tentative Hypotheses

The above analysis suggests two broad generalizations: there was an increasing modernization in the Chinese economy before 1937; and foreign trade and investment played an important role in bringing about such a development. If one takes the term "industrial revolution" to mean a sudden and drastic transformation from an agricultural to an industrial economy over a short space of time, obviously there was no such revolution in China (and one wonders whether one has ever occurred anywhere in the world). If one takes the term to mean gradual economic change toward industrialization, then China has long experienced such a change.

The crucial question is why the degree of economic modernization was so limited — or, why the diffusion processes (processes by which development of one sector leads to development of other sectors of the economy) were so slow and weak. Why was the modern sector confined chiefly, although with a declining tendency, to the treaty or open ports — a phenomenon that prompted Tawney to describe China's economic development as a modern fringe that was stitched along the hem of an ancient garment?[55] For instance, even the Chinese cotton mills were situated largely in Shanghai, Tsingtao, Wuhan, Tientsin, Wuhsi, and Nantung; all but the last were treaty or open ports.[56]

What were the factors retarding economic transformation in China? This question, of course, has been asked repeatedly. Unfortunately, solid knowledge is scarce. The following tentative hypotheses are presented in the hope that they may be useful in further research.[57]

A frequently given explanation for the slowness of China's economic response to the Western challenge is that there was no effective leadership on the part of the imperial government of the Manchu dynasty. It is suggested that in the closing decades of the Manchu regime "there was no enlightened despot, for the Manchu dynasty was already reaching its lowest ebb of racial vitality"; and there was "no enlightened nobility, for the Manchu nobility and the Manchu military caste were long weakened and ruined by two and a half centuries of easy and parasitic living." [58] During most of the last four decades of the Manchu regime the court was under the control of Empress Dowager Tz'u-hsi. Essentially devoted to conservative ends and personal power, the Empress Dowager even managed to crush the famous Hundred Days of the reform attempts of Emperor Kuang-hsü in 1898.

In Hu Shih's view the absence of government leadership was crucial, because nowhere else could leadership be located in China. Unlike Japan, where a powerful ruling class existed (in the person of the daimyo and the samurai), which provided all the members of the brilliant galaxy of statesmen of the early Meiji era and directed all the political and economic reforms, China had no such counterpart. Since the passing of the political and military feudalism more than two thousand years before, there had been no hereditary aristocracy that could last decades. There was no primogeniture to preserve large estates. The hereditary nobility descended from the imperial family was periodically swept away in the waves of the dynastic cycle. The civilian bureaucracy was an instrument of administration and could not assume decisive leadership. There were great statesmen from time to time, but their prominence and contributions were at the mercy of the throne.[59]

In the closing decades of the Manchu regime there were many men of foresight who saw the need to modernize the country, but they lacked the power to do anything on a large scale. Even Li Hung-chang, probably the most powerful leader in modernization attempts, had to admit in 1877, "My official duty is to command the military . . . Even if I wish to go beyond this and take up the more important and fundamental reforms, it is certain that I shall never be allowed to carry out my wishes." [60]

The view that the imperial court, being ineffective and conservative, retarded China's modernization undoubtedly carries a great deal of force.[61] Yet this is not tantamount to saying that the court, however ignorant, was simply uninterested in, or indifferent to, China's modernization. The modernization efforts in the industrial sector have already been noted. In agriculture, attempts to increase the area of cultivation and the output per acre by improved methods of cotton growing, animal husbandry, wool production, reforestation, scientific sericulture, water control, etc., were already being made in the 1860's.[62] These measures, though initiated by provincial officials, had to be sanctioned by the court; and taken together, they cannot be easily described as irrelevant or insignificant to economic development. Probably few would say that such measures as setting up armament factories and textile mills, opening coal and iron mines, building railroads, etc., would have had no important consequences on the Chinese economy if they had been carried out on a much larger scale.

Why were they not carried out on a larger scale? At least part of the answer lies in the fact that the fiscal system of the imperial government was not so structured as to make it possible to undertake large-scale modernization programs; and when this rigid system was faced with a decline of revenues because of civil war and an increase of expenditures because of the indemnity, the imperial government became bankrupt. The traditional sources of imperial revenue were the land tax, rice tribute, salt monopoly tax, and taxes on domestic commerce. Of the most important tax, the land tax (which probably accounted for two thirds of the total), the rate had been fixed by a series of edicts between 1712 and 1745 in which the imperial government promised never to raise it. The newly developed taxes, such as the likin and custom duties, though larger, were never large enough to close the budget deficit in the closing years of the Ch'ing regime.

The whole argument as to the effectiveness or ineffectiveness of the imperial government in attempting to modernize the country rests on the assumption that modernization depended on government action. Some have argued, though their reasons are not always clear, that comprehensive, large-scale, centrally-directed planning and control by the government was a necessary condition for economic development in China. This view is not only contradicted by the experience of many other countries but is not in accord with the fact that there was a limited degree of development in the Chinese economy at least partly as a result of the government's efforts. A milder view is that in the absence of effective government leadership, China had to follow a course of cultural response that Hu Shih calls "diffused penetration" or "diffused assimilation." [63] According to this theory, during all the years of cultural contact between China and the West, Western influences undeniably penetrated into almost every phase of Chinese life,[64] but the pressure for cultural changes sprang spontaneously from the people. The leadership came from private individuals who began as small minority advocates and gradually won over a larger following. Although this type of "diffused penetration and permeation" was at times rapid, in the main the changes were slow, evolutionary, and gradual.

Another more general and comprehensive hypothesis about China's limited degree of economic development is that the Chinese economy had reached by the mid-nineteenth century, the beginning of the modern period, a situation that may be described as a vicious circle. This circle was particularly hard to break because of two factors: (1) a cultural tradition of vitality, not entirely conducive to economic modernization, and (2) a series of external and internal disturbances that slowed down progress.

The notion of a vicious circle is a familiar one.[65] Briefly it means that the reason a country is poor is simply because it is poor. Since per capita income is low, savings are small, therefore net capital formation is negligible, and thus labor productivity and income remain low. Since income is low, consumption and education levels are low, which in turn keep labor productivity low (due to poor health, lack of knowledge, etc.). The relative scarcity of savings and land makes the interest rate (usury) and rent high, and such high returns tend to make potential investors shy away from modern industries, in which the rate of profit may not be as high because of low purchasing power of the people. Furthermore, the low level of income means a low tax base, and the low levels of government revenue makes it difficult to undertake social overhead projects such as railroads, which are so important to help provide an environment conducive to private capital formation. The vicious circle may, of course, be described in a number of different ways but the main idea is that the characteristics of an underdeveloped economy are such that they keep the economy underdeveloped.

To break this circle is a difficult task, although it may not be as difficult as suggested by advocates of the "minimum effort thesis." [66] According to this thesis, if the per capita income of an underdeveloped economy is to be raised permanently and continuously, a certain minimum effort or a certain minimum of the magnitude of the stimulant (investment, for instance) is necessary, the magnitude being such that the "income-raising forces" (the cumulative forces of development) will outgrow the "income-depressing forces" (principally population increase). The minimum effort thesis lends support to the notion that unless there are special circumstances or a large-scale investment, economic development is a painful and slow process.[67] Although the vicious circle may be broken by the processes of "economic gradualism," this cannot be achieved in a short time.

The economic condition of China in the latter part of the nineteenth century remains to be investigated, but it seems plausible to assume that conditions fitted the requirement of the vicious circle. The country was predominantly agricultural, but after an apparently rapid population increase in the eighteenth century the land–population ratio was extremely low — probably not much different from what it was in the 1930's, or about four acres of land per farm household of five or six persons.[68] (Official figures show that total population in China had already reached 430 million in 1850.)[69] With such a low land–population ratio, the margin between production and consumption, if any, must have been very small. Nonagricultural sectors such as commerce, international trade, mining, and industry were insignificant. Under such circumstances it is no wonder that the government preached and taught the people the ancient Confucian virtues of industry and frugality. Moreover, with such a low tax base there did not appear to be any way for the government to raise sufficient revenue to undertake large-scale social overhead projects and other modernization programs, although fiscal reform could undoubtedly have increased the government's revenue to some extent. The imperial government was not even able to provide enough funds to suppress internal rebellions, and during the Taiping and Moslem rebellions in the

1860's and 1870's the provincial authorities were forced to borrow from foreign merchants — a measure that was against tradition and would therefore never have been resorted to unless it was a matter of absolute necessity.

This does not mean that there was no wealthy class in China. There were wealthy landlords, merchants (especially in the salt industry and banking), and officials. How many there were and how much wealth they possessed remain fields for further exploration, but the following events may be worth mentioning. The demand by the powers in 1895–1903 for railroad concessions in China generated such indignation and resentment in the Chinese people that the latter finally demanded that the government oppose any more grants of railroad concessions and stop contracting foreign loans that would invite the powers to interfere in railroad administration. "Build railroads with our own capital" became a popular plea all over the country, particularly in Southeastern China.

Many measures to raise capital were attempted.[70] Different kinds of stocks were issued, with particular emphasis on smaller denominations in order to mobilize the savings of the lower-income classes. People were sent abroad to induce overseas Chinese to send money home. In some cases lotteries were conducted in such a way that the winners had to spend half the money in railroad investment. Local governments levied many kinds of surtaxes (such as land, rice, or salt) for the purpose of subscribing railroad stocks. Part of the surplus of public-owned enterprises was specifically designated for investment in railroads. Despite these efforts, the capital raised was too small to carry out even part of the plans. The only provinces that had some degree of success were Kwangtung, which was able to raise considerable capital among its prosperous emigrants in foreign countries, and Kiangsu and Chekiang, which benefited from their large foreign trade.[71]

This incident does not necessarily constitute proof that there were no private savings available for railroad development. It may well be that there were other more profitable investment opportunities in traditional fields such as land, usury, or handicrafts;[72] that a sound financial and banking system was lacking to mobilize scattered savings; or that there were more important institutional factors inhibiting investment in modern fields. One thing, however, is clear: it was hard to raise funds for modernization efforts.

What were the traditional institutions that retarded economic modernization in China? The most frequently noted are the low social status of the merchant; the highly self-sufficient village economy (and therefore the limited development of inter- and intra-regional trade); the absence of primogeniture; the government monopoly of large-scale economic activity; the official exactions and corruption; the preference for leisure instead of business pursuits; the fatalism and resignation; the overemphasis on Confucian classics by the intellectuals to the neglect of scientific studies; the preoccupation with the family (the extended family); and the lack of individualism.

These factors merit close and careful scrutiny. In the first place, did all of them really exist in traditional China, and if so, to what extent? Did they still prevail in the latter part of the nineteenth century when China began to modernize? In what specific manner and to what degree did they slow down China's modernization processes? Consider that much-emphasized institution, the family, for instance. The notion that the Chinese placed their family interests over and above all other obligations does not seem to have taken account of the Confucian image of the "superior man" or the "great man," who was also supposed to be loyal to the state, to public welfare, and to his fellow men. It is also not clear how the family system was particularly harmful to economic progress: the overseas Chinese have for the most part retained the traditional family system and yet have achieved important economic gains, especially in Southeast Asia.

There is one general fact about the Chinese cultural tradition that is not commonly emphasized and which, in our view, may have been an effective retarding force to economic modernization. It is often suggested that over the centuries the traditional Chinese order had become a strongly integrated, firmly knit, and thoroughly tested society, with a culture of great vitality. May it not be that this vitality, especially in the economic field, actually made progress toward modernization more difficult? As Tawney remarked some years ago: "She [China] had mastered certain fundamental arts of life at a time when the West was still ignorant of them. Like her peasants, who ploughed with iron when Europe used wood, and continued to plough with it when Europe used steel, she had carried one type of economic system and social organization to a high level of achievement, and was not conscious of the need to improve or supersede it." [73] Later, when China tried to supersede the traditional technology with modern technology, she found it a difficult task indeed.

Traditional technology had achieved a degree of sophistication that enabled it to satisfy many of the demands of the people, given their level of income and tastes, factor proportions, and prices. After modern technology was introduced, such products could still be produced as cheaply, or cheaper, by traditional technology because of the low cost of labor. This low labor cost constituted the most important factor of production in traditional technology. Therefore, modern technology had to concentrate on products beyond the reach of traditional technology. Since the range of goods that were beyond its reach and yet within the purchasing power of the masses was narrow, the introduction and use of modern technology was limited. The resisting power of traditional technology tends to diminish as purchasing power of the people grows greater and the wage rates grow higher, but this may take a long time. It is in this sense that the vitality of the traditional economic order may have made modernization difficult.

Few students of modern Chinese history would fail to note the frequency with which external as well as internal wars have been fought on Chinese soil, yet no serious studies have ever been made of their effects on the Chinese economy. If the modern period of Chinese history can be dated from 1840, then the very beginning was marked by an external war — the so-called Opium War (1839–1842) with Great Britain. The Taiping Rebellion, which is sometimes described as the greatest civil war in world history, broke out in 1851 and lasted until 1864, with no less than seven provinces seriously affected.[74] The Nien Rebellion took place in the Huai River area, southern Chihli, and western Shantung and lasted from 1853 to 1868. The Mohammedan Rebellion in Shensi and Kansu kept the government forces busy in both the 1860's and the 1870's.

In the meantime, on the pretext of the arrest by the Chinese of the crew of the Chinese lorcha *Arrow*, which had registered under the British flag, and the execution of a French priest, Great Britain and France joined forces and captured Canton in 1857. Further hostilities led to their capture of Tientsin and Peking and the burning of the Summer Palace in 1860. A war with France was fought in 1883–1885 and China lost her tributary state Annam. The humiliating war with Japan in 1894–1895 was disastrous to China, since she lost to Japan her protectorate, Korea, as well as Formosa, the Pescadores, and the Liaotung Peninsula in South Manchuria, not to mention the huge indemnity of 300 million taels. The anti-foreign Boxer Uprising in 1900 brought into Tientsin and Peking the armed forces of eight powers and resulted in an indemnity of 450 million taels (£67,500,000). The Russo-Japanese War of 1904–05 was fought neither in Russia nor in Japan but in Manchuria. The Revolution of 1911 ended the Manchu dynasty.

Wars did not cease with the Manchu dynasty, however. In fact, the whole period from 1912 to 1927 has been known as a period of civil wars or a period of warlordism. Even the most careful historian would have a hard time to trace the details of all the wars: who fought whom, where, and for what. In Szechwan, for instance, it has been recorded that over four hundred civil wars, large and small, were fought after 1911.[75] In Shensi, wars were recorded for every year except 1915 during the period 1912–1921.[76] The country was nominally united after the establishment of the National government in Nanking in 1927, but wars between the Nationalists and the Communists continued until 1936. Externally, the Manchuria Incident of 1931 resulted in the loss of Manchuria to Japan, to be followed by the latter's penetration into Inner Mongolia and North China. The eight-year war with Japan finally broke out in 1937.

The impact of these foreign and domestic wars on the Chinese economy must have been great and should be carefully examined. When more studies are made and more evidence is collected, it will most probably be found that these conflicts were among the most powerful obstacles to China's economic development. They exerted a double squeeze on the government — a decline in revenues and an increase in war expenditures — and both had the effect of reducing the government's financial ability to attempt modernization. (Throughout the era of the republic, war expenditures were always the largest item in the budget of the central government.) Wars interrupted planting and harvesting schedules, ruined much of the crop area, and wiped out part of the labor force,[77] thereby lowering agricultural output. They interrupted transportation, the flow of raw materials and commodities, and hence adversely affected production. Perhaps the most devastating effect, especially of the civil wars, was the breakdown of law and order in the interior provinces, thus confining the growth of modern industries to the treaty ports, which were least affected by civil wars. If the wars had a positive effect on economic development because of the demand for standardized mass provisions for war, as argued by Sombart, this probably only accentuated the development of the treaty ports, the stronghold of modern industries.

Chapter 7

A Dualistic Economy

A persistent argument in condemning foreign economic intrusion into China is that the "traditional" or "indigenous" sector of the economy was "hampered," "disrupted," or even "ruined." It is maintained that the handicrafts, small mines, native banks, junks, and coolie carriers were all helplessly depressed because of the competition from their respective counterparts in the modern sector of the economy. Some have asserted that the supposed decline in the traditional sector was a net loss to China in that the development in the modern sector was too limited for its gains to offset the losses in the traditional sector. Others have taken the more moderate view that the net effect of foreign economic penetration cannot be ascertained, since it is not possible to compare quantitatively the gains and losses in the modern and traditional sectors. In either case, however, the assertion is made that there was a decline in the traditional sector. The purpose of this chapter will be to examine the validity of such a contention.

Significance of the Traditional Sector

In the traditional sector of the Chinese economy were included those fields that made essentially the same goods and services in the 1930's as they had in, say, the 1840's, with essentially the same production techniques and organizations.[1] Agriculture, handicrafts, native banking, coolie transportation, most commerce and services — all belonged to the traditional sector. Not that in this sector there was no change whatever in the quality of the products or the production functions, but the changes, if any, were small, and by the 1930's the difference between the traditional and modern ways of doing things were still very distinct and could be easily recognized.

There is little doubt that in the 1930's the economy remained predominantly traditional. In agriculture, which accounted for over 60 percent of the net national product in 1933, the degree of modernization was negligible aside from an increasing extent of commercialization of crops, despite various attempts to improve it. In mining, on the other hand, modern coal and iron mines[2] made substantial progress: in 1912 they could produce no more than 57 percent of the coal, 31 percent of the iron ore, and 5 percent of the pig iron,[3] whereas in 1933 they had become overwhelmingly predominant, as shown in Table 34. For other minerals, however,

Table 34. Relative significance of traditional and modern sectors of the Chinese economy, 1933 (percent).[a]

Industry	Modern sector	Traditional sector
Coal	78	22
Pig iron	82	18
Iron ore	77	23
Manufacturing	28; 24	72; 76
Shipping	14	86
Transportation (all types)	42; 26	58; 74
Banking[b]	66; 64	34; 36
Exports (1930)	23[c]	77

Source: For coal, pig iron, iron ore, and exports, see Yen Chung-p'ing, ed., T'ung-chi tzu-liao, pp. 73, 104. For the first figures under manufacturing, shipping, transportation, and banking, see Ou Pao-san, "So-te hsiu-cheng," and Ou Pao-san, et al., Kuo-min so-te, I, 98, 114. For the second figures, see Liu and Yeh, pp. 141, 153, and Appendix H.

[a] Figures refer to the percentage share of the sector in the industry in terms of net product (value added). Alternative figures are given in some cases.

[b] Insurance companies not included.

[c] Including products of modern mines and factory-made manufactures or semi-manufactures.

small native mines remained important, even in the 1930's, although their exact share in total production can not be determined.[4]

With regard to Table 34, Ou includes in the modern sector all manufacturing firms of the factory type having both motive power and an employment of more than thirty persons, whereas Liu and Yeh include all manufacturing establishments using mechanical power regardless of the number of workers employed. Liu and Yeh do not include water and utilities in manufacturing, but Ou does. The relative importance of handicrafts varied considerably in different industries (as shown in Table 35).

Table 35. Share of handicrafts in total manufacturing in terms of net product (value added), 1933.[a]

Industry	Percent
Woodworking	95.1
Machinery	32.6
Metal	32.6
Electrical instruments	11.4
Transportation	91.8
Bricks, earthenware, etc.	78.5
Water, gas, electricity	—
Chemicals	37.4
Textiles	62.9
Clothing	83.2
Leather, rubber	73.6
Food, drink, tobacco	90.3
Paper, printing	70.6
Scientific and musical instruments	52.8
Miscellaneous	92.6
Weighted average	72.0

Source: Ou Pao-san, "So-te hsiu-cheng," pp. 130–133, 139–140.

[a] Total manufacturing includes both handicrafts and factories. A factory is defined as a manufacturing firm that has more than thirty employees and uses mechanical power.

Included in transportation in Table 34 are airlines, railroads, shipping, automobiles, tramcars, and human carriers. Inasmuch as animal-drawn carts and animal carriers are not included, Ou's figure on transportation underestimates the relative importance of the traditional sector. In shipping, which was the most important means of transportation in pre-1937 China in terms of its contribution to national income, there was often direct competition between modern and traditional means in the sense that both steamers and junks plied the same water; yet traditional means were still predominant in the 1930's, accounting for more than 85 percent of the total value added by shipping to the net national product in 1933.

The traditional sector of banking in Table 34 includes native banks (p'iao-hao, ch'ien-chuan, and yin-hao) and pawnshops. Native banks were active in all commercial centers of the country and were engaged in all types of financing, especially for internal trade and exchange with small merchants and business firms. Even in Shanghai, where modern banks grew most rapidly, the financial strength of native banks was equal to over one third of that of Chinese modern banks in the 1930's, according to one estimate.[5] It may also be noted that Ou's figure in Table 34 does not include the part of rural credit that was supplied by relatives, friends, landlords, and merchants, who were the greatest source of supply of rural credit.

In the field of foreign trade the largest part of Chinese exports were agricultural products. In 1930, for instance, the components of exports were: agricultural products, 45.1 percent; minerals, 4.6 percent; semimanufactured goods, 15.7 percent; and manufactured goods, 34.4 percent. Machine-made products accounted for only 23 percent of the goods in all of these categories.[6] However, in 1873 the share of machine-made products had not even been quite 2 percent.

The modern sector of the Chinese economy undoubtedly contributed relatively a very small part of the total national income in the 1930's. According to Ou's estimate, the total contribution by the modern sector to net national product in mining, manufacturing, transportation, and banking amounted to only 6.6 percent in 1933.[7] There was, of course, the modern element in other fields, such as construction, commerce, and professional services, but its share could not have been large. In their recent monumental study Liu and Yeh allow no more than 13 percent for the total contribution to national income by the modern sector in all fields of the economy in 1933.[8] The predominance of traditional elements in the Chinese economy appears unquestionable. It is interesting to note that even in Japan, where there has been rapid economic growth for decades, the "indigenous components" of the economy are still of considerable importance today.[9]

External Demand

The fact that the traditional sector dominated the Chinese economy in the 1930's does not necessarily reveal whether that sector had grown or declined. Obviously it had declined relative to the modern sector, for prior to the 1840's the traditional sector was almost identical with the total economy; the only modern element was imports from abroad, which were of very minor importance. However, the traditional sector could have actually increased, declined, or remained constant, depending on the changes in aggregate income. When faced with a declining or constant aggregate demand, an increase of goods and services imported from abroad or supplied at home by modern enterprises would mean an absolute decline of the traditional sector. The reason commonly given by those who assert that this is what happened is simply that there was an increase in both imports and modern production in China. Can it be assumed, however, that aggregate demand remained constant or even declined? Might it not be that the increase in exports and the development of the modern sector resulted in a net increase of aggregate demand? Might it not be that the modern products were consumed primarily in the treaty ports and that the consumption of such products in the rural sector was offset by the increase of its exports to the modern sector or foreign countries?

There was unquestionably a rise in external demand for traditional Chinese products. The physical quantity of China's commodity exports increased at a rate of 2.4 percent a year from 1867 to 1932.[10] While modern enterprises contributed more and more to China's exports, the traditional sector also showed an increase and remained the main source of supply. According to one estimate, the total exports contributed by the traditional sector amounted to Chin$1074 million in 1930 as compared with Chin$106 million in 1873.[11] Allowing for a general price increase, this means a rise of 433 percent, or an annual rate of growth of 2.6 percent.[12]

Using a rather strict definition of handicrafts, Herman reports that the value of Chinese handicrafts (at 1913 prices) increased from 8.8 million Haikwan taels in 1875 to 33.4 million in 1928 (an increase of about 2.6 percent a year), although their share in total commodity exports declined consistently from about 15 percent in the 1880's to about 5 percent in 1930.[13] Using a broader definition, a recent study shows that the total value of exports of sixty-seven handicraft articles, after being adjusted to changes in the general price level, also increased at 1.1 percent from 1912 to 1931, as shown in Table 36, although their share in total commodity exports declined from 42 percent in 1912 to 29 percent in 1913.[14]

Not every item of traditional exports witnessed an increase or even remained constant. The two most conspicuous examples are hand-reeled silk and tea. As filature silk gained increasing importance, hand-reeled silk not only experienced a drop in its percentage share of the total export of silk (from 71 percent in 1895 to 18 percent in 1929) but also suffered an absolute decline (at a rate of 7.6 percent a year from 1895 to 1932).[15] This took place during a period when the total export of silk continued to rise. However, if one goes back not just to the 1890's but all the way to the 1840's, when foreign economic invasion in China began, quite a different picture emerges, for prior to the 1840's the export of hand-reeled silk was around 8,000 piculs a year,[16] as compared with 19,300 piculs in 1932.

The same may be said of the export of tea. In 1830–1833 the yearly export of tea was about 330,000 piculs.[17] It increased to 2,167,000 piculs in 1888, and thereafter a slight downward trend developed. After the First World War there was a sharp drop; the bottom was reached in 1920 when total export was only 306,000 piculs. A recovery was made, and the export figure reached 926,-000 piculs in 1928. It was slightly less in the 1930's. The decline of China's tea export after the 1880's can hardly be attributed to whatever economic modernization was achieved in China. On the contrary, it was due to China's lack of progress in tea production as compared with her tea competitors, such as India and Ceylon. China's tea was still prepared almost entirely by the traditional method in the 1930's.

Domestic Demand

Given a rising external demand, the question whether there was an absolute decline in the traditional sector of the Chinese economy depends upon the change in domestic demand.[18] To what extent, if at all, did foreign imports and domestic modern production replace the demand for traditional products? In the absence of comprehensive data, a few individual industries may be examined.

Table 36. Annual rates of change for selected indicators of the traditional sector of the Chinese economy (percent).

Indicator	Annual rate of growth (+) or decline (−)[a]
Chinese junks entered and cleared in Chinese Customs:	
1864–1903	+6.3
1904–1914	+2.4
1904–1922	0.0
1914–1930	−4.4
Tonnage of Chinese junks in the Yangtze:	
1890–1919	+0.7
Coal production:	
1912–1923	+6.2
1914–1934	0.0
1923–1937	−1.6
Pig iron production:	
1912–1928	0.0
1928–1937	−1.6
Iron ore production:	
1912–1931	0.0
1929–1937	−4.3
Exports of selected handicrafts:	
1875–1928	+2.6
Exports of 67 handicrafts:	
1912–1931	+1.1
Exports:	
1873–1930	+2.6
Textile industry in Ting-hsien:	
1892–1899 (cloth production)	+6.6
1892–1933 (cloth production)	+2.5
1900–1913 (cloth exports)	+10.2
1912–1932 (number of improved looms)	+11.9
Hand looms in Kao-yang region:	
1912–1929	+19.3

Source: For Chinese junks in Chinese Customs, see Yang, Hou, et al., p. 140, and Bank of China, Statistics of China's Foreign Trade, 1912–1930 (Shanghai, 1931), p. 72. For Chinese junks in the Yangtze, coal, pig iron, iron ore, and textiles in Ting-hsien, see Yen Chung-p'ing, ed., T'ung-chi tzu-liao, pp. 70, 103, 235; Yen Chung-p'ing, Mien-fang-chih, p. 272. Data for exports of selected handicrafts were provided by Theodore Herman and deflated by the wholesale price index prepared by Franklin L. Ho (given in Yang, Hou, et al., p. 3). For exports of 67 handicrafts and exports (1873–1930), see Peng Tse-i, Vol. III, Appendix 3; the data were deflated by the index of wholesale prices of import and export commodities in China compiled by the Nankai Institute of Economics (as given in China: Ministry of Industries, Silver and Prices in China, pp. 2–4). For hand looms, see Wu Chih, p. 18.

[a] All but two of the annual rates of change are calculated on the basis of the values of the trends, which are all fitted by the freehand method. The two exceptions are exports (1873–1930) and cloth production in Ting-hsien (1892–1933), where the values of only the first and last years are taken.

In the shipping industry, which served domestic as well as external trade, Chinese junks displayed remarkable resistance to the competition of steamers. Tonnage of Chinese junks (vessels built and owned by the Chinese) entered and cleared in the Chinese Customs continued to rise from 1864 to 1914 and fluctuated around a rather constant trend line from 1914 to 1922. It did not drop to a low level until the 1920's. The same may be said of Chinese junks on the Yangtze River. The trend continued upward from 1890 to 1917 and then experienced a sharp drop in the early 1920's. A similar sharp decline occurred in the 1920's for Chinese junks plying the route from Nan-ning to Wu-chou. The reason for these sharp declines is not clear. It might be that modern steamers finally caught up with them or that the Chinese junks were hampered by internal wars. The interesting point is that for a few decades before the 1920's Chinese junks not only survived the competition of steamers but actually increased in business.[19] The growth of trade evidently created a demand for both steamers and native junks. The latter were used to carry bulky cargoes that did not easily deteriorate, such as rice, beans, salt, and timber. Moreover, the Chinese junks plying waters where modern steamers could not navigate must have also experienced a growth in view of the considerable increase in volume of trade. Although the railroads undertook an increasing share of the total volume of transportation, they were not so situated as to be a substitute for the numerous waterways suitable only for junks.

In mining, while modern mines grew rapidly in their share of total production, the small native mines nevertheless survived. The indigenous coal mines continued to grow from 1912 to 1923, when they experienced a downward trend. In 1936 their production was still 57 percent more than in 1912. With regard to iron ore and pig iron, indigenous mines maintained their production from 1912 to around 1930, when a decline occurred. However, the production level in 1936 was still 83 percent (for pig iron) and 87 percent (for iron ore) of that in 1912.[20]

One of the most developed industries in the modern sector of the Chinese economy before 1937 was cotton textiles. Cotton yarn spindles increased at a yearly rate of nearly 12 percent from 1897 to 1936. After a period of stagnation between 1897 and the First

World War, power looms entered a course of rapid growth: 13 percent a year from 1918 to 1936.[21] In addition, the trend of the import of cotton yarn was distinctively upward from 1867 to 1899 (at a rate of 15 percent a year), and then remained constant at the peak level until 1917. It was only after 1918 that a marked downward trend developed. For the import of cotton goods, the rate of increase was 2.4 percent a year from 1891 to 1928.[22]

However, it is interesting that in spite of all this modern development the handicraft textiles, especially weaving, stood up surprisingly well. In the case of hand weaving of cotton cloth, the experience of the Kao-yang and Ting-hsien areas in Hopei is most revealing.[23] The cloth of these two regions, which were among the most important hand-weaving centers in China before 1937, was sold in places where imported cloth or cloth made in factories in China was also available, yet the hand-weaving industry in both regions witnessed a rapid growth, as shown in Table 36.[24] The same appears true of Nantung, another center for hand weaving, which prospered despite its location in a province that was leading in its development of modern textiles.[25] In the case of hand weaving primarily for private consumption (a widespread phenomenon throughout the countryside of China), the resistance to competition from foreign or factory cloth must have been even greater. Since hand weaving was generally done in spare time, the important item of labor cost could be ignored.[26] High transportation costs would also have reduced the competitive power of modern textiles in the interior.

If hand weaving did not suffer a decline in the first three decades of the twentieth century, as evidenced by the development in Kao-yang and Ting-hsien,[27] it could hardly have declined during the latter half of the nineteenth century. Imported cotton yarns continued to increase from 1867 to 1900, and machine yarns made in China also showed some increase. Since very little machine yarn was exported or used on power looms, and since there was no significant decline, if at all, in the quantity of hand-spun yarn, it follows that the hand-weaving industry could not have declined.

The hand-spinning industry has become a classic example of how a handicraft can be destroyed by machine production. Yet even here the evidence that the industry actually suffered a severe decline in pre-1937 China is by no means conclusive. In the absence of production figures on hand-spun yarn for the early years, one may speculate on the fate of the industry on the basis of the production and consumption data on cotton. As shown in Table 37, estimates of cotton production in China around 1913 vary con-

Table 37. Three estimates of production and consumption of cotton in China (millions of pounds).[a]

Estimate	1913	1933[b]	1932–1936 (av.)[c]
1. Domestic production	1000 (100)	2054 (205)	2202 (220)
Export	116 (1904–1913)	115	77
Total available for domestic use	884	1939	2125
Consumption by factories	17	1357	980
Traditional consumption	867	582	1145
Direct consumption	—	320	533
Hand spinning	—	262	612
2. Domestic production	750 (100)	(273)	(294)
3. Domestic production	563 (100)	(365)	(391)

Source: For 1913, see Odell, p. 199. According to Odell, the two highest estimates of production were made by "a firm of cotton dealers and exporters that has branches in all the important cotton markets in China and operates a number of bale-pressing establishments." The lowest estimate was noted in an editorial note. For 1933, see Ou Pao-san *et al.*, *Kuo-min so-te*, II, 96, Vol. I, p. 25. For 1932–1936 domestic production and factory consumption, see Yen Chung-p'ing, *Mien-fang-chih*, p. 308. (Yen's estimate of production came from the National Agricultural Research Bureau, which gave an average of 16,514,000 piculs for 1932–1936. Yen converted this figure into 8,257,000 quintals, obviously using the ratio 1 quintal = 2 piculs. Actually one quintal is equal to 1.6534668 piculs.)

[a] Imported cotton not included because it was rarely used for hand spinning. Changes in inventory are assumed to have been small or offsetting for the various years. Figures in parentheses represent the index numbers.

[b] Manchuria included where an estimated total of 25 million pounds of cotton was produced.

[c] Manchuria not included.

siderably, ranging from 563 million pounds to 1000 million pounds. While the accuracy of these estimates is difficult to ascertain, in the light of the 1932–1936 production figure, it is not unreasonable to assume that the actual production of cotton in 1913 was somewhere near the highest estimate. Commodity terms of trade moved favorably from 1913 to 1936 for cotton growers vis-à-vis noncotton growers.[28] Cotton acreage almost doubled from 1904–1909 to 1929–1933.[29] Whether an increase of cultivated area meant a proportionate increase in production would depend on such factors as the scale of production and the quality of marginal land. Our knowledge of both of these is very limited. However, during this period there seems to have been some improvement in cotton seeds, which should have resulted in an increase of output per unit of land.[30]

With regard to the consumption of cotton by factories, the difference between Ou's estimate for 1933 and Yen's estimate for 1932–1936 is due in part to the difference in coverage (Ou includes Manchuria; Yen does not) and in part to the fact that 1933 may have been a good year for the Chinese textile industry in terms of yarn output.[31] There is, however, a real difference between Ou and Yen with regard to their estimates on cotton production. Covering the same area (all China except Manchuria) for the year 1933, Ou estimated cotton production at 15,139,000 piculs (1 picul = 133 1/3 pounds), whereas Yen estimated it at 16,595,000 piculs.[32] In view of a recent RAND study that placed cotton production in China in 1933 at 18,400,000 piculs, Yen's figure may be more acceptable. (The RAND figure does not include Manchuria and Sinkiang, but cotton production in those two regions was small.)[33]

Therefore, Yen's estimate of the amount of cotton available for traditional consumption for the first half of the 1930's may not be far wrong. However, his estimate of direct consumption, which was chiefly for wadding purposes, appears on the high side as compared with other estimates, the lowest of which is about 241 million pounds.[34] Yet a lower figure for direct consumption means a higher figure for hand spinning. If a constant "direct consumption" for 1913 and 1932–1936 is assumed, there was a substantial increase of cotton consumption by hand spinning during the period. Even if Yen's high figure for direct consumption is used, there was still an increase of cotton for hand spinning. Alternatively, if the proportion of cotton used for direct consumption and hand spinning is assumed to have been the same from 1913 to 1936, the figures in Table 37 for cotton available for traditional consumption would indicate the change in the quantity of cotton available or used for hand spinning during the period.

To what extent the figures cited in Table 37 and the various assumptions made above are realistic will remain unanswered until new evidence is brought to light. However, the data presented here seem to provide grounds to question the widely held assertion that the hand-spinning industry suffered a severe decline during the period under discussion.[35]

It has been estimated by Ou Pao-san that handicrafts contributed, in terms of value added, no more than 12 percent to the total value of the cotton-spinning industry in 1933.[36] This seems an underestimate of hand spinning, inasmuch as Ou underestimates domestic cotton production and takes the cotton consumption of hand spinning as a residual. According to Yen's estimate, hand-spun yarn was about 35 percent of the total in 1934–1935 in terms of weight.[37] There is no question that factory yarn, whether in terms of value or weight, was far more important than hand-spun yarn in the 1930's. If there was no decline in hand spinning, does the increase in machine-made yarn imply an equal increase in total yarn consumption in China? To answer this, one has to look into the import figures for cotton yarns. In 1901–1903 the average annual import of cotton yarns amounted to 331 million pounds.[38] It dwindled to an insignificant amount in the 1930's, as shown in Table 38. Thus, the increase in factory production of cotton yarn since 1913 was, to no small degree, import-replacing.

For the years before 1913 there are even fewer statistics on the fate of the hand-spinning industry. In terms of cotton production and consumption it is highly unlikely that the industry had suffered any serious decline. There was probably an increase in cotton production, partly because of the various private and governmental efforts to improve cotton production (especially by using American cotton seeds),[39] and partly because of the increase of cotton crop area in certain provinces. Moreover, export of cotton was negligible in the nineteenth century, especially before 1890, and the quantity of domestic cotton used for machine spinning was small.

On the other hand, the rapid increase of yarn imports was a serious threat to hand spinning. The total import of cotton yarn

Table 38. Consumption of machine-made yarn on hand looms in China, 1913–1935 (millions of pounds).

Machine-made yarn	c.1913	1930	1934–1935 (av.)[a]
Production	200	982	1088
Import	358	23	3
Total	558	1005	1091
Export	0	44	46
Total available for domestic use	558	961	1045
Consumption on power looms	15	207	418
Hand looms and other uses	543	754	627
Index	100	139	115

Source: For 1913, see Odell, p. 185. For 1930, see Fang Hsien-ting, *Mien-fang-chih*, p. 276. For 1934–1935, see Yen Chung-p'ing, *Mien-fang-chih*, Chap. 8, p. 309; Yen Chung-p'ing, ed., *T'ung-chi tzu-liao*, p. 74.

[a] Manchuria not included.

was only 20 million pounds in 1880. It increased to 144 million pounds in 1890 and soared to the all-time peak of 364 million pounds in 1903. Thereafter it stabilized somewhat at a lower level until 1915, when a marked downward trend developed. To what extent imported cotton yarn (especially during 1890–1903) replaced hand-spun yarn — and to what extent it represented a net increase in domestic consumption, especially in the treaty ports — can not be ascertained in terms of available data. (During 1890–1903 there was also an increase of imports of cotton goods.)

If it can be assumed that the hand-spinning industry did not suffer any serious decline from the 1910's to the 1930's, one can go further and speculate on the fate of the hand-weaving industry nationally. Available data indicate an increase during this period in the amount of machine-spun yarn available for hand weaving and "other uses," as shown in Table 38. Since the other uses, which refer to knitting and miscellaneous purposes, were small, the consumption of machine-spun yarn on hand looms may be regarded as having increased. Assuming a constant yarn–cloth ratio, the hand-weaving industry must have witnessed a growth.

Sociological Dualism

The foregoing evidence suggests that the traditional sector existed quite well alongside the modern sector of the Chinese economy. Such a phenomenon may also be found in other underdeveloped countries. Indeed, since it is considered so universal, it is now given a name and referred to as economic dualism.[40]

Boeke has suggested that economic dualism is really a matter of social dualism — a result of the clashing of an imported social system with an indigenous social system of another style.[41] In the case of Indonesia, for which Boeke's theory was primarily intended, the imported system is capitalism, representing the modern sector of the society. When capitalism is imposed upon a culture possessing such noncapitalist features as limited needs, absence of profit motive, aversion to capital accumulation, fatalism, and resignation, a dualistic society is bound to occur. Such a dualism, according to Boeke, exists not only in Indonesia but is typical of the countries in Southern and Eastern Asia.

In trying to explain the forces of economic retardation in China, Weber links religious beliefs with economic mentality.[42] In his view the lack of capitalist development in China was primarily due to the teachings of Confucianism, Taoism, and Buddhism, for they prevented what he regards as the "proverbial" and "intense" acquisitiveness of the Chinese from developing into a Calvinist, growth-promoting economic mentality.

Weber has recently been criticized by Chiang on the grounds that it is incorrect to link economic mentality with Chinese religion because Confucianism, the orthodoxy, had only a limited sphere of influence and Taoism and Buddhism, the heterodoxy, had no means of presenting doctrine through preaching.[43] Chiang attempts to trace economic mentality by studying the Chinese proverbs, which he believes reflected the mentality of the masses. He concludes that their economic mentality was not growth-promoting. They did not regard wealth acquisition as a worthwhile goal in life, and they even stressed the futility of wealth per se. They were resigned to fate and relied more on "indirect appeals to supernatural forces than on direct exertion of human effort in business pursuits."[44] Once in possession of wealth, they spent large sums for ceremonial and social functions and for support of members of their sprawling families, leaving little for capital accumulation.

If Weber and Chiang were correct in their analyses of the Chinese economic mentality, their theories would be comparable to Boeke's and could be readily borrowed to explain the phenomenon of economic dualism in China. The latter would be basically a sociological phenomenon, culturally determined — the modern sector was a product of imported capitalism while the traditional sector was a heritage of the noncapitalist tradition. The difficulty with their views, however, is that a large gap may have existed between what the religions or proverbs taught on the one hand and how the people actually behaved on the other. While the economic behavior of the Chinese people in the past remains an inviting topic for research, the following facts may be noted: private ownership remained a leading feature of economic life; land concentration or consolidation was recurrent; there was always a sizable group of rich merchants who were sufficiently "acquisitive" to be commonly labeled as treacherous; and the choice of crops was often a response to price changes, which were essentially determined by forces in the market. Furthermore, inasmuch as there were also many proverbs that were quite in accord with the "spirit of capitalism," as Chiang himself admits, it is difficult to determine which proverbs had greater effect, if at all, on the Chinese mentality.

Technological Dualism

The question as to what economic mentality the Chinese people actually had or how important it was in shaping the economy does not have to be solved here, for fortunately there is no need to resort to sociological or cultural differences to explain economic dualism. The latter can be explained on economic grounds; and contrary to Boeke's belief, Western economic theory is quite useful in the analysis of an Eastern economy.

In economic terms, the coexistence of traditional and modern sectors of an economy is primarily a matter of factor prices and factor proportions dictated by technology. In the traditional sector the technology employed makes use of more labor relative to capital, while in the modern sector more capital intensive technology is employed. If the price of labor is low relative to that of capital, as in the case of an underdeveloped economy, the unit cost of production in the traditional sector may not be any higher than that in the modern sector, even though labor productivity in the former is lower than that in the latter. A demonstration of this has been ably given by Eckaus or Hirschman.[45] Their analysis is facilitated by the assumption that wage rates (relative to productivity) are lower and the price of capital is higher in the traditional sector than in the modern sector because of various imperfections (labor unions, social legislation, etc.).

Whether there were wage differentials in the two sectors is hard to substantiate in the case of China, except in cases where labor in the traditional sector was performed in spare time, that is, at zero wage rate. In both sectors considerable differentials existed within an industry; and in the traditional sector wages were often paid in kind and a substantial number of apprentices were employed without pay, except for room and board. This makes it difficult to compare the wage levels in the two sectors, given the available data.[46]

A wage differential would certainly help the competitive power of the traditional sector of an economy, but it is not always necessary. In the early 1930's there were a large number of hand looms in the Shanghai area and no less than 50,000 people earned their living by hand weaving in the International Settlement in Shanghai, a leading center of the modern textile industry.[47] Such a coexistence can not be very well accounted for by a difference in wage levels.

A situation in which wage rate is the same and yet labor-intensive technology is able to compete with capital-intensive technology is demonstrated in the graph.

The ordinate measures capital and the abscissa labor, both in physical units. The expansion path of a production process is M in the modern sector (capital-intensive) and T in the traditional sector (labor-intensive). Both processes require a certain fixed proportion of inputs.[48] Wage rate and price of capital are assumed to be the same for both sectors. OC and OD represent the same level of output. AB is the constant-expenditure line, meaning the same total cost for OC and OD. It may readily be seen that the equality

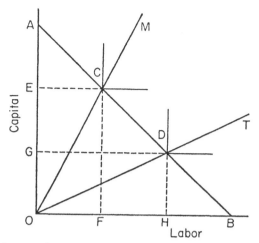

Same unit cost with different factor proportions.

of total cost for OC and OD is maintained when $i/w = HF/EG$, where i is the price of capital, w the wage rate, HF the difference in the quantity of labor, and EG the difference in the quantity of capital as used in the two production processes.

The fact that hand weaving or even hand spinning could survive in China can be explained in terms of the above analysis. Given low wage rates and the high price of capital, modern technology had no advantage over traditional technology in terms of the unit cost, which reflects not only the productivity of labor and capital but also their price. As a consequence, modern technology could do no more than concentrate on products that were beyond the reach of traditional technology. Whereas hand weaving and hand spinning produced coarse cloth and yarn, their modern counterparts specialized in finer products. The Chinese masses continued to use the coarse products not simply because of their tradition-determined tastes but because they could not afford the finer, more expensive products. In the area of the products that they could afford, traditional technology could well compete with modern technology and hence survive.

This analysis does not exclude other factors that help the traditional sector of an economy survive. High transportation costs strengthen the competitive power of traditional production if modern development is located, as it was in China, in a certain small part of a country. Consumption habits that can be satisfied only by traditional products are not easily altered. For instance, a large number of Chinese, both poor and rich, illiterate and educated, continued to use certain traditional medicines that were free from competition by modern drugs either because of a certain secret formula or because of a centuries-old reputation.

It is interesting to note that the vitality and competitive power of the Chinese handicrafts and traditional technology were discovered early by foreigners. Richthofen observed in the early 1880's that modern technology could compete only in rare cases with the traditional Chinese technology, which used little capital and took advantage of the low wage rates.[49] He specifically noted the good quality of the Shansi iron and iron products, which he believed that the Chinese would prefer to Western products, given the same price.[50] According to another report, "all Chinese tools and instruments had in the course of long generations become perfectly adapted to their uses; and were, moreover, turned out extremely cheaply, probably more cheaply even than by machines."[51]

With regard to textiles, British consuls in China reported in the 1870's that "the great obstacle to China's becoming a consumer of English fabrics . . . is the fact she herself can produce an article of more durable quality and better suited to the wants of the people, at an equal or lower cost."[52] Commenting on the quality of Chinese cloth, they noted that "a coat made of native woven cotton will outlast two or three made from the ordinary Manchester fabrics."[53] Of course, the British manufacturers could have turned out a cloth that was thick and durable, but "the prices of raw cotton and freight will not allow."[54] Because of this difficulty, it was suggested that the best opportunity "for foreign manufactures was not in direct general competition with native manufactures, but in meeting special and limited demands"[55] — demands of the well-to-do, or demands of the poor for certain products for certain occasions (dresses to wear at a funeral or a wedding, for instance).

It is not suggested, of course, that a country like China is doomed forever to a dualistic economy. The basis of survival of traditional technology is cheap labor and the low purchasing power of the masses. This basis gradually weakens as the economy develops.

The purchasing power of the people grows, enabling them to buy goods that are beyond the traditional technology to produce; and wage rates push higher, lessening the competitive power of traditional technology. However, this may take a very long time.

The resistance of traditional technology tends to retard modern development to the extent that no capital, whether domestic or foreign, is likely to enter or stay for long in a field where tough competition is expected from the traditional products. The question arises, if traditional technology can take care of the demand for a certain product, would it not be better for new capital to develop new products that are beyond the capabilities of traditional technology? The difficulty is that, given the low income and purchasing power of the masses, it may not be easy or may take a long time to develop a market for new products. In this situation technological progress should include creative adaptation of the traditional methods rather than concentrating entirely on purely modern technology.

In the case of China, it is true that the masses showed great interest in such new products as kerosene oil, lamps, matches, needles, window glass, Western socks, towels, and fine cloth, to name a few. They showed sufficient interest around the turn of the century to cause Cheng Kuan-ying to issue his famous warning that the Chinese would soon lose their livelihood.[56] However, even in the 1930's these new products still formed a very minor part of the consumption of the masses. It was simply another case of the vicious circle described earlier.

Spread Effects

The effects on the traditional sector of the development of the modern sector need not always be destructive. In the case of China there is ground to believe that the modern sector in some ways actually helped the traditional sector to survive. The building of railroads, for instance, created a demand for many goods and services provided by the traditional sector. Many modern products such as matches, soap, and cigarettes were imitated by the handicrafts. The development of the modern sector itself meant an increasing demand for a variety of traditional products that still constituted an essential part of the consumption of even the urban residents.

For certain industries the most important contribution of the modern sector had to do with supply. It provided the traditional sector with certain goods and services necessary for its growth and also with certain technological improvements that strengthened its competitive power. The most illustrative case is the hand-weaving industry. The yarn consumed on the hand looms in the Kao-yang area, for instance, was largely supplied first by imports and then by textile factories established in China. Without such a regular and reliable source of supply, the hand-weaving industry would probably never have been able to develop as it did in Kao-yang. In the country as a whole machine-made yarn was an important supplier for hand weaving in the 1930's. The hand-weaving industry also relied upon the modern sector for other materials, such as dyes.

An essential factor responsible for the growth of hand weaving in many areas, including Kao-yang, Ting-hsien, and Pao-ti, is believed to have been the introduction of the iron hand loom to replace the age-old wooden type.[57] These more efficient iron looms were first made available by import from Japan. The technical knowledge for operating them was spread to the masses in the early twentieth century by the establishment of scores of Bureaus of Industry and Art in various places in Hopei. Such establishments were a part of the "self-strengthening" efforts made by the imperial government, its officials, and the people in response to what was regarded as a foreign economic invasion of China.

Improvements in technology may also be found, though on a very limited scale, in other handicraft industries, such as silk reeling, oil pressing, soap manufacturing, flour milling, or cotton fluffing and ginning. The improvement was made sometimes because of severe pressures of competition from the modern sector, sometimes because of participation in the investment by foreign as well as Chinese merchants. In rare cases the improvement was such that a handicraft was completely converted into a modern factory.[58]

In the case of shipping, Chinese junks benefited from the growth of trade in ports or places that foreign steamers could not enter.[59]

They also benefited from the fact that "the presence of foreign steam vessels, gunboats, etc., had put a marked check on piracy, particularly in the Southern China seas." [60]

Backwash Effects

The favorable effects or spread effects of the modern sector, to use the phrase coined by Myrdal, were undoubtedly weak in China.[61] The traditional sector, though improved, was far from being modernized, and it experienced little if any significant growth. However, it is very doubtful that the spread effects were outrun by what is called the "backwash effects," another phrase coined by Myrdal.[62]

In Myrdal's analysis the development of one region (the modern sector in the Chinese case) tends to have, in balance, an unfavorable effect on the undeveloped regions (the traditional sector in the Chinese economy). The net unfavorable effect may take the form either of an increasing share of national income accrued to the developed region or of an absolute decline in the undeveloped regions. The unfavorable effects are brought about by the penetration of products from the developed region, by emigration of labor and capital, by a change in the commodity terms of trade, or by a decline in public revenue and hence public investment in undeveloped regions.

In the case of China a great deal of research remains to be done on all of these unfavorable effects. The matter of competition with modern products has been discussed above. With regard to the emigration of capital, it is significant that industrial capital in China was supplied primarily by compradores, treaty-port merchants, officials, and foreign investors. Landlords, though also participating in industrial development, were of very modest importance.

Undoubtedly there was an emigration of labor to the modern sector, though not on any large scale.[63] While it may be true that those who emigrated to the cities were abler and more enterprising than those who remained in the country, whether the talents of the former would have been utilized in the country is quite another matter. Moreover, emigration might also have relieved to some degree whatever disguised unemployment existed in the country. The fact that the Chinese, however far from home, rarely severed their ties with their home, may have served as a useful channel between the modern and traditional sectors, promoting the flow of modern knowledge or habits to the traditional sector.

The change in the terms of trade of the traditional sector vis-à-vis the modern sector is difficult to analyze,[64] as are the consequences of the change. A deterioration of the single factoral terms of trade may mean a decline in real income, but an increase in price of the products of the traditional sector may force the modern sector to look elsewhere for its sources of supply.[65] In the Chinese case, the trend of the commodity terms of trade (the prices Chinese farmers received relative to the prices they paid) was favorable to the farmers from 1906 to 1930 and then dropped sharply in the next three years.[66] However, the question of the terms of trade may not be very important here. As noted previously, the share of the modern sector in national income was small, suggesting that the traditional sector was by and large self-sufficient. Of course, Chinese peasants consumed certain items from the modern sector, but those items constituted a rather small proportion of their total budget. On the other hand, the modern sector's demand for the products of the traditional sector appeared to increase, at least for certain industrial raw materials, especially cotton.

In response to Western economic penetration the Chinese government undoubtedly undertook or attempted to undertake certain measures toward economic modernization, but these measures were not taken at the expense of the traditional sector, which the Chinese government also tried to improve. The attempts to raise agricultural output in the 1860's have been noted. Around the turn of the century the imperial government again attempted measures to improve agriculture, such as establishing agricultural societies and schools in order to spread scientific knowledge, translating Western books on agriculture, founding experiment stations, introducing Western seeds, improving farming tools and techniques, and establishing industrial bureaus to improve the handicrafts. Similar measures were tried by the Peking government and the National government.[67] It can not be denied that few of these measures had any significant effect, but further research is necessary to determine why or how they failed.

The government probably paid more attention to the modern sector than to the traditional sector. For instance, factory-made products were exempted from the likin, the troublesome transit tax; agricultural and handicraft products were not. Yet it is doubtful that the burden of the modernization efforts was assumed unduly by the traditional sector. In fact, farm taxes, an important burden to the peasant, did not rise as fast as farm prices from 1906 to 1933.[68]

Productivity and Income

Although there is reason to doubt the widely held assertion that the traditional sector witnessed a severe decline before 1937, this does not mean that every handicraft survived modern competition. For instance, the wide use of kerosene certainly displaced much of the vegetable oil for lighting, and modern needles displaced the traditional ones. In localities near the treaty ports many handicrafts fell victims to their modern counterparts. At the same time, there is evidence to suggest that when one handicraft was threatened, people began to turn to other fields. The shift from cotton spinning to weaving in Kwangtung,[69] or from textiles to strawbraid manufacture in Shantung,[70] are cases in point.

If it can be said that the traditional sector did not decline as a result of the development of the modern sector, the latter was obviously a net gain to the Chinese economy and had a positive effect on raising China's national income.[71] What would have been the net effect on China's national income if the conventional view is taken that the traditional sector did decline? The answer is uncertain. To illustrate, let us take a hypothetical case.

Assume that the total real income contributed by rural industries is 1000 units, with 100 people participating in the work; five hundred units are sold to or consumed by the workers themselves, while the other half are sold to the urban residents. Then, modern factories are established or imports are increased to furnish the same goods at the same price but of a better quality. The modern factories can produce 500 units with only 30 workers. At this point the urban residents shift their consumption entirely from handicraft products to modern products. If the rural industries can still sell 500 units to the rural workers themselves, under constant cost conditions there will be 20 rural workers who are unemployed (assuming that 30 persons have gone to the modern factories). The net effect of the modern development will be a decline in handicrafts, an increase in factory production, an increase in rural unemployment, and an increase in labor productivity; but total national income will remain the same. (Real income might be considered to rise in the sense that there is an improvement in the quality of goods.)

National income will decline, however, if the rural industries can no longer sell 500 units to the rural population. If the handicraft production is carried out at home in spare time, the farmers will probably continue to produce and consume 500 units. But if such production is carried out in organized workshops where workers are employed, as was the practice in many places in China, a displacement of handicraft products by factory products will mean the closing of some of the handicraft workshops and an increase in unemployment. The unemployed workers will most likely cut down their consumption of handicraft products if they are unable to find other employment and will become surplus labor or what is called "disguised unemployment."

In the Chinese case, some of these consequences undoubtedly occurred. Certainly there was a migration of labor from the country to the cities, and there was also an increase of labor productivity. The workers in modern industries enjoyed a much higher productivity than they did in rural industries. However, there are no data to measure the trend of rural disguised unemployment, if such unemployment existed at all.[72] Nor are there any data to measure the trend of labor productivity in the traditional sector.

Chapter 8

External Aspects
of Foreign Investment in China

Export Development and External Instability

When the records of China's external trade are examined, they reveal some important features that differentiate China from many other underdeveloped countries. In physical terms external trade grew at the compound rate of about 2.5 percent a year from 1867 to 1932, reaching its peak in 1928–1929. At peak level the total volume was about US$1500 million. Thereafter China's external trade dropped to US$724 million in 1933 and US$809 million in 1936, partly because of upward tariff revisions in China and partly because of world-wide depression.[1] In the year 1933, for which a comprehensive estimate of China's national income is available, total external trade formed about 9 percent of total national income.[2] Since there was an unfavorable trade balance, total exports were about 3 percent of national income for that year.[3]

Undoubtedly trade volume was substantially higher in the 1920's than in the 1930's. For 1929–1931 the average volume of exports was Chin$1464 million and of imports was Chin$2082 million. At this peak level total trade was no more than 12 percent of total national income (estimated to be Chin$29.41 billion). Prior to the 1920's trade volume was smaller than in the 1930's, and since it is highly unlikely that the rate of growth of national income exceeded that of foreign trade, the trade–income ratio must have been even smaller in the earlier years than in the 1930's. Therefore, as compared with other underdeveloped countries, China was among those with the lowest ratios of foreign trade (especially exports) to national income.[4]

Along with the increase in volume China's foreign trade also became diversified.[5] In the early years imports consisted chiefly of two categories, opium and textiles (cotton and woolen piece goods). In 1867 they accounted for no less than 77 percent of total imports.[6] While the import of opium followed a declining course, cotton manufactures remained important. As late as 1920 they still accounted for 32 percent of imports. Then their importance began to wane in the 1920's and 1930's. Opium and textiles were replaced among imports not by any particular group of goods,[7] but by a number of different commodities. Consequently, in the first half of the 1930's no single item formed more than 10 percent of China's imports, with the exception of raw cotton (1930 and 1931).

The same may be said of exports. In the early years exports consisted primarily of two items, tea and silk, which accounted for nearly 92 percent of total exports in 1842. The tea trade assumed a downward course after the 1840's, while silk maintained its importance (30–40 percent) until 1908. By 1931 silk accounted for no more than 14 percent and tea accounted for no more than 4 percent of China's total exports. The place of silk and tea was taken largely by what used to be known as "chow-chow" cargo or "muck and truck." For example, beans and bean cakes assumed increasing importance in China's exports after 1908. Prior to 1908 they had never formed more than 6 percent of the total. Their share continued to increase, reaching 21 percent in 1931 and 22 percent in 1936.[8] Apart from silk, beans, and bean cakes (and tea before 1915), no other commodity constituted more than 10 percent of China's, total exports in the twentieth century (up to 1937). In contrast, in 1938 a number of underdeveloped countries had 50 percent or more — as much as 92 percent in the case of Venezuela — of their exports concentrated in one primary commodity.[9]

What brought about the increasing diversification in China's external trade? The relative decline of the import of cotton manufactures was evidently a result of development of the textile industry in China. Increasing contact between Chinese and Westerners may have broadened the former's taste for Western products. Energetic promotion efforts by trading firms and the development of transportation also contributed to lengthening the list of imported items, which increased by nearly 300 from 1912 to 1931.[10] The last two factors must also have helped a number of Chinese products to realize their absolute or comparative advantages in the international market. The number of exported items increased by 157 from 1912 to 1931.[11]

As for the lack of export concentration, one important factor has to be emphasized. Unlike the case in many underdeveloped countries, foreign capital in China was not generally used for export development. Although much of it was employed in fields that had the effect of promoting trade, little went to the direct development of the export commodities. Virtually no foreign-capital went into tea, sericulture, beans, or other agricultural products, which made up most of China's exports. The amount of foreign capital in mining was also relatively small, and minerals were not among the important items on China's export list. In terms of gross product, only 5 percent of the total foreign investments in manufacturing was invested in industries for export in 1933 (such as eggs and egg products, tea, hides, leather and skins, tung oil, linen, silk and silk piece goods, bean oil and bean cakes).[12]

China also compared favorably with many other underdeveloped countries as regards the magnitude of fluctuations in exports. According to a United Nations study, the average year-to-year fluctuation in the prices of 46 commodities that underdeveloped countries exported from 1901 to 1950 was 14 percent per annum.[13] The average year-to-year fluctuation in the quantity of 18 commodities exported by these countries in 1901–1950 was 19 percent, while the same fluctuation in total proceeds from these commodities was 23 percent.[14] When the value of exports fluctuates widely — a phenomenon chiefly due to economic instability in the industrial countries — a primary-producing country finds it difficult to control money supply, investment, national income, and rate of development. It is this instability in export markets that has been used as one of the arguments against specialization in primary production.

There was, of course, instability in China's exports. The average year-to-year fluctuation in total proceeds from all exports from 1864 to 1931 was 8.8 percent (Table 39). For 67 percent of the years covered, the total proceeds of exports were rising with an average year-to-year change of 9.5 percent. For one third of the years covered there was a decline in the value of exports, with an

Table 39. Frequency distribution of year-to-year fluctuations in China's exports (percent).[a]

Year-to-year change	Proceeds[b]			Quantity index			Price index		
	Rise	Fall	Total	Rise	Fall	Total	Rise	Fall	Total
			1867–1931						
0–4.99	14.9	13.4	28.3	21.9	12.5	34.4	31.3	25.0	56.3
5–9.99	17.9	10.4	28.3	32.8	10.9	43.7	17.2	9.4	36.6
10–14.99	19.4	6.0	25.4	7.8	4.7	12.5	7.8	6.3	14.1
15 and over	14.9	3.0	17.9	4.7	4.7	9.4	3.0	0.0	3.0
Total	67.1	32.8	100.0	67.2	32.8	100.0	59.3	40.7	100.0
Average (mean)	9.5	7.2	8.8	7.0	7.3	7.1	5.9	4.7	5.4
			1932–1936						
Average (mean)	12.5	16.5	14.5	12.5	3.0	7.8	10.0	10.5	10.0

Source: For proceeds (1864–1931), see China: Maritime Customs, *Decennial Reports, 1922–1931.* For 1932–1936, see Cheng Yu-kwei, Appendix 1. For quantity index, see *Nankai Social and Economic Quarterly* (July 1937), pp. 346–347. For price index (the adjusted Nankai index), see Table 52.

[a] A year-to-year fluctuation is the percentage change from one year's value to that of the next, with the higher value of the two being the denominator.

[b] In Haikwan taels, beginning in 1864.

average year-to-year decline of 7.2 percent. The average year-to-year change in quantity (rise and fall) was 7.1 percent, while that in prices was 5.4 percent.[15] The year-to-year percentage changes for 1932–1936 (when Manchuria was not included) appear to be greater than in 1867–1931, but the period was too short to permit generalizations. Therefore, the extent of instability of China's exports as a whole was relatively small as compared with that of the leading primary commodities in the world market, although for certain individual Chinese items, such as tea (after 1914), cotton, carpet wool, feathers, and weasel fur (undressed), the magnitude of fluctuation was large.[16] It may be that when the industrial centers on the gold standard were in the midst of an economic contraction, silver prices in the centers tended to fall along with other prices, but to a greater extent.[17] However, a decline in the purchasing power of silver in the industrial centers tended to have a stimulating effect on China's exports when she was still on the silver standard. Because of the relatively small share held by exports in China's national income and the relatively high degree of diversification of the exports, it seems that the burden of external instability on the total economy was not as severe as in many other countries.

Nevertheless, the impact of external instability on the producers of certain exported commodities can not be ignored. A large proportion of the total production of some minerals was for export, as shown in Table 40, although these minerals were never im-

Table 40. Export of minerals as percentage of production.[a]

Period	Tungsten	Antimony	Tin	Iron ore	Pig iron
1912–1931	—	—	—	—	44
1922–1931	—	—	—	40	—
1933	96	99	113	51	—
1934	73	97	79	73	—
1935	51	93	83	80	—
1936	72	92	87	71	—

Source: For all minerals except iron ore (1922–1931) and pig iron, see Yen Chungp'ing, ed., *T'ung-chi tzu-liao*, p. 79. For iron ore (1922–1931) and pig iron, see Ku Yuan-t'ien, pp. 722–724.

[a] Manchuria not included except for iron ore (1922–1931) and pig iron. Virtually all iron ore and pig iron exports went to Japan.

portant in China's total exports. Except in the case of iron ore and pig iron, foreign capital was insignificant in the production of the minerals listed in Table 40. Foreign capital was important in coal mining, but a relatively smaller proportion of coal was used for export.[18]

For certain agricultural commodities such as raw silk, bean cakes, wood oil, and sheep's wool, which were among China's relatively important exports, the impact of external instability must also have been significant. As shown in Table 41, a high proportion of these products was sold abroad;[19] a fluctuation in the export markets must have affected the spending and income of the producers. For instance, in Wuhsin, a typical sericultural district in Chekiang where silk culture was primarily for export, the revenues for silkworm raising and mulberry growing represented no less than 70 percent of the total income of the rural families in the years around 1921, when the silk industry was at its peak, while

Table 41. Export and estimated total production of agricultural products.

Product	Exports (1928–1931 av.) (thousands of piculs)	Production (1933) Estimate I (thousands of piculs)	Estimate II (thousands of piculs)	Exports/ Estimate I (percent)	Exports/ Estimate II (percent)
Raw silk	164	223	320	73.5	51.3
Tea (processed)	1	2,400	3,000	0.0	0.0
Soybeans[a]	39,905	172,000	236,300	23.2	16.9
Bean cakes	20,724	36,722	47,300	56.4	43.8
Groundnuts	2,670	46,056	66,900	5.8	4.0
Raw cotton	918	15,400	19,000	6.0	4.8
Bean oil	1,352	5,233	7,700	25.8	17.6
Groundnut oil	572	5,757	6,600	9.9	8.7
Wood oil	1,049	2,035	3,000	51.5	35.0
Sheep's wool	454	937	—	48.5	—

Source: For exports, see China: Maritime Customs, Decennial Reports, 1922–1931, pp. 185–193 (the figure for sheep's wool is increased by 40 percent because of the exclusion of Sinkiang and Mongolia); Ou Pao-san et al., Kuo-min so-te, II, 110. For Estimate I, see ibid., I, 28–30, and II, 103, 142, 144. For Estimate II, see Liu and Yeh, pp. 300, 521, 523, 527, 529, 532.
[a] Including other beans that were not significant.

the revenues from rice cultivation amounted to only 30 percent. When the silk industry was at a low point in 1934, the income from sericultural activities was 30 percent, while that from rice cultivation was 70 percent.[20] These figures suggest that the consumption, investment, and financial market in Wuhsin and related regions was affected by export instability. Likewise, a sustained change in export prices and proceeds must also have had an important bearing on the allocation of agricultural resources and the shift of rural occupation. These processes of adjustment remain to be investigated, however.

Terms of Trade

The only existing series of the Chinese terms of trade[21] was prepared by the Nankai Institute of Economics under the direction of Franklin L. Ho. It was first published in English in 1930.[22] In 1932 it was revised twice and published in a Chinese journal.[23] In the first revision corrections were made for a number of years, and the revised figures for 1867–1912 became the final figures of the Nankai series. The second revision was made for 1915–1930, but these figures were again revised in 1936.[24] The series (1867–1936) that appeared in *Nankai Index Numbers, 1936*,[25] and in *Nankai Social and Economic Quarterly* (July 1937) represents the final product of all the previous revisions.[26]

The revisions were made because of technical computational errors; the basic method of construction of the series (explained by Ho in his original publication) remained the same. The basic data are from the Chinese customs returns. The prices used are derived prices; that is, they were obtained by dividing the known quantity of each of the commodities into its total declared value (in other words, unit value is used). Not all commodities as reported in the customs returns are included, but about two thirds of them are, in terms of value. The chain base method is used; and for weighting, Fisher's ideal formula is employed.

The reliability of the Chinese trade statistics has often been a source of debate. Remer, among others, has advanced the criticism that the export figures of China were undervalued.[27] He made a comparison of the total value of goods entered into China's international trade both as reported by the Chinese customs and as reported in the official trade statistics of the chief foreign countries trading with China. He concluded that for every Chin$100 in goods that the Chinese statistics reported as having been sent out in 1928 and 1930, the foreign countries reported that they had received Chin$138 in the first case and Chin$175 in the second. He suspects that the main reason for this gap was the fall in price of silver in the world market. The value of exports from China was expressed in silver, while the value of imports into the various foreign countries from China was expressed in foreign currencies. The Chinese customs, Remer suspects, may have failed to adapt themselves immediately to the true situation and hence undervalued exports. He offers no evidence to show that the actual silver price of export commodities in China was higher than the customs valuation.

As C. M. Li argues, however, if the trade returns of China and the foreign countries with which she traded are compared, a number of technical difficulties are encountered that render the comparison fruitless — difficulties such as the selection of appropriate exchange conversion, the time lag required for transportation, and the matter of transit trade and re-exports.[28] Of course, adjustments should still be made for the Chinese trade statistics because of the problems of smuggling and unrecorded trade.

Whether the Chinese imports and exports were overvalued or undervalued need not affect the accuracy of the terms of trade if the bias, whether upward or downward, was consistent. Except for a change in the method of valuation in 1904, there is little evidence to suggest an irregularity in the valuation of China's trade by the Chinese customs. There is evidence that the prices used by the customs returns in Shanghai followed closely the prices that prevailed in the wholesale market in Shanghai with regard to Chinese imports and exports. Furthermore, there is evidence to discount Condliffe's suspicion that the local divergencies of products and prices would make any index of import or export prices a less meaningful average than is usually the case.[29] Despite serious transportation difficulties, price changes in China followed quite a similar pattern all over the country, at least in the 1930's.[30]

With regard to the change in 1904 in the valuation method, prior to 1902–1904 Chinese imports were valued by the customs at the market price prevailing at the port of landing. This price included import duties and all other charges incurred in delivering the imported goods to the market. Exports were also valued at the market price prevailing at the port of shipping, but this price did not include export duties and all charges incurred in delivering the goods to the water's edge. During the period 1902–1904 this method of valuation was gradually revised, and beginning in 1904 the value of imports was recorded on the basis of c.i.f. and the value of exports was recorded on the basis of f.o.b. at the port of export. Therefore, in order to render the trade statistics comparable before and after 1904, it is necessary to subtract from the recorded value of imports before 1904 import duties and "other charges" and to add to the recorded value of exports before 1904 export duties and "other charges."

As far as can be ascertained, the above change was not taken into consideration in the Nankai series.[31] The failure to do so, however, does not hamper the usefulness of the series in any significant way, at least for the period 1867–1904. The terms of trade as calculated in the Nankai series (which defines terms of trade as the ratio of the prices of imports to the prices of exports relating to a base period) were obviously overvalued before 1904 (because import price was overvalued and export price undervalued), but this overvaluation does not affect the yearly changes or the trend of the terms of trade for the period 1867–1904. Import and export duties remained stable, and the "other charges" were always assumed by the Chinese customs to be 7 percent of the duty-paying value in the case of imports and 8 percent in the case of exports.

However, when a comparison is made of the terms of trade for the years before and after 1904, adjustment to take into account the 1904 changes in method seems in order — especially if one is interested in the trend over the entire period from 1867 to 1936. The adjustment certainly lowers the position of the trend line for 1867–1904 and affects the trend for the entire period 1867–1936. Therefore, the method of adjustment used by the Chinese customs is followed in Table 42 — the adjusted as well as the unadjusted Nankai series are presented.[32]

The secular trend of the terms of trade was against China over the period 1867–1936. For the years from 1867 to 1900 the trend appears to have been fairly stable. Only after the turn of the century did it become noticeably unfavorable. By 1936 the relative prices of imports, as calculated by the trend, had increased by 40 percent, which means that at the end of the period 1867–1936 a given quantity of exports would pay for only 71 percent of the imports that it had bought at the beginning of the period.[33]

Furthermore, the terms of trade fluctuated with distinct cyclical movements. It seems that there were seven cycles from 1867 to 1936, excluding the downswing ending in 1867, which appears to have been part of a previous cycle not covered in the period.[34] On the average, the cycles had a duration of 8.6 years, with about 5 years of deterioration and 3.7 years of improvement.

While China was on the silver standard until 1934, most of her trading partners were on gold. The world price of silver in terms of gold experienced a secular decline from 1867 to 1936, and this decline was not accompanied by a decline in general price level in the gold-standard countries. Consequently, the purchasing power of silver (in terms of all goods and services) declined in the gold-standard countries.[35] Such a decline was equivalent to exchange depreciation for China.

Table 42. Terms of trade of China, 1867–1936 (1913 = 100).

Year	Nankai series	Adjusted series	Ratio of adjusted to Nankai series	Year	Nankai and adjusted series
1867	104.0	79.0	76	1904	94.1
1868	90.7	69.2	76	1905	89.8
1869	100.2	76.1	76	1906	83.2
1870	101.3	76.5	76	1907	84.3
1871	100.4	75.9	76	1908	101.4
1872	95.2	71.1	75	1909	105.1
1873	93.3	70.8	76	1910	111.7
1874	83.9	62.8	75	1911	111.7
1875	86.9	65.3	75	1912	112.9
1876	71.8	54.4	76	1913	100.0
1877	87.0	65.2	75	1914	103.3
1878	88.8	66.3	75	1915	104.8
1879	85.2	63.9	75	1916	104.6
1880	93.2	69.7	75	1917	123.4
1881	97.8	72.8	74	1918	128.4
1882	103.9	76.7	74	1919	134.1
1883	100.8	75.1	75	1920	155.6
1884	112.8	83.6	74	1921	142.3
1885	112.4	83.3	74	1922	117.7
1886	122.7	91.4	75	1923	109.1
1887	83.0	62.4	75	1924	105.4
1888	83.2	62.7	75	1925	103.5
1889	83.1	63.0	76	1926	98.6
1890	79.0	59.8	76	1927	108.6
1891	74.0	56.1	76	1928	100.4
1892	77.0	58.8	76	1929	93.1
1893	88.0	67.0	76	1930	102.5
1894	118.9	91.1	77	1931	116.0
1895	123.6	96.4	78	1932	128.6
1896	116.3	91.0	78	1933	142.7
1897	108.6	85.7	79	1934	136.1
1898	115.4	91.2	79	1935	122.9
1899	86.2	68.5	80	1936	109.4
1900	103.7	82.3	79		
1901	106.7	85.4	80		
1902	95.5	82.6	87		
1903	99.2	85.5	86		

Source: For Nankai series, see *Nankai Social and Economic Quarterly* (July 1937), pp. 346–347. Terms of trade are defined as P_i/P_e, that is, the price of imports over the price of exports relative to a base year. The method of adjustment is as follows. First, correct the value of imports before 1903 as recorded in the customs returns by deducting from the recorded value the import duty plus 7 percent of the recorded value for "other charges." Correct the value of exports before 1903 as recorded in the customs returns by adding to the recorded value the export duty (duty on native produce exported to foreign countries) plus 8 percent of the recorded value for "other charges."

There is no necessary relationship between exchange depreciation and the terms of trade. It depends on the price elasticities of supply and demand with regard to imports and exports. The classical position is that depreciation will worsen the terms of trade, but this is based on the assumption that the supply and demand elasticities of imports are higher than those of exports. In other words, the classical position assumes that as a supplier, a country enjoys some degree of monopoly power, whereas as a buyer, it is only one of the many perfectly competitive buyers in the world market.

In the case of China, the decline of the purchasing power of silver in the gold-standard countries undoubtedly raised the price level of both imports and exports as expressed in Chinese currency. The question is whether it exerted more upward pressure on the import prices. If the answer is in the affirmative, then the decline may be said to have been a contributing factor to the deterioration of China's terms of trade.

The fact that the secular deterioration of the terms of trade was associated with a secular decline of the purchasing power of silver in gold-standard countries does not suggest any causal or even correlational relationship. After a close look at the year-to-year changes of the two series, it seems reasonably clear that no definite and consistent relationship can be found between them. The decline of the purchasing power of silver was sometimes associated with a

---

Table 42 (continued)

The Chinese Customs made the above corrections for the years 1888–1903, and they may be found in the yearly *Returns of Trade and Trade Reports* and in C. M. Li, "China's International Trade Statistics: An Evaluation." The corrections for 1867–1877 are my own; the figures for import and export duties are from China: Maritime Customs, *Returns of Trade and the Treaty Ports, 1877,* and *Returns of Trade and Trade Reports, 1889.* The latter volume provides an explanation for the corrections.

To compute the adjusted price index of imports, let a stand for uncorrected value of imports and b stand for corrected value of imports. Then $(b/a)P_i$ = adjusted price index of imports, where P_i is the price index of imports used by the Nankai series. The ratio of the corrected value over the uncorrected value of imports for most of the years from 1867 to 1903 is 87 percent. For 1887 no appropriate data are available for the import duty and the opium likin; the b/a ratio is assumed to be 87 percent. Compute the adjusted price index of exports by the same procedure as for imports. The ratio of the corrected value over the uncorrected value of exports for most years from 1867 to 1903 ranges from 112 to 115 percent. The ratio of the adjusted price index of imports over the adjusted price index of exports is the adjusted terms-of-trade index.

deterioration of the terms of trade (as, for instance, in 1891–1895 or 1906–1911), and sometimes with an improvement of the terms of trade (as, for instance, in 1920–1929). This lack of correlation was especially true after the turn of the century.

The Chinese case is obviously not in accord with the classical position, but this can be explained. There is reason to believe that China, both as a buyer and a seller in the world market (especially after the turn of the century), was not significant enough to affect world prices by changing her demand for foreign goods or by altering the supply of her own products. In other words, China was, to use Metzler's expression, a price taker rather than a price maker. Under such conditions exchange depreciation would equally affect import and export prices (expressed in Chinese currency) and have no effect on the terms of trade.[36]

It is not difficult to see why China was a price taker in her imports. Her principal imports were manufactures, although their share in total imports declined over a period of time. In 1913 manufactures, including manufactured foodstuffs and semimanufactures, accounted for nearly 90 percent of the total, while in 1931 their share dropped to about 70 percent. During the 1930's imports consisted of numerous commodities, with none taking a large share of the total. The fact that China's imports never amounted to more than US$1 billion per year, even for the peak years, would seem to make it certain that China's demand for any one item was insignificant in the total world demand for that commodity. Even in the latter part of the nineteenth century, when her imports consisted of relatively few commodities, her demand would have had no appreciable effect on world price, for the total value of Chinese imports was still small in the world market.

The case of exports is more complicated. China's exports consisted mainly of raw materials and foodstuffs, which accounted for more than 80 percent of total exports, although there was an increasing degree of diversification. Before the turn of the century tea and silk were the two most important items. Together they accounted for nearly 90 percent of the total in the 1870's and more than 50 percent in the closing years of the nineteenth century. Their share continued to decline, but was still nearly 30 percent before the First World War. Only in the 1930's did their combined share drop to less than 15 percent.

In the case of tea, China's exports almost monopolized total world exports prior to the 1860's, because Great Britain obtained her tea almost entirely from China and the United States bought about two thirds of her tea from China.[37] After the middle of the 1870's China gradually lost her American tea market to Japan and Ceylon. Until the turn of the century China still supplied half of the tea that the United States imported, but the share declined to less than 20 percent after 1915.[38]

In the British tea market it was the Indian and Ceylon teas that made rapid progress, supplying half of the tea in the closing years of the 1880's and virtually replacing Chinese tea after the turn of the century. Russia remained the chief importer of Chinese tea throughout the end of the nineteenth century and up to the 1930's. Just before the First World War China's share in the total world export of tea was still significant, close to 30 percent.[39] After the First World War it dropped sharply reaching 10 percent or so by the 1930's.[40] Since the largest part of China's tea went to Russia, which in turn primarily imported her tea from China, there is reason to believe that foreign, or at least Russian, demand for Chinese tea was not perfectly elastic.

In the case of silk, China's supply in the world market was also significant in the nineteenth century, although the exact percentage share is difficult to estimate. It was reported that in the season 1877–1878 raw silk from Central China constituted 52 percent of the export of raw silk from the East.[41] During the years 1885–1900 China still exported annually about twice as much raw silk as did Japan, accounting for about 42 percent of the supply in the Western markets.[42] Thereafter Japan rapidly overtook China and became the leading supplier of silk in the world market. In 1913 Japan furnished 44 percent of the total silk supplied to the Western world, whereas China furnished no more than 31 percent.[43] In the 1930's Japan supplied nearly three quarters of the total, while China supplied just about 10 percent.[44]

Therefore, the situation of Chinese exports in the nineteenth century seems to be in accord with the classical assumption that

China specialized in exports. An exchange depreciation would have lowered the export price as expressed in foreign currency. If China is regarded as having generalized in imports, as noted before, exchange depreciation would have brought no change in the import price (as expressed in foreign currency). Thus the net result of exchange depreciation would have been to worsen China's terms of trade.

However, if one compares China's terms of trade and the purchasing power of silver in London in the latter part of the nineteenth century, he finds little in the way of support for the above theoretical conclusion. From 1877 to 1887 the purchasing power of silver in London went up, but China's terms of trade worsened rather than improved (1876–1886). From 1890 to 1902 the long-run purchasing power of silver showed a continuous decline, whereas China's terms of trade showed a deterioration from 1891 to 1895 but an improvement from 1895 to 1899.

It is not possible to explain conclusively this gap between the actual and the theoretical relationships. It may be speculated, however, that in the closing decades of the nineteenth century world demand for both tea and silk was greatly increased on the one hand, and China had to compete with an increasing number of rivals on the other. The adjustment to the structural change in supply and demand was further complicated by the fact that China's tea and silk trade was primarily handled by giant foreign trading firms in China whose pricing practices were likely to follow those under imperfect competition. Exchange depreciation, therefore, might not be accompanied by a lower price for China's exports (as expressed in foreign currency), if depreciation took place at a time when world demand was increasing or if price rigidity existed due to market imperfections.

If China was not a price taker for her exports in the nineteenth century, there is reason to believe that she became one in the twentieth century. As noted before, although her share in the world supply of tea and silk greatly declined, she now had a large share in the world supply of a few other commodities. China had a virtual monopoly over tung oil and tungsten; but these products constituted only a very small proportion of her exports, and the change in their prices would not have appreciably affected her terms of trade. In the case of beans and bean cakes, China's export undoubtedly constituted a large proportion of the world supply (about 80 to 90 percent for soybeans in the 1930's),[45] so that she could hardly be regarded as a price taker, even though the demand was probably rather elastic because of substitutes. Here again it should be noted that beans and bean cakes never assumed the same importance in China's total exports that tea or silk had in the nineteenth century. It was not until after the 1920's that they became important, accounting for more than 15 percent of the total exports. Therefore, it may be said that China was, on the whole, a price taker in her exports after the turn of the century. Coupled with the fact that she was also a price taker in her imports, this leads to the conclusion that the terms of trade after the turn of the century were independent of the exchange depreciation.

The relation between capital transfer and the terms of trade is a complicated one. If the transfer is effected through price changes alone, as classical theory assumes, the terms of trade will turn against the capital exporter in favor of the importer. If income changes are introduced, as modern income theory suggests, the effect on the terms of trade will by no means be certain. It depends on a number of variables, such as the marginal propensities to save in the two countries, the accelerators, the marginal propensities to import, and the supply elasticities.

The effect of foreign investment on China's terms of trade can be analyzed in terms of both the short run and the long run. In the short run, to the extent that foreign loans and direct investment were directly used for imports of equipment, machines, and so on, and to the extent that foreign supplies of such goods were almost perfectly elastic from the viewpoint of China (since the demand was so small compared with the total), the terms of trade could hardly have been affected by the capital inflow. In the long run, foreign investment undoubtedly increased China's demand for foreign commodities, since it promoted external trade, contributed to industrial development, and helped develop the taste of the Chinese for Western products. Foreign investment also increased the supply of exports, especially through the efforts of the trading firms and the reduction in internal transportation costs. However, since her share in world trade was generally small, a change in either supply or demand, or both, on her part would not have had any appreciable effect on world prices. It may be concluded that China's terms of trade, in both the short run and the long, were independent of foreign investment in China. In other words, the terms of trade were primarily determined by forces in the world market, especially after the turn of the century.[46]

Obviously the direct gains from trade will decrease as the terms of trade deteriorate, more goods having to be given up in exchange for a given quantity of imports. However, a deterioration of the terms of trade is compatible with a greater volume of total gains if, during the period of deterioration, the total volume of trade increases and the terms of trade have not worsened to a point equal to the limiting ratio as set by comparative costs. To use a formula developed by Viner, the index of total gain from trade increased from 100 in 1867–1871 to 316 in 1928–1932, indicating that China reaped a substantial increase of direct gains from trade despite the unfavorable movement of the commodity terms of trade.[47] The increase in import prices relative to export prices evidently did not lessen China's capacity to import. In fact, the "income terms of trade," which measures changes in the quantity of imports obtainable through the sale of exports, increased from 100 in 1867–1871 to 273 in 1928–1932.[48] A higher level of export prices would probably have increased even more the capacity to export and hence to import, but price was not the only determining factor. As noted before, the development of transportation and the energetic promotion activities of the trading firms were, among others, most instrumental in broadening China's absolute or comparative advantages.

If the deterioration of a country's terms of trade is brought about by the reduction of the production cost of exports, it is possible that real income will increase rather than decline because more exports will be produced by a given quantity of the factors of production and more imports will be received in exchange, even at unfavorable terms of trade. In other words, real income depends on the quantity of imports per unit of the factors of production of exports (this is, of course, Viner's single factoral terms of trade).[49]

There are no productivity data for China's export industries. It is probable that their productivity did not increase much, if at all; exports consisted mostly of agricultural products, and there is little evidence to suggest any significant improvement in their production during the period under discussion. However, there is evidence that the development of railroads and shipping, for which foreign investment was largely responsible, reduced the cost of transportation, and hence the cost and the price of exports.[50] The reduction of transportation costs should have had the same effect on the terms of trade as an increase of productivity. Similarly, there is no adequate measurement for the changes in quality of imports and exports. Most likely the improvement, if any, in the quality of exports was small as compared with that of imports.

It is clear that the deterioration of the terms of trade, though undesirable from the Chinese viewpoint, did not necessarily preclude any gains from trade. However, was the movement of the terms of trade a really important factor in China's economic development? The import buyers and the export producers would certainly have been better off if there had been a favorable movement of the terms of trade. To the extent that some exports were handled by a relatively small number of large foreign trading firms capable of paying a rigid price to the numerous suppliers, especially in the earlier years, an increase in world price would have enlarged the profit margins of these firms; and to the extent that these firms reinvested part of their profits in China, a favorable change in export price would have been beneficial to China's economic development. It is doubtful, however, whether the producers of exports, who were mainly the numerous small farmers, would have increased their savings and investments because of a better price for their products. The same may be said of the buyers of imports. Inasmuch as most of China's imports were for consumption, the beneficiaries of a relatively lower price would have been the numerous individuals whose marginal propensity to consume was likely to be high.[51] Although their real income would have increased, it is doubtful that they would have increased their savings to any important extent, especially when their expenditure on imported goods was a small proportion of their total budget. It is a matter of speculation whether the government could have employed various fiscal or other measures to channel the gains from the improvement in the terms of trade into economic development.

Finally, it may be argued that a higher level of import prices might have served as an incentive to develop import-substitute industries.

Foreign Investment and Balance of Payments

It has recently been suggested by Cheng that "the bulk of China's passive trade balance in her modern history had in fact been counterbalanced by foreign investments in China."[52] To support this view, Cheng points out that the cumulative value of the unfavorable balance of merchandise trade amounted respectively to US$461.8 million, US$1598.3 million, and US$2909.9 million in 1900, 1914, and 1930. The value of total foreign investments in China was US$787.9 million, US$1610.3 million, and US$3242.5 million in the corresponding years.[53] He further suggests that the parallelism between foreign investment and the adverse balance of merchandise trade can also be found in the individual nations that invested in, and traded with, China.[54]

While it is true that in the final analysis international capital movements represent movements of goods and services, the value of foreign investment at a given point of time has to be distinguished from the movement or flow of foreign capital. As Cheng himself recognizes, the value of foreign investment in China represented the result of not only the inflow of foreign capital but also the reinvestment of profits and the appreciation of the value of properties owned by foreign interests in China. Therefore, if one is to find out how the chronic trade deficit was financed, the capital-inflow figures (rather than the amounts of foreign investment) are relevant.

For the entire period 1864–1937 there were only six years (1864, 1872–1876) when China did not have an adverse trade balance. If Remer's estimates on the inflow of capital are tolerably acceptable, there seems little doubt that the inpayments on account of total foreign investments (government loans and direct investments) played a significant role in financing the trade balance in the years before 1914.

For the period 1894–1901 the annual trade deficit averaged Chin$83 million.[55] The average annual inpayment on account of foreign loans to the Chinese government was, according to Remer, Chin$21 million, and the annual inpayment on account of foreign direct investments may have been as high as Chin$60 million.[56] Even when one allows for a wide margin of error on the inpayment figure for foreign direct investments, the inflow of capital still appears significant as compared with the trade deficit. The same may be said of the period 1902–1903, as shown in Table 43. In those

Table 43. Annual inpayment and outpayment on foreign investments, import excess, and current income of China's balance of payments, 1902–1936 (Chin$ millions).[a]

Period	Inpayment on foreign investments	Import excess	Outpayment on foreign investments	Income on current account[b]
1902–1913 (average)	113.8	188.2	158.5	635.2
1914–1930 (average)	97.4	272.0	209.7	1276.6
1928	100.0	306.9	242.0	2036.7
1929	170.0	375.1	277.6	2134.5
1930	202.0	622.4	309.4	2033.3
1931	43.6	583.8	222.4	2365.7
1932	60.0	746.0	146.0	1533.0
1933	30.0	807.2	117.0	1293.0
1934	80.0	568.7	127.6	1045.5
1935	140.0	467.0	162.4	1072.2
1936	60.0	329.9	197.8	1381.6

Source: See Table 21.

[a] Manchuria not included after 1932.

[b] Current income does not include net exports of gold and silver, which are estimated as follows (in Chin$ millions):

1902–1913	0.0
1914–1930	3.3
1928	0.0
1929	3.0
1930	24.9
1931	211.9
1932	215.4
1933	203.6
1934	391.4
1935	357.4
1936	335.2

early years there was a rapid increase of foreign investment in China, and the largest part of the foreign loans to the government during 1898–1911 was raised abroad for railroad development. As a consequence, there was a large amount of capital inflow to China.

The situation changed significantly after 1914. The trade deficit continued to grow, but not the inflow of capital. Much of the increase in the value of direct investment was due to higher price levels and reinvestment of profits. Part of the increase in foreign loans to the Chinese government was due to interest in arrears; and part was due to the fact that some loans, especially the unsecured ones, were advanced by foreign banks in China, especially the Japanese, which brought no inpayments to China.[57] Furthermore, some of the loans were raised to pay interest on previous loans. Therefore, although they increased from US$525.8 million in 1914 to US$710.6 million in 1931, no corresponding amount of capital inflow resulted. The inflow of foreign capital did not resume its importance until 1937, when new direct investments were made, and large amounts of railroad loans were contracted from abroad in 1936 and 1937.[58]

While foreign investments in China did not make a significant contribution to the inpayments of the balance of payments, especially after 1914, did they also impose a serious burden on China's balance of payments? Part of the profit on direct investments was remitted to the investing countries, and amortization and interest payments had to be made on the foreign loans to the government. The total outpayments on account of foreign investments are shown in Table 42. For the entire period 1902–1936 the total outpayments overbalanced the inpayments.

To answer the question whether the net balance of outpayments endangered China's balance of payments, the investment-service ratio may be prepared. It is defined as the ratio of foreign investment income payments to total receipts on the current account of the balance of payments. Foreign investment income payments include interest charges and amortization of foreign loans as well as the remittance of profit on direct investments. If the ratio is small, the portion of current income that goes for servicing foreign investment is small. Investment service will not result in any serious balance-of-payments difficulties even if, for instance, current income falls as a result of a decline in exports. On the other hand, if the ratio is large, a fall in current income may result in serious problems. If the country is unable to raise capital from abroad to pay investment service, it may have to restrict imports and thus obstruct economic development, or it may have to default on foreign debts at the expense of the national credit.

As shown in Table 44, investment service averaged 25 percent of China's current income for the years 1902 to 1913. In the period 1914–1930 the ratio became 16 percent, and it was smaller in later

Table 44. Investment service ratio of China, 1902–1936 (percent).[a]

Period	Government loans	Direct investment	Total
1902–1913	14.04	10.91	24.95
1914–1930	5.55	10.87	16.42
1928	3.09	8.79	11.88
1929	3.71	9.30	13.01
1930	5.48	9.76	15.24
1931	5.72	3.69	9.41
1932	5.87	3.65	9.52
1933	7.19	1.86	9.05
1934	10.77	1.43	12.20
1935	10.02	5.13	15.15
1936	9.25	5.07	14.32

Source: Tables 21 and 43.
[a] Income from exporting gold or silver not included in current income.

years, partly because of the default on foreign loans in the 1920's (largely due to internal wars) and partly because of the continuous increase in current income. The generally adverse economic conditions in China after 1931 also reduced the profit margins and therefore the remittance of profits on direct investments.[59] The rising outpayments on government loans in the 1930's reflected the efforts of the Nationalist government to readjust China's foreign debts.

The investment-service ratio appears high in the period 1902–1913, but the steady increase in current income without marked fluctuations made it possible to service foreign investments with ease. For the entire period 1902–1903 there were only three years (1905, 1911, and 1912) when there was a decline in the value of total exports, with the largest decline being no more than 5 percent from the previous year. In the period from 1913 to 1930 there were two mild recessions (1913–1914 and 1926–1927) and one deep slump (1919–1921) in the value of China's exports in terms of United States dollars, but their value increased substantially in this period as compared with the previous period. The annual amount of overseas remittances also increased and became the second largest source of current income. The fact that foreign capital increased the capacity for exports and that China's exports were subject to relatively less violent fluctuations seems to have made the task of servicing foreign investment less difficult than it appeared.

Chapter 9

Summary and Conclusion

Foreign investment in China, defined as a source of income owned by a foreigner or non-Chinese, reached US$788 million in 1902, $1610 million in 1914, and $3243 million in 1930, according to Remer. According to a Japanese source, the amount was US$3483 million in 1936. At current prices, foreign capital in China doubled between 1900 and 1914, and redoubled between 1914 and 1931. Deflated by the available wholesale price index, it increased by nearly 90 percent during the twelve years from 1902 to 1914, then increased by only about 20 percent during the seventeen years from 1914 to 1931.

Foreign direct investment in China was always predominant, becoming more so as time went on. In 1931 no less than 78 percent of total foreign investment was direct investment. Its steadily increasing importance was accompanied by a decline in foreign borrowing by the Chinese government, which accounted for 36 percent of the total in 1902 and 22 percent in 1931. Foreign borrowing by private individuals and firms remained negligible throughout. In 1931, when the total direct investments of Great Britain, Japan, Russia, and the United States accounted for more than 90 percent of direct investments of all countries, 46 percent of their investment was situated in Shanghai, 36 percent in Manchuria, and 18 percent in the rest of China.

Great Britain, Russia, Germany, and France were the chief investing countries in China during the last century. During the present century (until 1937), while Great Britain maintained its important position, the other countries were replaced by Japan. In 1931 Great Britain accounted for 37 percent and Japan 35 percent of total foreign investments.

The Chinese government began to borrow from foreigners in

China as early as 1861 for the purpose of crushing internal rebellions. Large-scale borrowing did not begin until 1895, when
China had to raise funds abroad to pay the indemnity imposed
upon her by Japan. During 1898–1911 China also raised large
sums abroad, chiefly for railroad construction. Loans for general
administrative and political purposes dominated the period 1912–
1926. After a period of inactivity after the National government
was established in 1927, large railroad loans were sought in 1936
and 1937. During the entire period from 1861 to 1938, 44 percent
of the foreign loans to the government, as expressed in constant
prices, were for military and indemnity purposes, 20 percent for
general administrative purposes, 5 percent for industrial purposes,
and 31 percent for railroads.

The rate of interest on China's foreign loans varied a great deal,
because loans were contracted for different purposes or at different
times. The rate of interest on all loans was 8–9 percent for 1864–
1886, and 5.3–7.0 percent for 1886–1894. From 1895 to 1915, it
ranged from 4.5 to 5.8 percent, with 5 percent being the most
common. From 1916 to 1929 most of the loans were contracted at
7.5 to 9.5 percent. In 1931–1937, 5 to 6 percent was most common.
These rates do not include the discount, which was the difference
between the par value of the principal that China borrowed and
was obligated to repay and the amount that was received by
China and was available for spending. In most cases, especially for
railroad loans, the discount was between 5 and 10 percent (that is,
the issuing price was 90–95 percent of the par value).

The rate of interest was considerably lower in 1895–1915 and
1931–1937. Loans during these two periods were raised primarily in
foreign markets, and the rate of interest that China had to offer
was a little higher, but not too much higher, than that offered by
other countries borrowing from England. For other periods, such
as 1864–1893 and 1916–1927, the loans were made primarily by
foreign banks in China, which charged an interest rate reflecting
the Chinese money market.

Most of the railroad and industrial loans gave the right of construction to the foreign agencies, which charged a 2 1/2–5 percent
commission on the total cost of construction for acting as purchasing
and constructing agent. In most contracts the interest payments

were handled by the foreign banks or agencies concerned, and a 1/4 of 1 percent commission was charged. Some of the railroad contracts before 1907 granted foreign agencies the right to receive 20 percent of the net profit until the loans were paid.

Almost all the foreign loans contracted by the Chinese government before 1914 were secured loans. For railroad loans the security consisted of a first mortgage upon the entire property and, in most cases, the net revenue of the railroad concerned. For general loans the customs and salt revenues were the main resources to be pledged as security. All railroad loans before 1908 placed the management of the railroads in the hands of the lender during the period of the loan. The Maritime Customs, which was administered by foreigners from 1853, played the leading role in controlling the taxes that were pledged as security. Salt revenues, which were first pledged as security for foreign loans in 1895, came under foreign control in 1913.

Apart from their indirect benefits, the Chinese railroads were barely profitable enough to pay the interest charges on the loans with which they had been built. Little of the income from the other loans was used in a way that increased the government's capacity to service its foreign debts, for loans were raised as a result of necessity, inasmuch as the government was in financial trouble. The debt services imposed a heavy burden on the budget; and many of the loans were in default in the 1920's, when civil wars were being fought recurrently in China.

From the beginning, foreign direct investments in China were made largely in fields associated with foreign trade. The first economic contact between foreigners and Chinese was through trade, and it was not long before shipyards were built to repair the ships used for trade. Banks were opened to finance the trade, export and import processing was developed, and public utilities were founded. Mines were worked to supply the coal used for steamers as well as for export; to transport the minerals, railroads also had to be developed. The increase of imports established a market for many articles, which were then produced in China, taking advantage of the cheap local labor or raw materials. In 1931 about 40 percent of foreign direct investments in China was in import and export trading, shipping, banking, and mining; 18

percent was in real estate and public utilities; and 15 percent was in manufacturing, mainly to replace imports. Direct investment in railroads, which was clearly politically motivated, accounted for 16 percent.

On a per capita basis, the amount of foreign investment in China was very small (less than US$8 in 1936) as compared with that in other underdeveloped countries. It was also small in terms of its contribution to China's national income. In terms of capital inflow, the amount was smaller than the increase of investments might indicate. A large part of the increase of foreign direct investments (measured at constant price) was due to plowing back the profits. Some foreign loans to the Chinese government were provided by foreign banks or merchants residing in China, and some were used to pay interest on previous loans borrowed abroad. If allowance is made for remittances of interest and profits on foreign investments, not only was there no net inflow of capital but there was a considerable net outflow throughout the period 1902–1936. (For the period 1902–1931 the inflow–outflow ratio was 57 percent.)

Why was the amount of foreign investment and capital inflow small? It is true that, historically, foreign investment has never constituted a sizable proportion of capital formation or national income of a large country, but in the Chinese case there seem to have been special factors responsible for the small amount of foreign investment. An examination of the history of international capital movements provides two broad generalizations. First, the golden age of international capital movement occurred in the few decades before 1914, when Great Britain, the chief creditor of the world, invested abroad about 4 percent of her national income. However, the capital went chiefly to the so-called "regions of recent settlement": the spacious and virtually empty plains of Canada, the United States, Argentina, Australia, and other new countries in the world's temperate latitudes. The export of capital to these places was also accompanied by a migration of about sixty million people, including many trained and enterprising persons from Europe. Only about a quarter of the British capital exported went to what are known today as the low-income, underdeveloped economies. The second generalization is that the capital that did go to the underdeveloped countries was induced primarily by primary production for export to the industrial countries. This has become known as the "colonial" type of investment.

China obviously did not possess the characteristics of the "regions of recent settlement." She was densely populated, and there was no appreciable immigration to China. She also differed from many of the other underdeveloped countries in that, although she was a target of Western exploitation, China never became a colony of any power. Because of the international power struggle, she managed to maintain her sovereignty, however intruded upon in certain respects. For economic activities such as trading and manufacturing, foreign investors enjoyed the fullest degree of freedom, but only in the trading ports. For economic activities that had to take place outside the treaty ports, such as railroad construction, mining, and plantations, they had to negotiate with the Chinese government. Despite setbacks, China was generally successful in stopping foreign economic penetration of the interior. The restrictive mining regulations (requiring Sino-foreign joint ownership, etc.) were not repealed or substantially modified, despite foreign demands. Foreign nationals, with the exception of missionaries, were not permitted to own or lease land outside the treaty ports. For these reasons, there was relatively little foreign capital in primary production in China.

In the treaty ports, where foreigners were protected by extraterritorial rights, foreign investments were made largely in fields associated with foreign trade. Such investment could not have grown large because of the small volume of trade, a concomitance of the low level of national income. No substantial amount of foreign investment was made in manufacturing because it was not as profitable as it appeared. For the products that the Chinese masses could afford to buy, traditional handicrafts proved to be a stubborn and effective competitor of modern technology. For the products that were beyond the reach of traditional technology, the market was limited because of the poverty and low purchasing power of the masses. As for the foreign borrowing by the government, the amount seems to have been restricted by the terms of the loans — especially the "control clause," which, however desirable from the viewpoint of the investors, was deeply resented by the Chinese. The international power struggle and the political implications of the loans also limited the choice or willingness of the government to borrow abroad.

Although small in amount, foreign capital played a significant role in bringing about whatever economic modernization existed in China before 1937. The most obvious link between foreign investment and China's economic modernization was that the former not only performed the pioneering entrepreneurial function of introducing modern technology into a number of fields but also accounted for a large share of the modern sector of the economy. Most of the railroads were built with foreign capital. It was predominant in water transportation as well. Foreign capital was present in virtually all modern iron mines and works, through either Sino-foreign joint ownership or loans. More than one half of the total output of coal from 1912 to 1937 was produced by mines that were either completely foreign-owned or foreign-controlled by means of co-ownership or large loans.

In each of a number of manufacturing industries of the factory type — such as sawmills, shipbuilders, water, gas, and electric works, tanners, cigarette, soda water, and egg producers — foreign-owned firms accounted for more than 50 percent of the total output in 1933, although for such industries as a whole the ratio was only 35 percent. In cotton textiles, the most important light industry in China before 1937, foreign mills accounted for more than 40 percent of total yarn spindles and nearly 70 percent of all looms in the 1930's. The largest part (perhaps as high as 90 percent as late as 1930) of the import–export trade and other international transactions was handled by foreign banks and trading firms in China.

The growth of the modern sector of the economy was not the product of foreign capital alone, however. Chinese capital and entrepreneurship also contributed to the growth. In the nineteenth century the Chinese government figured significantly in efforts toward economic modernization. These efforts were to a large extent a response to the Western challenge, a symbol of which was foreign economic penetration. Fearful of foreign domination, politically or economically, the government tried to develop in the 1860's the manufacture of ammunition and weapons for the purpose of defending the country against invasion. In the 1870's it was realized that to counterbalance foreign economic penetration it was necessary to adopt economic countermeasures. In addition to establishing enterprises by itself, the government adopted the formula of "official supervising and merchant undertaking," according to which the government exercised initiative and supervision while the private businessman supplied capital and management. The total number of enterprises that were either entirely government-owned or under state supervision was pitifully small, but the total expenditure of officials funds for these enterprises constituted a heavy burden to the government budget.

The government did not limit itself to establishing such enterprises. It also adopted or tried to adopt a host of other measures to promote development, such as founding language and technical schools, sending students abroad, exempting Chinese machine-produced goods from the troublesome likin, granting monopoly rights to certain types of manufactures, awarding official ranks to certain entrepreneurs, and guaranteeing dividends to stockholders of certain industrial corporations. It is doubtful that any of the measures had a really important impact, but they helped to create an atmosphere that encouraged the efforts of private individuals to undertake economic modernization. In the few years from 1903 to 1908, when the movement called Recovering Economic Interests, a symbol of growing nationalism, was at its peak, a number of corporations were formed by private individuals with the stated purpose of resisting foreign economic influence.

Therefore, foreign investment — a symbol of foreign invasion — supplied the fuel for nationalism, and the nationalistic spirit provided the will to develop modern industries. Moreover, foreign investment helped to establish an environment in which profits could be expected from industrial undertakings. Foreign factories were the precursors of many Chinese industries, and they were the training ground for Chinese to acquire modern techniques. Foreign investment provided much of the social overhead (banking, public utilities, railroad, etc.) that facilitated the development of Chinese-owned enterprises. Finally, the entire treaty port system, a concomitance of foreign investment in China, provided a degree of law and order in the treaty ports where the Chinese-owned modern enterprises were chiefly located.

When the Treaty of Shimonoseki was concluded with Japan in 1895, granting Japanese nationals (and other foreign nationals by virtue of the most-favored-nation clause) the right to manufacture in the treaty ports, a widespread anxiety was expressed that the Chinese modern enterprises would not be able to develop. It was feared that foreign firms would outcompete their Chinese counterparts. Available evidence shows, however, that the Chinese share in the modern sector remained remarkably stable in the long run. In the main there was a persistent coexistence between Chinese and foreign enterprises in the modern sector during the years before 1937. As a group, Chinese enterprises were able to grow as fast as foreign firms over the long run. Such a performance suggests that the various advantages that foreign firms are supposed to have enjoyed — such as strong financial backing, better technical and managerial skill, and immunity from Chinese laws, taxes, and official abuse — may have been exaggerated. There may also have been forces working to the advantage of the Chinese enterprises, such as nationalism, boycotts, the "buy-Chinese" appeal, labor relationships, local knowledge, and location. It is likely that in many cases the market was divided between Chinese and foreign firms, thereby eliminating or keeping at a minimum severe competition between them.

The often-held assertion that the traditional or indigenous sector of the Chinese economy (handicrafts, small mines, junks, etc.) suffered a severe decline as a result of foreign economic intrusion lacks factual support. The traditional sector remained overwhelmingly dominant, even in the 1930's. Although its relative share in the economy decreased, there is little evidence to suggest that it suffered an absolute decline. On the contrary, in cases such as coal mining, shipping, and cotton weaving it may even have grown, although at a low rate.

How did the traditional sector manage to survive modern competition (imported and factory-made products)? One important explanation is that the traditional technology employed more labor relative to capital, as compared with the modern sector, where more capital intensive technology was used. Since the price of labor relative to that of capital was low, the unit cost of production by traditional technology may not have been higher than that by modern technology, although labor productivity in the traditional sector was lower than that in the modern sector. As a consequence, modern technology could do no more than concentrate on products that were beyond the reach of traditional technology. Since these products were more expensive, they were also beyond the purchasing power of the Chinese masses.

Although cheap labor and the poverty of the masses were the basis of survival of the traditional sector, the development of the modern sector also had favorable effects on the traditional sector with regard to supply and demand. There was a persistent increase in internal and external demand for traditional products; for instance, the increase of trade also increased the demand for native junks. Moreover, the modern sector supplied the traditional sector not only with goods and services necessary for its growth but also with a technology that strengthened its competitive power. The hand-weaving industry in Kao-yang is a case in point.

China's external trade, growing in physical terms at the compound rate of about 2.5 percent a year from 1867 to 1932, constituted approximately 9 percent of her national income in 1933. The growth in volume was accompanied by an increasing diversification in both imports and exports. The lack of export concentration may be explained in part by the fact that little foreign capital was used in the development of primary production. While there was instability in exports (in quantity, price, and proceeds), the degree of instability appears relatively mild compared with that of many leading primary products exported by the underdeveloped countries. The external market for China's leading exports was a small proportion of the total domestic production. Although there were a number of commodities that were produced primarily for export, these commodities were not important in total exports.

The trend of the commodity terms of trade moved against China from 1867 to 1936. At the end of the period, a given quantity of exports could pay for only 71 percent of the imports that it could have bought at the beginning of the period. The trend appeared fairly stable in 1867–1900 but became noticeably unfavorable after 1900. This change was determined primarily by forces in the world market. Since China was a price taker as both a buyer and a supplier in the world market, especially after the turn of the century, her commodity terms of trade were not appreciably affected by capital transfer or by the declining trend of the purchasing power of silver (for all commodities) in the countries with which she had trade relations. (China was on the silver standard.) Both the total gain from trade (measured by Viner's index) and the capacity to import (measured by the income terms of trade) were improved, despite the deterioration of the commodity terms of trade. There is also evidence that the development of railroads and shipping reduced the cost of transportation and therefore the cost of exports.

The inflow of capital in gross terms was significant in China's balance of payments before 1913. It was not much less in magnitude than the unfavorable balance of the merchandise trade. After 1914 the inpayments on foreign investments were small, even compared with China's trade deficit on merchandise account. For the entire period 1902–1936 the total outpayments on foreign investments outbalanced the inpayments. Total foreign investment service (remittance of profits on direct investments, and interest and amortization on government loans) average 25 percent of the total receipts on current account of China's balance of payments for the years 1902–1913. The ratio was 16 percent in 1914–1930 and smaller in later years.

These, then, are the broad findings of this study. It can be said that foreign investment played an important role in bringing about whatever economic modernization or "preconditions" for development China experienced, that the Chinese-owned enterprises and the traditional sector survived the destructive effects of foreign competition, and that foreign investment did not result in a lopsided export development and all its accompanying evils, such as excessive external instability. Can the conclusion then be drawn that foreign investments were all to the benefit of China and that their pattern should be repeated in countries resembling China? The answer is hardly yes, for only certain aspects of the impact of foreign investment on China have been examined, and no claim is made that all the possible or even all the important aspects have been scrutinized. In forming a judgment on the effects of foreign investment, one has to examine not only the economic consequences but also the psychological, social, and political consequences.

These forces are mutually determining and reinforcing, especially for a country that embarks on a new road to modernization and has to make all the necessary adjustments. For example, did the treaty port system under which foreign investment took place lessen or promote political instability? Did it hinder or foster democratic tendencies in China? Did it weaken the Chinese government? How did it affect the social structure, the social psychology, and the traditional values and institutions? Did it obstruct or facilitate the process of adjustment to the modern age? In short, what would have happened to the Chinese society if there had been no external intrusions associated with foreign trade and investment? Speculation on these questions may be necessary to form a final judgment on the over-all effect of foreign investment on China; but such speculation can not be made here.

On the other hand, it is equally true that no analysis of Chinese modern history or social change is complete that fails to take account of foreign economic impact. The conclusions reached in this book regarding the effects of foreign investment on the Chinese economy are for the most part different from those that have been widely held. It would be presumptuous to suggest that the analyses and findings presented here are always correct, but an important purpose will have been served if, as a result of this study, the validity of the traditional views on foreign investment is questioned rather than taken for granted by the students of social change.

From the viewpoint of general theory of international investment, our findings tend to support the classical position (as recently expounded by Haberler) rather than the Singer-Prebisch-Myrdal thesis. Foreign trade and investment were innovating forces in whatever economic modernization or "preconditions" for development China had. It is not possible to ascertain whether China or the West obtained the greater benefit from their economic contact. Development in China was basically a matter of change in the attitude of the government toward economic affairs, in the direction in which savings were employed, and in the level of technology and inventiveness. Changes of this kind are hardly subject to quantitive measurement and may not be reflected in the level of per-capita income in the short run. The Singer-Prebisch-Myrdal thesis is thus not applicable to the Chinese experience, though it may still apply to other underdeveloped countries, especially those where there has been an export development. The underdeveloped countries are by no means homogeneous, and it is dangerous to make generalizations.

APPENDIX

NOTES

INDEX

Appendix

Table 45. Type of foreign investments in China by country
(US$ millions; percent in parentheses).

Year	Direct investments		Obligations of Chinese government	Total
		Great Britain		
1902	150.0	(57.6)	110.3 (42.4)	260.3
1914	400.0	(65.8)	207.5 (34.2)	607.5
1930	963.4	(81.0)	225.8 (19.0)	1189.2
1936	1059.3	(86.8)	161.5 (13.2)	1220.8
		Japan[a]		
1900	1.0	(100.0)	0.0	1.0
1914	192.5	(87.6)	9.6 (4.4)	219.6
1930	874.1	(76.9)	224.1 (19.7)	1136.9
1936	1117.8	(80.2)	241.4 (17.3)	1394.0
		United States		
1875	7.0	(100.0)	0.0	7.0
1900	17.5	(88.8)	2.2 (11.2)	19.7
1914	42.0	(85.2)	7.3 (14.8)	49.3
1930	155.1	(78.8)	41.7 (21.2)	196.8
1936	244.6	(81.9)	54.2 (18.1)	298.8
		Russia		
1903	220.0	(89.4)	26.0 (10.6)	246.0
1914	236.5	(87.8)	32.8 (12.2)	269.3
1930	273.2	(100.0)	0.0	273.2
		France		
1902	29.6	(32.5)	61.5 (67.5)	91.1
1914	60.0	(35.0)	111.4 (65.0)	171.4
1931	95.0	(49.4)	97.4 (50.6)	192.4
1936	142.0	(60.7)	92.1 (39.3)	234.1
		Germany		
1902–1904	85.0	(51.7)	79.3 (48.3)	164.3
1914	136.0	(51.6)	127.6 (48.4)	263.6
1931	75.0	(86.2)	12.0 (13.8)	87.0
1936	59.1	(39.8)	89.4 (60.2)	148.5
		Belgium		
1931	41.0	(46.0)	48.0 (54.0)	89.0
1936	13.8	(23.6)	44.6 (76.4)	58.4
		Netherlands		
1931	10.0	(34.8)	18.7 (65.2)	28.7
		Italy		
1931	4.4	(9.6)	42.0 (90.4)	46.4
1936	7.8	(10.8)	64.5 (89.2)	72.3
		Scandinavia		
1931	2.2	(71.0)	0.9 (29.0)	3.1

Table 45 (continued)

Source: For years before 1931, see Remer, *Foreign Investments*, Pt. 2. For 1936, see Table 1, notes. Note that for individual countries, as shown in Tables 45 and 46, Remer gives 1900 and 1930 among other varying years dating foreign investment in China. In Tables 1–4 where Remer's summary figures appear, however, the years were made uniform at 1902 and 1931.

ᵃ Japanese totals include loans to private Chinese parties, estimated as follows: 1914, US$17.5 million (4.4 percent); 1930, $38.7 million (3.8 percent); 1936, $34.8 million (2.5 percent).

Table 46. Industrial distribution of foreign direct investments by country, 1914–1936
(US$ millions; percent in parentheses.)

Year	Transportation	Communications, public utilities	Mining	Manufacturing	Banking, finance	Real estate	Import-export	Sundry	Total
				Great Britain					
1930	134.9 (13.9)	48.2 (5.0)	19.3 (2.0)	173.4 (18.0)	115.6 (12.0)	202.3 (21.0)	240.8 (25.1)	28.9 (3.0)	963.4 (100)
1936	61.4 (5.8)	48.6 (4.6)	15.8 (1.5)	179.8 (17.0)	302.4 (28.5)	202.3 (19.1)	243.9 (23.0)	5.1 (0.5)	1059.3 (100)
				Japan					
1914	68.3 (35.5)	3.5 (1.8)	29.1 (15.1)	10.6 (5.5)	6.4 (3.3)	8.5 (4.4)	42.5 (22.1)	23.6 (12.3)	192.5 (100)
1930	204.5 (23.4)	15.7 (1.8)	87.4 (10.0)	165.2 (18.9)	73.4 (8.4)	73.4 (8.4)	182.7 (20.9)	71.6 (8.2)	874.1 (100)
1936	558.7 (50.0)	3.9 (0.3)	22.2 (2.0)	328.3 (29.4)	95.7 (8.6)	8.6 (0.8)	45.5 (4.1)	55.0 (4.9)	1117.8 (100)
				United States					
1930	10.8 (7.2)	35.2 (23.4)	0.1 (0.1)	20.5 (13.7)	25.3 (16.8)	8.5 (5.6)	47.7 (31.8)	2.1 (1.4)	150.2 (100)
1936	6.1 (2.5)	70.0 (28.6)	0.0	9.4 (3.8)	53.4 (21.8)	8.5 (3.5)	94.5 (38.6)	2.7 (1.1)	244.6 (100)
				Russia					
1930	210.5 (77.0)	0.0	2.1 (0.8)	12.8 (4.7)	0.0	32.5 (11.9)	12.2 (4.5)	3.1 (1.1)	273.2 (100)
				France					
1936	33.1 (23.3)	11.4 (8.0)		2.0 (1.4)	60.4 (42.5)	21.7 (15.3)	13.3 (9.4)	0.1 (0.1)	142.0 (100)
				Germany					
1936	3.8 (6.5)	0.1 (0.2)	0.4 (0.7)	7.1 (12.0)	12.4 (21.0)	0.0	35.2 (59.6)	0.0	59.1 (100)
				Italy					
1936	2.0 (25.6)	0.0	0.0	0.0	4.0 (51.3)	0.0	1.8 (23.1)	0.0	7.8 (100)
				Belgium					
1936	0.0	3.8 (27.5)	3.5 (25.4)	0.0	4.9 (35.5)	0.0	1.6 (11.6)	0.0	13.8 (100)
				Others					
1936	4.5 (12.1)	0.5 (1.3)	0.0	0.0	15.4 (41.4)	0.0	14.4 (38.7)	2.4 (6.5)	37.2 (100)

Source: See Table 45.

Table 47. Contractions of foreign loans to the Chinese government by use, 1861–1937 (£ thousands; percent in parentheses).[a]

Year[b]	Military, indemnity	Administrative	Railroad[c]	Industrial	Total
1861	100 (100)	0	0	0	100
1862	253 (100)	0	0	0	253
1864	80 (100)	0	0	0	80
1866	107 (100)	0	0	0	107
1867	1,067 (100)	0	0	0	1,067
1874	634 (100)	0	0	0	634
1875	977 (100)	0	0	0	977
1877	1,500 (100)	0	0	0	1,500
1878	521 (100)	0	0	0	521
1881	1,108 (100)	0	0	0	1,108
1883	560 (100)	0	0	0	560
1884	2,563 (100)	0	0	0	2,563
1885	1,000 (100)	0	0	0	1,000
1886	750 (80)	192 (20)	0	0	942
1887	0	250 (51)	243 (49)	0	493
1888	0	462 (100)	0	0	462
1889	0	0	440 (100)	0	440
1893	0	197 (100)	0	0	197
1894	1,635 (100)	0	0	0	1,635
1895	20,820 (100)	0	0	0	20,820
1896	16,000 (100)	0	0	0	16,000
1898	16,000 (70)	0	6,800 (30)	0	22,800
1900	0	0	0	210 (100)	210
1901	0	0	0	48 (100)	48
1902	0	0	1,600 (100)	0	1,600
1903	0	0	1,000 (100)	0	1,000
1904	0	0	2,250 (100)	0	2,250
1905	1,000 (29)	0	2,400 (71)	0	3,400
1907	0	267 (9)	2,790 (91)	0	3,057
1908	0	0	4,715 (83)	1,000 (17)	5,715
1909	0	67 (3)	2,320 (97)	0	2,387
1910	0	0	3,220 (100)	0	3,200
1911	0	267 (4)	7,000 (90)	500 (6)	7,767
1912	397 (4)	7,000 (73)	2,150 (23)	0	9,547
1913	3,500 (9)	25,000 (66)	5,401 (14)	4,000 (11)	37,901
1914	1,302 (16)	5,705 (71)	1,016 (13)	0	8,023
1915	0	120 (18)	500 (76)	42 (6)	662
1916	0	441 (19)	1,911 (81)	0	2,352
1917	4,161 (76)	232 (4)	650 (12)	450 (8)	5,493
1918	2,014 (12)	9,639 (60)	1,507 (9)	3,066 (19)	16,227
1919	1,869 (25)	3,235 (44)	798 (11)	1,436 (20)	7,338
1920	73 (1)	330 (4)	5,579 (74)	1,588 (21)	7,570
1921	0	147 (3)	4,395 (93)	181 (4)	4,723
1922	0	271 (3)	7,077 (81)	1,420 (16)	8,768
1923	0	780 (100)	0	0	780
1924	0	1,619 (100)	0	0	1,619
1925	130 (2)	6,287 (96)	144 (2)	3 (—)	6,564

Table 47 (continued)

Year[b]	Military, indemnity	Administrative	Railroad[c]	Industrial	Total
1926	0	530 (100)	0	0	530
1928	0	0	1,027 (87)	150 (13)	1,177
1929	0	0	156 (34)	307 (66)	463
1931	0	189 (100)	0	0	189
1932	0	0	0	50 (100)	50
1933	0	5,408 (87)	671 (11)	127 (2)	6,206
1934	0	0	3,401 (80)	875 (20)	4,276
1935	0	471 (51)	450 (49)	0	921
1936	0	1,090 (10)	10,017 (90)	0	11,107
1937	0	853 (9)	8,636 (87)	411 (4)	9,900

Source: For 1861–1893, see T'ang Hsiang-lung, "Min-kuo i-ch'ien kuan-shui tan-pao chih wai-chai." For military, indemnity, administrative, and industrial loans, see Coons, Tables A and C; Chia Shih-i, *Hsü ts'ai-cheng shih*, IV, 84–192; Chia Te-huai, pp. 319, 336; *China Yearbook, 1938*, pp. 502–511; Kao P'ing-shu, pp. 55, 58.

For railroad loans (1894–1926), see Cheng Lin, pp. 24–57; for 1927–1937, see *China Yearbook, 1938*, pp. 500–509; Bank of China, *Chinese Government Foreign Loan Obligations*, table of the foreign loans of China compiled by E. Kann and J. Baylin; Chang Chia-nau, pp. 94–148. See also Yen Chung-p'ing, ed., *T'ung-chi tzu-liao*, table of railroad loans; Tōa kenkyūjo, *Shogaikoku no tai-Shi tōshi*, Vol. 2; *T'ieh-tao nien-chien* (Railroad yearbook; 1933), Vol. 1.

[a] The different currencies are converted as follows:

> £1 =   4.8665 U.S. dollars
> 10 yen (before 1926)
> 17 yen (1935)
> 25 French francs (before 1916)
> 30 French francs (1919)
> 83.4 French francs (1933)
> 60 Belgian francs (before 1920)
> 147.456 Belgian francs (1936)
> 12.1 Netherland florins
> 20 marks (before 1914)
> 13 marks (1934)
> 16.5696 yuan or CNdollars (1935–1937)
> 1 tael = 1.5 silver dollars (of various sorts).

The different taels are all treated like Haikwan taels. (When contracted in taels, Chinese foreign loans were mostly contracted in the K'up'ing tael, which was nearly the same as the Haikwan.) These conversion rates are very close to the actual yearly averages of the current exchange rates for the years when the loans were contracted. Since the foreign loans were largely contracted in pounds sterling, the rates should not distort the picture in any significant way.

The classification of loans is based, insofar as possible, on the actual utilization of the funds. For instance, loans that were contracted for railroad or industrial purposes, but were actually used for administrative purposes, are included in the latter category. Loans about which the actual use is not known are classified according to the original purpose for which they were contracted. Loans contracted for the repayment of previous loans that have already been included in the totals are not included. For instance, a large part of the Peking-Hankow railroad redemption loan of 1908 is not included

Table 47 (continued)

because it was used to redeem the Lukouchiao-Hankow railroad loan of 1898, already recorded. However, where it is doubtful whether the previous loans are recorded, loans contracted for the repayment of previous debts are included. For instance, quite a portion of the Reorganization Loan of 1912 was disposed of to pay for previous debts, but, since it can not be determined whether the previous loans are recorded, we include the total amount of the loan. For the same reason we include about £2.2 million that was contracted between 1912 and 1926 for the payment of previous debts. Loans that were contracted but not issued are not included.

 b For the years omitted, no loans are known to have been contracted.

 c The list of railroad loans for 1894–1926 provided by Cheng Lin is corrected as follows: the Nanking-Shanghai railroad loan (first issue) of 1904 should be £2,250,000; the Tientsin-Pukow railroad loan (first issue) of 1908 should be £3 million; the fourth issue of the Tientsin-Pukow railroad loan of 1910 was not issued; the Ssupingkai-Changchitun railroad loan of 1915 should be 5 million yen; the Chuchow-Chinchow railroad loan of 1916 should be US$1,150,000; the Kirin-Chungchun railroad loan (revised) of 1917 should be 6,500,000 yen; the Kaomi-Suchow-Shunte-Tsonan railroad loan of 1918 was used for administrative purposes.

Additions to Cheng's list include: the Tangshan-Hsukochweng railroad loan of 1887 (1 million taels); the Tientsin-T'ungchow railroad loan of 1889 (2 million taels); the Sha-Hsing railroad loan of 1914 (£50,000); the Lung-Hai railroad 7 percent notes of 1916 (10 million Belgian francs); the Peking-Suiyuan railroad loan of 1918 (3 million yen); the Peking Suiyuan railroad loan of 1922 (silver $300,000). Also added to the list are the Canton-Kowloon railroad advances of 1913 (£50,000) and the various railroad material and supply loans as reported in Chia Shih-i, *Hsü ts'ai-cheng shih*, Vol. 4. The dates given by Chia for these loans may not be entirely accurate since the amounts of some of them were cumulative. To the railroad loans for 1927–1937 are added the French material loan of 1933 (56 million francs) and the French material loan of 1935 (£450,000).

Table 48. Holdings of Chinese government obligations by country, 1902–1936 (percent).ᵃ

Country	1902	1914	1930	1936
Great Britain	38.7	39.5	31.8	21.1
Japan	0.0	1.8	31.5	31.5
Germany	27.9	24.3	1.7	11.7
France	21.6	21.2	13.7	12.0
Belgium	0.0	0.0	6.8	5.8
Italy	0.0	0.0	5.9	8.4
United States	0.8	1.4	5.9	7.1
Russia	9.3	6.2	0.0	0.0
Netherlands	0.0	0.0	2.6	0.0
Others	1.8	5.6	0.1	2.4
Total	100.0	100.0	100.0	100.0
Total obligations (in US$ millions)	284.7	525.8	710.6	766.7

Source: See Table 45.

ᵃ Percentages may not total 100 because of the rounding of numbers.

Table 49. Distribution of foreign railroad loans to the Chinese government by country (US$ millions; percent in parentheses).[a]

Country	1914	1931	1935
Great Britain	88.5 (45.0)	70.4 (28.3)	64.9 (19.8)
Japan	11.0 (5.6)	83.6 (33.6)	92.1 (28.1)
Belgium	13.6 (6.9)	37.5 (15.1)	53.6 (16.4)
Germany	37.2 (18.9)	0.0	53.6 (16.4)
France	38.7 (19.7)	13.9 (5.6)	12.3 (3.8)
United States	7.5 (3.8)	15.0 (6.0)	11.3 (3.4)
Netherlands	0.0	18.2 (7.3)	39.3 (12.0)
Others	0.0	9.9 (4.0)	0.0
Total	196.5 (100.0)	248.5 (100.0)	327.1 (100.0)

Source: For 1914, Kao P'ing-shu, p. 24 (US$1 = Chin$2); for 1931, Remer, *Foreign Investments*, pp. 140, 143 and 531; for 1935, Chang Chia-nau, p. 172 (£1 = US$4.92). Remer's estimate of US$63.1 million for Japanese railroad loans in Manchuria in 1931 is added to Chang's estimate for Japan in 1935. Foreign railroad loans totaling US$93.3 million were contracted by the government in 1936 and 1937. By country, they were: Great Britain, US$47.7 million; Belgium, 15.3 million; Germany, 13.9 million; France, 13.4 million; Czechoslovakia, 1.4 million; United States, 1.5 million. (See Chang Chia-nau, Pt. 2.)
[a] Percentages may not total 100 because of the rounding of numbers.

Table 50. Production of iron mines in China, 1918–1937 (percent).[a]

Period	Hanyeh-p'ing	Anshan	Miao-Er-Kou	Others	Total	Thousands of metric tons
			Iron Ore			
1918–1923	36	9	5	50	100	1623
1924–1927	16	20	5	59	100	1639
1928–1931	18	31	6	45	100	2333
1935–1937	17	41	10	32	100	3237
			Pig Iron			
1915–1918	41	0	11	48	100	354
1919–1925	27	18	12	44	100	388
1926–1931	0	47	16	37	100	441
1935–1937	0	60	18	21	100	735

Source: For 1915–1931, Ku Yuan-t'ien, p. 706. For 1935–1937, *Chung-kuo k'uang-yeh chi-yao*, No. 7:100–102.
[a] Manchuria included. Percentages may not total 100 because of the rounding of numbers.

Table 51. Foreign capital in the coal production of China by country, 1918–1937 (percent).[a]

Year	Japanese	British	German	Russian	Chinese	Total	Millions of metric tons
1918	20.2	22.0	3.5	0.9	53.4	100	18.4
1920	20.9	23.9	2.0	1.4	51.8	100	21.3
1922	24.9	20.2	2.3	0.9	51.7	100	21.1
1924	27.6	20.4	2.0	0.9	49.1	100	25.8
1926	32.7	16.8	1.5	1.2	47.8	100	23.0
1928	33.1	19.8	1.1	2.3	43.7	100	25.1
1935	35.0	8.7	0.6	0.0	55.8	100	35.8
1936	34.5	7.9	0.6	0.0	57.0	100	39.3
1937	40.2	7.8	0.6	0.0	51.4	100	36.9

Source: For 1918–1928, see Wu Pan-nung, p. 37. In foreign shares, Wu only states that the production of all mines in which foreign capital participated is included. He probably includes the total production of the Sino-foreign mines in the foreign shares. For 1935–1937, see *Chung-kuo k'uang-yeh chi-yao*, No. 7. For these three years the capital ratio is used in calculating the share of foreign capital in the production of Sino-foreign mines.

[a] Manchuria included. Both modern and small mines included. Percentages may not total 100 because of the rounding of numbers.

Table 52. Statistics on China's foreign trade.[a]

			Exports				Imports	
Year	Total value in Haikwan taels (millions)	Year-to-year change in value[b] (percent)	Quantity index (1913 = 100)	Year-to-year change in quantity (percent)	Price index (1913 = 100)	Year-to-year change in price (percent)	Quantity index (1913 = 100)	Price index (1913 = 100)
1864	48.7	—	—	—	—	—	—	—
1865	54.1	+10	—	—	—	—	—	—
1866	50.6	− 6	—	—	—	—	—	—
1867	52.2	+ 3	31.9	—	52.2	—	24.7	41.2
1868	61.8	+16	33.7	+ 5	59.5	+12	25.4	41.2
1869	60.1	− 3	35.4	+ 5	55.3	− 7	26.4	42.1
1870	55.3	− 8	33.3	− 6	53.3	− 3	25.9	40.8
1871	66.9	+17	39.4	+15	54.7	+ 2	28.1	41.5
1872	75.3	+11	43.3	+ 9	56.4	+ 3	27.9	40.1
1873	69.5	− 8	39.1	−10	57.1	+ 1	27.3	40.4
1874	66.7	− 4	40.1	+ 2	53.4	− 7	31.5	33.5
1875	68.9	+ 3	42.2	+ 5	47.2	−12	33.8	30.8
1876	80.9	+15	42.8	+ 1	54.2	+13	36.3	29.5
1877	67.4	−17	40.8	− 5	47.5	−12	36.1	31.0
1878	67.2	− 1	41.4	+ 1	46.9	− 1	34.9	31.1
1879	72.3	+ 7	43.2	+ 4	48.0	+ 2	40.8	30.7
1880	77.9	+ 7	47.2	+ 8	47.9	− 0	36.2	33.4
1881	71.5	− 8	43.5	− 8	47.6	− 1	40.8	34.7
1882	67.3	− 6	45.9	+ 5	42.6	−10	36.4	32.7
1883	70.2	+ 4	47.2	+ 3	43.0	+ 1	35.0	32.3
1884	67.1	− 4	50.6	+ 7	38.6	−10	34.5	32.3

Table 52 (continued)

			Exports				Imports	
Year	Total value in Haikwan taels (millions)	Year-to-year change in value[b] (percent)	Quantity index (1913 = 100)	Year-to-year change in quantity (percent)	Price index (1913 = 100)	Year-to-year change in price (percent)	Quantity index (1913 = 100)	Price index (1913 = 100)
1885	65.0	− 3	47.6	− 6	39.9	+ 3	40.5	33.2
1886	77.2	+16	54.2	+12	41.3	+ 3	35.3	37.8
1887	85.9	+10	41.2	−24	60.0	+31	41.6	37.4
1888	92.4	+ 7	43.6	+ 6	60.3	+ 1	50.3	37.8
1889	96.9	+ 5	45.2	+ 4	61.1	+ 1	44.0	38.5
1890	87.1	− 10	42.0	− 7	58.9	− 4	54.8	35.2
1891	100.9	+14	47.9	+12	59.6	+ 1	60.8	33.5
1892	102.6	+ 2	49.8	+ 4	58.5	− 2	59.9	34.5
1893	116.6	+12	57.2	+13	57.3	− 2	59.4	38.4
1894	128.1	+ 9	60.1	+ 5	59.4	+ 4	45.3	54.2
1895	143.3	+11	66.3	+ 9	60.0	+ 1	45.8	57.8
1896	131.1	− 9	56.4	− 5	64.7	+ 7	53.2	58.8
1897	163.5	+20	61.6	+ 8	73.5	+12	49.7	63.0
1898	159.0	− 3	63.4	+ 3	69.4	− 6	51.3	63.3
1899	195.8	+19	62.5	− 1	86.7	+20	69.2	59.4
1900	159.0	− 19	54.9	−12	80.1	− 8	49.5	65.9
1901	169.7	+ 6	59.8	+ 8	78.2	− 2	62.5	66.8
1902	214.2	+21	65.1	+ 8	90.1	+13	70.9	74.4
1903	214.4	+ 0	59.8	− 8	98.1	+ 8	65.1	83.9
1904	239.5	+10	64.0	+ 7	92.7	− 5	69.2	87.2
1905	227.9	− 5	62.5	− 2	90.4	− 2	96.6	81.2
1906	236.5	+ 4	64.6	+ 3	90.6	+ 0	95.3	75.4
1907	264.4	+11	67.1	+ 4	97.6	+ 7	88.7	82.3
1908	276.7	+ 4	73.0	+ 8	94.1	− 4	72.7	95.4
1909	339.0	+18	92.9	+21	90.5	− 4	77.1	95.1
1910	380.8	+11	102.9	+10	91.8	+ 1	79.2	102.5
1911	377.3	− 1	102.1	− 1	91.5	− 0	80.9	102.2
1912	370.5	− 2	103.8	+ 2	88.6	− 3	82.8	100.0
1913	403.3	+ 8	100.0	− 4	100.0	+11	100.0	100.0
1914	356.2	− 12	83.8	−16	105.4	+ 5	91.6	108.9
1915	418.9	+15	96.5	+13	107.8	+ 2	70.3	113.0
1916	481.8	+13	102.3	+ 6	117.0	+ 8	73.7	122.4
1917	462.9	− 4	108.3	+ 6	106.2	− 9	73.4	131.0
1918	485.9	+ 5	105.5	− 3	114.5	+ 7	66.1	147.0
1919	630.8	+23	140.0	+25	112.0	− 2	75.4	150.2
1920	541.6	− 14	119.3	−15	112.9	+ 1	75.9	175.7
1921	601.3	+10	126.9	+ 6	117.6	+ 4	94.7	167.4
1922	654.9	+ 8	130.5	+ 3	124.7	+ 6	112.6	146.8
1923	752.9	+13	137.3	+ 5	136.3	+ 9	108.5	148.7
1924	771.8	+ 2	136.6	− 1	141.2	+ 3	119.6	148.8
1925	776.4	+ 1	132.9	− 3	145.9	+ 3	109.9	151.0
1926	864.3	+10	141.1	+ 6	152.9	+ 5	130.5	150.8
1927	918.6	+ 6	154.1	+ 8	148.9	− 3	109.8	161.7
1928	991.4	+ 7	156.1	+ 1	158.4	+ 6	131.5	159.1
1929	1015.7	+ 2	149.2	− 4	169.8	+ 7	139.9	158.1
1930	894.8	− 12	131.1	−12	170.4	+ 0	131.0	174.7
1931	909.5	+ 2	136.5	+ 4	166.3	− 2	129.9	192.9
1932	492.6	−36	100.8	−26	140.0	−16	106.0	180.1
1933	392.7	−20	124.7	+19	121.4	−13	97.5	173.2
1934	343.5	− 13	118.6	− 5	111.6	− 8	85.1	151.9
1935	369.6	+ 7	126.7	+ 6	112.4	+ 1	83.6	138.1
1936	453.0	+18	125.6	− 1	139.2	+19	77.9	152.3

Source: The value of exports is the recorded value of the Chinese custom trade returns. Figures after 1931 are taken from Cheng Yu-kwei, Appendix I. The quantity indices are Nankai's indices, and the price indices are adjusted Nankai's indices. For the adjustment, see Table 42.

ᵃ Manchuria not included after 1931.
ᵇ For definition, see Table 39.

Notes

Some of the preliminary findings of this study were published in *Economic Development and Cultural Change*, October 1961; *Journal of Asian Studies*, August 1961; and *Journal of Economic History*, September and December 1963. I wish to express my appreciation to the publishers for permission to incorporate those findings in this book.

INTRODUCTION

1. Mao Tse-tung, "The Chinese Revolution and the Chinese Communist Party," in *Selected Works of Mao Tse-tung* (Bombay, 1954), III, 77.

2. *Ibid*, p. 79.

3. Chiang Kai-shek, *China's Destiny*, tr. Wang Ch'ung-hui (New York, 1947), pp. 63–64.

4. *Ibid.*, p. 66.

5. *Ibid.*, p. 75.

6. Sun Yat-sen, *San min chu i*, tr. Frank W. Price (Shanghai, 1928), p. 37.

7. *Ibid.*, p. 54.

8. Sun Yat-sen, *The International Development of China* (New York, 1922).

9. For an understanding of the reactions of high Chinese officials to the West in the latter part of the nineteenth century, see Teng Ssu-yü and John K. Fairbank, *China's Response to the West: A Documentary Survey, 1839–1923* (Cambridge, Mass., 1954); Knight Biggerstaff, "The Secret Correspondence of 1867–1868: Views of Leading Chinese Statesmen Regarding the Further Opening of China to Western Influence," *Journal of Modern History*, 22.2:122–136 (June 1950); also, Chao Feng-t'ien, *Wan-Ch'ing wu-shih-nien ching-chi ssu-hsiang shih* (Economic thought during the last fifty years of the Ch'ing period; Peiping, 1939).

10. See Cheng Yu-kwei, *Foreign Trade and Industrial Development of China* (Washington, D.C., 1956), p. 41.

11. For a recent evaluation of Hobson and Lenin, see D. K. Fieldhouse, "Imperialism: An Historiographical Revision," *Economic History Review*, 14.2:187–209 (Dec. 1961). Hobson argued, in brief that the export of capital by capitalist countries was a device to solve the domestic problem of surplus capital due to underconsumption; that the capitalists exercised control and influence over the government, by force if necessary, in finding markets for their surplus capital; and that the indigenous people of the colonies of the European powers were invariably exploited by the appropriation of their land or their use as cheap labor — forced or nominally free — in mines, farms, and factories. Lenin differed from Hobson only in that he considered the export of capital to be not only a device to solve a domestic problem but also a necessary and inevitable tool for attempting to save capitalism.

12. H. W. Singer, "The Distribution of Gains between Investing and Borrowing Countries," *American Economic Review, Papers and Proceedings*, 40:473–485 (May 1950); Paul Prebisch, "Commercial Policy in the Underdeveloped Countries," *ibid.*, 49:251–273 (May 1959); United Nations, *The Economic Development of Latin America and Its Principal Problems* (New York, 1949); Gunnar Myrdal, *Rich Lands and Poor: The Road to World Prosperity* (New York, 1957).

13. Gottfried Haberler, *International Trade and Economic Development* (Cairo

Egypt, 1959); also his "Critical Observations on Some Current Notions in the Theory of Economic Development," *L'industria*, No. 2:8 (1957).

14. Haberler, *International Trade*, p. 5.

15. *Ibid.*, p. 11.

16. For a discussion of the controversy over the terms of trade, see Hou Chiming, "The Terms of Trade of China, 1867–1936," in Carl J. Friedrich and Seymour E. Harris, eds., *Public Policy, 1961* (Cambridge, Mass., 1962), pp. 341–365.

CHAPTER I

1. Earl H. Pritchard, *The Crucial Years of Early Anglo-Chinese Relations, 1750–1800* (Washington, D.C., 1936), pp. 391–396. H. B. Morse, *The Chronicles of the East India Company Trading to China, 1635–1834* (Oxford, 1926), Vol. 4. A summary of statistics on China's early external trade may be found in Yen Chung-p'ing, ed., *Chung-kuo chin-tai ching-chi shih t'ung-chi tzu-liao hsüan-chi* (Selected statistics on the modern economic history of China; Peking, 1955), p. 3.

2. See Chapter 3

3. C. F. Remer, *Foreign Investments in China* (New York, 1933), p. 66.

4. *Ibid.*, p. 66.

5. Yen Chung-p'ing, *T'ung-chi tzu-liao*, p. 244.

6. *Ibid.*, p. 134.

7. Remer, *Foreign Investments*, p. 70.

8. See Chapter 2.

9. Remer, *Foreign Investments*, p. 95.

10. This index may be found in Yang Twan-liu, Hou Hou-pei, *et al.*, *Statistics of China's Foreign Trade during the Last Sixty-Five Years* (National Research Institute of Social Sciences, Academia Sinica, 1931), p. 3.

11. Nan-k'ai ching-chi yen-chiu so (Nankai Institute of Economics), *Nan-k'ai chih-shu tzu-liao hui-pien* (Collection of Nankai's indices; Peking, 1958), p. 11.

12. Needless to say, the increase in various fields was uneven.

13. The institute's results were published in three huge volumes: Tōa kenkyūjo (East Asia Research Institute), *Shogaikoku no tai-Shi tōshi* (Foreign investments in China), Vol. 1 (Tokyo, 1942), Vols. 2 and 3 (Tokyo, 1943). For a summary, see Tōa kenkyūjo, *Rekkoku tai-Shi tōshi gaiyō* (An outline of foreign investments in China; Tokyo, 1943). These volumes do not include Japanese investments, which appear in Tōa kenkyūjo, *Nihon no tai-Shi tūshi* (Japanese investments in China; Tokyo, 1943). For a summary of Japanese as well as other investments, see Tōa kenkyūjo, *Rekkoku tai-Shi tōshi to Shina kokusai shūshi* (Foreign investments in China and China's balance of payments; Tokyo, 1944).

14. For instance, according to Remer, British investments in Hong Kong in 1929 amounted to US$89 million, and the public debt of the Hong Kong government in 1931 was estimated at about US$4 million, which was probably all in British hands. British investments in Hong Kong in 1931 were therefore in the neighborhood of US$93 million. According to the East Asia Research Institute, however, British investments in Hong Kong reached US$458.5 million. (See *Rekkoku tai-Shi tōshi to Shina kokusai shūshi*, pp. 198–201. Exchange rate at: Hong Kong $1 = US$0.3176.) In all likelihood, the increase was partly due to the different methods used by Remer and the institute in estimating investments, especially in banking and finance. The institute included all assets of the banking concerns,

whereas Remer included only certain kinds of assets. The inherent difficulty in allocating assets between Hong Kong and the rest of China must also be a reason for the large discrepancy.

15. The matter is further complicated by the conversion from yen to United States dollars. According to the *Japan Yearbook 1943–1944* (p. 965), Japanese investment in Manchuria was ¥1,700 million in 1931 and ¥2,863 million in 1936. In 1931 the exchange rate was US$1=¥2, while in 1936 it was US$1=¥3.45. Therefore, in United States dollars the investment figure was US$850 million in 1931 (considerably higher than Remer's figure of US$550 million) and US$830 million in 1936. Wholesale prices in Japan increased about 30 percent from 1931 to 1936. It is probable that the exchange rate in 1936 did not reflect accurately the internal and external purchasing power for the year. Foreign exchange control had been exercised by Japan since 1932. Of course, it is also possible that the 1931 estimate given by the *Japan Yearbook* was too high.

16. For the 1931 figure, Remer wrote: "Taking into account the errors in any such estimates, it may still be said with some certainty that the total falls between US$3000 million and US$3500 million." Remer, *Foreign Investments*, p. 58.

17. Employing a different definition of the term foreign investment, but relying principally on the Remer and Japanese estimates, Wu Ch'eng-ming arrived at some larger figures, as follows:

Foreign investment in China (US$ millions)

Country	1902	1914	1930	1936
Great Britain	344.1	661.6	1047.0	1045.9
United States	79.4	99.1	285.7	340.5
France	211.6	282.5	304.8	311.9
Germany	300.7	385.7	174.6	136.4
Japan	53.6	290.9	1411.6	2096.4
Russia	450.3	440.2	0.0	0.0
Others	69.6	92.7	263.9	354.3
Total	1509.3	2255.7	3487.6	4285.4

See Wu Ch'eng-ming, *Ti-kuo chu-i tsai chiu Chung-kuo ti t'ou-tzu* (Investments of imperialistic powers in Old China; Peking, 1958), p. 45. Wu defines foreign investment in China as the total amount of assets that foreigners "controlled." (In other words, the total assets instead of the owner's equity or proprietorship of a foreign firm are included.) All Sino-foreign enterprises are regarded as foreign enterprises. All indemnity payments are included in foreign debts of the Chinese government; and remissions of the Boxer indemnity are treated once more as foreign investments. The properties of all foreign religious, cultural, and philanthropic institutions are considered the same as those of foreign business firms, for they are all regarded as instruments of imperialism. For a detailed explanation of the methods of estimation, see his Appendix, pp. 147-188. Wu also lists in the appendix other estimates of foreign investment in China.

18. Remer, *Foreign Investments*, p. 395.

19. *Ibid.*, Chap. 17.
20. *Ibid.*, Chap. 18.
21. *Ibid.*, Chap. 19.
22. *Ibid.*, Chap. 20.
23. *Ibid.*, Chap. 15.
24. For a statistical summary of the nature of investments made in China by various countries before 1936, see Tables 45 and 46.

CHAPTER 2

1. There are variations in reports of China's early borrowings from foreign sources. The accounts given here are primarily those of T'ang Hsiang-lung, "Min-kuo i-ch'ien kuan-shui tan-pao chih wai-chai" (The foreign loans secured on the Customs revenue before 1911), *Chung-kuo chin-tai ching-chi-shih yen-chiu chi-k'an*, 3.1:1–49 (May 1935). See also C. John Stanley, *Late Ch'ing Finance: Hu Kuang-yung As an Innovator* (Cambridge, Mass., 1961), Chap. 5.

For other accounts of this period see Chia Shih-i, *Min-kuo ts'ai-cheng shih* (The financial history of the Republic of China; Shanghai, 1917), Vol. 2; S. R. Wagel, *Finance in China* (Shanghai, 1914); Ch'i Shu-fen, *Ching-chi ch'in lüeh hsia chih Chung-kuo* (China under economic exploitation; Shanghai, 1925); F. E. Lee, *Currency, Banking and Finance in China* (Washington, D.C., 1926); H. B. Morse, *The International Relations of the Chinese Empire*, Vol. 3, *The Period of Submission, 1894–1911* (London, 1918), Appendix A.

2. Chia reports that China first became involved in foreign loans in 1865, when she borrowed about £1,400,000 from an English bank to pay a war debt to Russia in accordance with the Treaty of Ili. See Chia Shih-i, *Ts'ai-cheng shih*, II, 1069.

3. Cheng Lin, *The Chinese Railways, Past and Present*, rev. ed. (Shanghai, 1937), p. 37. Also Yen Chung-p'ing, *T'ung-chi tzu-liao*, Chap. 5, Table 7.

4. This sum consisted of: the Hong Kong and Shanghai Bank silver loan of 1894 — 10 million Kuping taels (£1,635,000); the Hong Kong and Shanghai Bank gold loan of 1894 — £3 million; the Cassel loan of 1895 — £1 million; and the Arnhold, Karberg & Co. loan (or the Nanking loan) of 1895 — £1 million.

5. They were: the Franco-Russian gold loan of 1895 — 400 million francs (£15,820,000); the Anglo-German loan of 1896 — £16 million; and the Anglo-German loan of 1898 — £16 million.

6. They were: the Anglo-Danish telegraph loan of 1900 — £210,000; the supplementary Taku-Chefoo cable loan of 1901 — £48,000; and the advance on Anglo-Danish cable loan of 1911 — £500,000.

7. A. G. Coons, *The Foreign Public Debt of China* (Philadelphia, 1930), p. 15.

8. In 1923 Japan agreed to use the balance of the indemnity to promote cultural activities in China, but did not abandon her claims on the indemnity. China never received reports as to how the funds were employed. See *Ts'ai-cheng nien-chien* (Public finance yearbook; Shanghai, 1935), II, 1432.

9. Coons, p. 60; and Chia Shih-i, *Ts'ai-cheng Shih*, II, 1087–1097.

10. Remer, *Foreign Investments*, p. 540.

11. In these two years a total of ¥194 million (or £19.4 million) was borrowed from Japanese sources. Coons reports that the total amount of the Nishihara loans has been estimated by other than Chinese authorities to be as high as 200 million yen. Coons, p. 92.

12. Tōa kenkyūjo, *Nihon no tai-Shi tōshi*, Pt. 3.

13. Chia Shih-i, *Min-kuo hsü ts'ai-cheng shih* (The financial history of the Republic of China, Supplement; Shanghai, 1932–1934), Vol. 4.

14. Eugene Staley, *War and the Private Investor* (Garden City, N.Y., 1935), p. 13.

15. H. Frankel, *Capital Investment in Africa* (London, 1938), p. 374.

16. Edwin P. Reubens, "Foreign Capital and Domestic Development in Japan," in Simon Kuznets, W. E. Moore, and J. L. Spengler, eds., *Economic Growth: Brazil, India, Japan* (Durham, N.C., 1955), pp. 223–226. On the other hand, after noting that "it was a rather successful case of foreign borrowing," Lockwood has stated that "just what contribution was made by this borrowing episode to Japan's actual economic development is more difficult to determine. It was war and armament more than anything else which created the need, and absorbed the bulk of the funds placed at the government's disposal." See William W. Lockwood, *The Economic Development of Japan* (Princeton, 1954), p. 258.

17. Royal Institute of International Affairs, *The Problem of International Investment* (London, 1937), p. 270.

18. The foreign loans of Japan (1870–1929) were also floated considerably below par. The actual yield after discounts and commissions is estimated to have been about 90 percent of the face value. See H. G. Moulton, *Japan: An Economic and Financial Appraisal* (Washington, D.C., 1931), p. 390. The large profit margin may have been a result of the imperfection of the capital market. Or it may have been necessary to induce the middlemen to underwrite the loans. In the case of China both forces were perhaps at work.

19. Royal Institute of International Affairs, *The Problem of International Investment*, p. 161.

20. A. K. Cairncross, *Home and Foreign Investment, 1870–1913* (Cambridge, England, 1953), p. 227.

21. Royal Institute of International Affairs, *The Problem of International Investment*, p. 162.

22. Article XIII of the agreement of the loan stipulates that "the price of this present loan or of any series thereof to the Chinese Government shall be the price of its issue to the public on the London market less a deduction by the Banks of six percent (%) of the nominal value of the bonds. The issue price in London is not less than eighty-four percent (84%) for the entire loan. The Banks shall be responsible for all expenses connected with the issue of the loan except the printing and/or engraving of the bonds." See John V. A. MacMurray, ed. *Treaties and Agreements with and concerning China, 1894–1919* (New York, 1921), I, 1012. If the actual issue price was 84 percent, the effective rate of interest was about 6 percent. The loan was for 47 years.

23. Ch'i Shu-fen, Chap. 5.

24. Bank of China, *Chinese Government Foreign Loan Obligations* (Shanghai, 1935), Appendix, p. 130.

25. Lee, p. 51. Another authority commented: "Before and during the Great War there were several occasions when the Inspector General felt bound to protest against the rates quoted for certain loan settlements, but as a rule the banks have not taken an unfair advantage of China's disability to go on the open market for the settlement of her foreign loan installments." Stanley F. Wright, *The Collection and Disposal of the Maritime and Native Customs Revenue since the Revolution of 1911* (Shanghai, 1927), p. 71.

26. In many instances railroads were required to deposit with the serving banks

all of the net revenue up to an amount sufficient to cover the following year's installment of interest and principal. In some cases all receipts and earnings of the railroads had to be deposited in the creditor's banks.

27. J. R. Baylin, *Foreign Loan Obligations of China* (Tientsin, 1925), pp. 85–96.

28. Lo Tsung-yü, "Wo-kuo t'ieh-lu chai-k'uan kai-yao" (A general statement on China's railroad loans), *Chung-hang yüeh-kan* (Bank of China monthly review), 14.5:1–14 (May 1937). Also Bank of China, *Chinese Government Foreign Loan Obligations*, Table of Chinese government secured foreign loans, outstanding December 31, 1934.

29. Chia Shih-i, *Hsü ts'ai-cheng shih*, IV, 261.

30. *Ibid.*

31. Previously the railroads had sometimes been used for transportation of troops, but there was no major interference with their commercial operation. From 1924 to 1927 commercial operation was often disrupted; rolling stock was destroyed or carried away, and the permanent equipment of the railroads was often damaged.

32. "In these days, the provincial satraps who had hitherto remitted revenues to the Central Government kept them for themselves. This financial disintegration brought about heavy deficit in the Central treasury. Thus, official salaries were in arrears and the diplomatic and consular representatives and the government students abroad had to finance themselves. Such a pathetic state of affairs continued until the last day of the defunct Peking Government. It is not a surprise that all debts, internal and external, were not to be serviced." S. Y. Liu, "China's Debts and Their Readjustment," *Chinese Economic Journal*, 5.3:736–737 (Sept. 1929).

33. For a list of the secured foreign loans that were in default and those that were serviced continuously in the 1920's, see Bank of China, *Foreign Loan Obligations*, tables on Chinese government secured foreign loans, compiled by E. Kann and J. Baylin. Information on the default of unsecured loans is lacking, but apparently most of them were in default after the 1920's. The Financial Readjustment Commission of the Chinese government estimated that unsecured foreign loans amounted to silver $792 million (or US$396 million) as of the end of 1925. See *Ts'ai-cheng nien-chien*, II, 1460. Of the above amount, however, a total of silver $147 million (or US$73.5 million) was in secured loans according to Chia Shih-i, *Hsü ts'ai-cheng shih*, IV, 371–372. The unsecured loans amounted to US$365.8 million as of June 1935.

34. E. Kann, "On the Refunding of China's Foreign Loan Obligations," *Chinese Economic Journal*, 11.1:33–39. (July 1932); Chia Shih-i, *Hsü ts'ai-cheng shih*, IV, 359–388.

35. Bank of China, *Foreign Loan Obligations*, pp. 87–95; P. T. Chen, *Recent Financial Developments in China, 1934–1936* (Nanking, 1936), pp. 763–766. Chang Chia-nau (Chang Kia-ngau), *China's Struggle for Railroad Development* (New York, 1943), Pt. 3.

36. All the figures are from China: Ministry of Railways, *Statistics of Chinese National Railways* (issued annually after 1915).

37. For a better understanding of Tables 10 and 11 a brief explanation of the accounting procedures of the Ministry of Railways may prove useful. Two kinds of accounts were distinguished. The first set was the operating account. While operating revenues (such as transportation revenue) appeared on the credit side,

operating expenses (such as traffic, running, maintenance of equipment and buildings) appeared on the debit side. The balance was the net operating revenue, which was then transferred to the second set of accounts, called the income account. On the credit side appeared, in addition to net operating revenue, items such as income from securities, interest income, profit on industrial investment, and rents receivable. On the debit side were interest on funded debt, contractual dividends, government interest, loss on industrial investment, amortization of discount on funded debt, taxes, rents payable, discount on depreciated currency, contributions, etc. The difference between the credits and debits of the income account was called profit or loss.

38. See Chapter 4. Capital investments in railroads are usually greater than the cost of road and equipment.

39. Chang Chia-nau, p. 310.

40. T'ang Hsiang-lung, "Min-kuo i-ch'ien ti p'ei-k'uan shih ju-ho ch'ang-fu ti" (A study of the indemnity payments before 1911), *Chung-kuo chin-tai ching-chi-shih yen-chiu chi-k'an* (Studies in the modern economic history of China), 3.2:271 (Nov. 1935). According to Robert Hart's estimate, the interest and repayment of foreign loans amounted to 24 million taels in 1901. See Wagel, p. 347.

41. T'ang Hsiang-lung, "Min-kuo i-ch'ien," p. 273.

42. For the various estimates see Albert Feuerwerker, *China's Early Industrialization: Sheng Hsuan-Huai (1844–1916) and Mandarin Enterprise* (Cambridge, Mass., 1958), pp. 42–43, 264.

43. T'ang Hsiang-lung, "Min-kuo i-ch'ien," p. 280.

44. Lo Yü-tung, "Kuang-hsu ch'ao pu-chiu ts'ai-cheng chih fang-ts'e" (The governmental policies for meeting the financial crisis during the Kuang-hsü period) *Chung-kuo chin tai chin-chi-shih yen-chiu chi-k'an*, 1.2:260 (May 1933).

45. T'ang Hsiang-lung, "Min-kuo i-ch'ien," p. 273.

46. Coons, p. 121. The actual payment was Chinese $96 million, p. 122.

47. The 1934 budget of the National government set aside Chin$49.4 million for servicing foreign loans and Chin$38.9 million for the Boxer indemnity. However, only the secured loans under the care of the Ministry of Finance were included. Railroad loans, industrial loans, and all unsecured loans were excluded. See *T'sai-cheng nien-chien, 1935*, I, 143.

48. The annual revenue reported to Peking in the 1890's and 1900's has been estimated as follows (in million taels):

Land tax	25.1
Grain tribute	6.6
Salt gabelle (including salt likin)	13.7
Likin	13.0
Maritime customs (1893)	22.0
Native customs	1.0
Duty and likin on native opium	2.2
Miscellaneous	5.5
Total	89.1

See Feuerwerker, p. 42.

49. Sir Robert Hart's estimate of the expenditures of the imperial government in 1901 includes the following items (in million taels):

Imperial household and central government	12.5
Navy	5.0
Embassies and legations	1.0
Interest and repayment of foreign loans	24.0
Railroad construction	0.8
River conservancy works	0.9
Customs, lighthouses, and revenue cruisers	3.6
Provincial administration	20.3
Reserve funds	3.0
Total	101.1

See Wagel, p. 347.

50. Stanley Wright, pp. 127–129.

51. The loan was later canceled by an edict, partly because of the poor public reception and partly because of the compulsory methods used by some officials to sell the bonds.

52. Coons, pp. 6-7.

53. MacMurray, I, 41.

54. Coons, pp. 10–11.

55. W. W. Willoughby, *Foreign Rights and Interests in China*, rev. ed. (Baltimore, 1927), II, 991–992.

56. Remer, *Foreign Investments*, p. 543.

57. For an account of the political aspects of China's foreign railroad loans, see Chang Chia-nau; E-tu Zen Sun, *Chinese Railways and British Interests, 1898–1911* (New York, 1954); Tseng K'un-hua, *Chung-kuo t'ieh-lu shih* (History of Chinese railroads; Peking, 1924; Shanghai, 1929).

58. E-tu Zen Sun, p. 165.

59. For instance, the Chinese always considered the control clause an infringement of Chinese sovereignty and a foreign instrument for exercising political control. On this point, Willard D. Straight observed in 1912: "In the present negotiations with China for the reorganization loan, as in fact in all loan negotiations during the past few years, the banking groups have found their greatest difficulty in the settlement of the question of control." See his "China's Loan Negotiations," in George H. Blakeslee, ed., *Recent Developments in China* (New York, 1913), p. 131.

CHAPTER 3

1. For a list of foreign trading firms in China (except those of the Japanese), together with their capital and fields of activity, see Tōa kenkyūjo, *Shogaikoku no tai-Shi tōshi*, Vol. 1, Pt. 2.

2. See, for instance, G. C. Allen and A. G. Donnithorne, *Western Enterprise in Far Eastern Economic Development: China and Japan* (London, 1954), Chaps. 3–5.

3. For instance, Wu Yu-kan, *Chung-kuo kuo-chi mao-yi kai-lun* (A study of China's foreign trade; Shanghai, 1930), pp 579–585.

4. Tōa kenkyūjo, *Shogaikoku no tai-Shi tōshi*, Vol. 1, Pt. 2.

5. Information on the degree of concentration of power of foreign trading firms in China is scattered. Of the import of cotton, three Japanese trading firms (Toyo Menkwa Kaisha, Nippon Menkwa Kabushiki Kaisha, and Gosho Kabushiki Kaisha) accounted for 70 percent of the total imports from Japan and

50.4 percent of the total imports from India in 1928, although more than 40 foreign trading firms were engaged in the business. See Fang Hsien-ting (H. D. Fong), *Chung-kuo chih mien-fang-chih yeh* (China's cotton textiles; Shanghai, 1934), p. 57. Fang also reports (p. 58) that more than 40 foreign firms handled the export of cotton at Tientsin, with the 19 Japanese firms predominant. Yen states that these Japanese firms acted together to fix prices to the disadvantage of Chinese sellers. See Yen Chung-p'ing, *Chung-kuo mien-fang-chih shih-kao* (Draft history of Chinese cotton spinning and weaving; Peking, 1955), pp. 181–182.

Of the tung oil trade, 19 firms in Hankow and 7 firms in Shanghai were purchasing it for export (presumably in the early 1930's). Most of these firms were foreign-owned. There were sharp fluctuations in prices. See Li Chang-lung, *Chung-kuo tung-yu mao-i lun* (A study on China's tung oil trade; Shanghai, 1934), pp. 117 and 143.

Of the export of Chinese silk, there were more than 30 foreign trading firms in Shanghai in 1916–1917, with Jardine, Matheson & Co. the largest exporter. It exported about 10,000 piculs out of a total of 76,000 piculs during the period June 1, 1916 to May 1, 1917. For the period June 1, 1925 to May 31, 1926, there were 35 foreign trading firms handling the export of raw silk, amounting to 88,000 piculs. The largest exporter handled 19,000 piculs, and the rest were exported by others without marked concentration. For the last seven months of 1930 a total of 41,000 piculs of raw silk was exported by 38 firms in Shanghai, 33 of which were foreign owned. The largest exporter handled no more than 4,000 piculs. A total of 67,000 piculs of raw silk was exported from Kwangtung by about 17 firms in the period May 1, 1925 to April 1, 1926. Of this total, 17,000 piculs were handled by one foreign firm, and the rest were handled somewhat evenly by the others. See Mao Chung-hsiu, "Erh-shih-nien-lai chih tsan-ssu yeh" (The silk industry in the past twenty years), *Kuo-chi mao-i tao-pao* (Foreign trade Journal), 2.1:7, 9, 16, 19, 30 (1931).

6. T. H. Chu, *Tea Trade in Central China* (Shanghai, 1936).

7. *Ibid.*, p. 227.

8. For the price fluctuations, see Chang Tien-shou, "Kuo-ch'ü shu-shih-nien chih hua-ch'a ch'u-k'ou chia-ko" (The prices of tea exports in the past few decades), *Kuo-chi mao-i tao-pao*, Vol. 1, No. 5 (1930).

9. One student has reported that most of the foreign trading firms in China actually served as purchasing agents for the tea merchants in foreign markets and were paid on a commission basis (usually 3 percent). See Wu Chüeh-nung, "Shang-hai ch'a-yeh kai-k'uang" (The tea market in Shanghai), *Kuo-chi mao-i tao-pao*, 1.2:2 (1930). This would seem to add another element to the price formation of China's exports, which by and large is still little understood.

10. For the history of foreign banking in China, see for instance two articles by Kuo Hsiao-hsien: "Shang-hai ti wai-kuo yin-hang" (Foreign banks in Shanghai) *Shang-hai shih t'ung-chih-kuan ch'i-k'an* (Journal of the Shanghai Gazetteer Office), 2.2:547–602 (Sept. 1934); "Shang-hai ti chung-wai ho-pan yin-hang" (Sino-foreign banks in Shanghai), *ibid.*, 2.4:1339–1354 (Mar. 1935). For an English version of the first article, see "Foreign Banks in Shanghai," *Chinese Economic Journal*, 16.1:63–95 (Jan. 1935). See also "Foreign Banks in Tientsin," *ibid.*, 17.4:399–405 (Oct. 1935); Bank of China, *Ch'üan-kuo yin-hang nien-chien* (Bankers' yearbook; 1937); Wu Ch'eng-hsi, *Chung-kuo ti yin-hang* (Banking in China; Shanghai, 1934); Hsü Chi-ch'ing, *Tsui-chin Shang-hai chin-yung shih* (A recent his-

tory of banking and finance in Shanghai; Shanghai, 1932); Frank M. Tamagna, *Banking and Finance in China* (New York, 1942).

11. They were the Cathay Company (American, dominated by the Guaranty Trust of New York), the International Banking Corporation (American, called the National City Bank of New York since 1927), Banque Belge Pour L'Etranger (Belgian), and Netherlandsche Handel Maatschappij (Dutch).

12. Chen Kuang-fu, "Chan-shih t'ing-chih hou yin-hang chieh chih hsin shih-ming" (The new mission of Chinese banks after the war), *Yin-hang chou-pao* (Bankers' weekly), 16.13:2 (Apr. 12, 1932). Citing R. Feetham's *Report to the Shanghai Municipal Council* (Shanghai, 1931), Allen and Donnithorne state (p. 110) that "even as late as 1930 it was estimated that at least 90 percent of China's foreign trade was financed through the foreign banks."

13. Ellsworth C. Carlson, *The Kaiping Mines, 1877–1912* (Cambridge, Mass., 1957), p. 51.

14. For a list of such loans, see Yen Chung-p'ing, *T'ung-chi tzu-liao*, p. 137.

15. Wu Ching-hsi, p. 103. He did not include the surplus accounts.

16. Tamagna, p. 99.

17. For customs revenue, see *The Chinese Yearbook, 1936–1937*, p. 553; for salt revenue, see *The Chinese Yearbook, 1940–1941*, p. 512. For the history of the handling of customs and salt revenues by foreign banks, see Stanley Wright, Chap. 1.

18. The Imperial Bank of China was founded in 1897. The Hu-pu Bank, founded in 1904, was reorganized in 1908 as the Ta-Ching Bank, and again in 1912 as the Bank of China. The Bank of Communications was founded in 1907.

19. For a description of the development of paper currency in China, see Chang Chia-hsiang, *Chung-hua p'i-chih shih* (History of the monetary system in China; Peking, 1926), pp. 101–298; also "Paper Currency in China," *Chinese Economic Journal and Bulletin*, 18.4:545–558 (Apr. 1936).

20. The right of warships to visit Chinese ports, whether or not opened by treaty, was also first granted to the United States in 1844.

21. China: Ministries of Communications and Railways, *Chiao-t'ung shih: Hang-cheng p'ien* (History of communications: Shipping; Nanking, 1931), VI, 2671.

22. For the history of this company, see Liu Kwang-Ching, *Anglo-American Steamship Rivalry in China, 1862–1874* (Cambridge, Mass., 1962).

23. *Ibid.*, Chap. 4.

24. The capital of the firm was 8,100,000 yen in 1907. The government subsidy was 800,000 yen per year for five years. See Tōa kenkyūjo, *Nihon no tai-Shi tōshi*, pp. 430–431.

25. Allen and Donnithorne, pp. 124, 131. Also, Liu Kwang-Ching, Chaps. 2 and 4.

26. Tōa kenkyūjo, *Shōgaikoku no tai-Shi tōshi*, II, 408; *Nihon no tai-Shi tōshi*, p. 455.

27. Yen Chung-p'ing, *T'ung-chi tzu-liao*, p. 229.

28. For a description of the development of railroads in China, see Cheng Lin; also Chang Chia-nau.

29. In a memorial to the throne in 1881, Liu Hsi-hung presented the argument against railroads. The eight reasons that railroad operation would not be feasible were: (1) China did not have corporations, and it would therefore be difficult to raise large capital; (2) the government did not have the necessary funds; (3)

railroad construction would disturb the gods and spirits and thereby invite droughts, and floods; (4) corruption opportunities would be afforded to officials; (5) officials were lacking to supervise railroad repairs; (6) railroad property would be lost due to theft; (7) it would be difficult to maintain a regular schedule because of the bother of the multifarious likin stations; and (8) people carried so much luggage when traveling that they could not afford to buy tickets at a rate profitable to the railroads.

The eight reasons that railroads would not be profitable were: (1) they could transport goods only from one province to another, involving an exchange of goods and wealth only between one province and another, so that there would be no gain to the country as a whole; (2) Chinese goods for export were very limited and small in amount; (3) the Chinese people were content to stay at home and did not like to take long trips (as opposed to foreigners, who loved to travel and move, and even brought along their wives and children, for foreign women did not like to stay at home); (4) China had to pay high interest to borrow abroad, and it was not possible for railroads to make enough profit to pay such interest charges; (5) Chinese history fully illustrated that there was no need to rely upon railroads in order to supervise officials in the frontier provinces; (6) the argument that railroads would make it possible to station troops in the capital instead of in the provinces, thereby saving government expenditures, was unsound because it was necessary to station troops in the provinces to gain local knowledge and support; (7) it was not necessary to build railroads for mining purposes, for mining had long been developed in China without such assistance; (8) it was not necessary to rely upon railroads to transport food to the capital, even in emergencies when water transportation failed, for there were other means.

The nine reasons that railroads would be harmful were: (1) they would take land away from cultivation; (2) silver would be lost to foreign countries because of the necessary purchase of materials from abroad and the employment of foreign technicians; (3) the easy movement of, and access to, goods would make people live more luxuriously, eroding their industrious and frugal traditions; (4) the high cost of railroad transportation would make things more expensive; (5) the construction of railroads would make China more vulnerable to foreign attack, for the railroads would reduce natural strategic positions like mountain barriers to thoroughfares for locomotives and wagons; (6) they would make it possible for foreigners to penetrate the interior and either bribe the people over to their side or else make themselves so familiar that the people would be unwilling to fight them in case of war; (7) foreign domination would prevail should China borrow and fail to pay back foreign railroad loans; (8) railroads would make it easier for internal rebellion; (9) since China did not have the financial resources to build a network of railroads and it would be a sheer waste to build only one railroad, China would be trapped in endless financial misery. See China: Ministries of Communications and Railways, *Chiao-t'ung shih: Lu-cheng p'ien* (History of communications: Roads), I, 29.

30. Chang Chia-nau, p. 2. The Chinese opposed steam locomotives not only for fear that they would disturb the spirits or spoil the *feng-shui* (good luck) of their ancestral tombs, but also for fear that their unprecedented speed and noise would be a source of disturbance to pedestrians and animal herds.

31. At first the company was allowed to construct the railroad on the condition

that no steam locomotives, only horses and mules, be used to pull the trains. Soon it was found that animal power was not adequate, and a small locomotive was used instead.

32. Among the advocates, Li Hung-chang and Tso Tsung-tang emphasized the value of railroads in national defense, while Chang Chih-tung stressed their importance in economic development.

33. Cheng Lin, p. 21. Kent made a similar statement in 1908. See P. H. Kent, *Railway Enterprise in China: An Account of Its Origin and Development* (London, 1907), p. 93.

34. For the Yunnan Railway, see T. W. Overlach, *Foreign Financial Control in China* (New York, 1919), p. 132. Overlach does not give the period of time when the railroad suffered a loss. For the Chinese Eastern Railway, see Tsao Lien-en, *The Chinese Eastern Railway: An Analytical Study* (China Ministry of Industries, 1930), pp. 60–61. The railroad suffered losses from 1897 to 1922.

35. Cheng Lin, p. 88.

36. *Ibid.*, pp. 38, 45, 46.

37. The total mileage in 1911 was 5,796 miles. *Ibid.*, p. 46. The total in 1937 was 13,042 miles, including railroads in Manchuria. See Yen Chung-p'ing, *T'ung-chi tzu-liao*, p. 190.

38. Remer, *Foreign Investments*, p. 90.

39. Yen Chung-p'ing, *T'ung-chi tzu-liao*, pp. 185–190.

40. Leonard G. Ting, "The Coal Industry in China," *Nankai Social and Economic Quarterly*, 10.1:38 (Apr. 1937).

41. Sun Yu-tang, ed., *Chung-kuo chin-tai kung-yeh shih tzu-liao, 1840–1895* (Source materials on the modern industrial history of China, 1840–1895; Peking, 1957), I, 201.

42. *Ibid.*, p. 227.

43. *Ibid.*, II, 590.

44. In 1890 Liu Ming-ch'uan resubmitted his proposal and this time lost not only his proposal but also his job.

45. Thirty-seven mines were opened and 25 were planned. For a list, see Wang Ching-yü, ed., *Chung-kuo chin-tai kung-yeh shih tzu-liao, 1895–1914 nien* (Source materials on the modern industrial history of China, 1895–1914; Peking, 1957), I, 140–147.

46. MacMurray, I, 30.

47. *Ibid.*, pp. 911–914. According to modern accounting principles, the second item should be deducted in calculating profits.

48. H. Y. Hsieh, *Foreign Interest in the Mining Industry in China* (Shanghai, 1931), p. 14.

49. MacMurray, I, 661–662.

50. *Ibid.*, pp. 658–659.

51. H. Y. Hsieh, p. 11.

52. For the texts of the 1909 and 1911 agreements, see W. W. Rockhill, *Treaties and Conventions with or concerning China and Korea, 1894–1902* (Washington, D.C., 1904), pp. 790–792.

53. *Chung-kuo k'uang-yeh chi-yao* (General statement on the mining industry), Special report of the Geological Survey of China, 7th issue (1945), p. 629.

54. "If the net income available for distribution resulting out of the proceeds of a mining enterprise would allow for a yearly dividend of more than 5 percent

figured on the share capital paid up and expended for such enterprise the tax to be paid for that year to the treasury of the Government of Kiauchou shall be: from the amount exceeding 5% up to 7% the twentieth part; from the amount exceeding 7% up to 8% the tenth part; from the amount exceeding 10% up to 12% the third part; and from the amount exceeding 12% one half." See MacMurray, I, 254.

55. For the terms of the agreement, see *ibid.*, I, 131–134.

56. Hsü Keng-sheng, *Chung-wai ho-pan mei-t'ieh-k'uang-yen shih-hua* (Histories of Sino-foreign jointly-managed coal and iron mines; Shanghai, 1946), pp. 76, 96.

57. *Ibid.*, p. 76.

58. H. Y. Hsieh, p. 43.

59. Hsü Keng-sheng, pp. 117–119.

60. For the history of this enterprise, see Carlson; Wei Tzu-ch'u, *Ti-kuo chu-yi yü K'ai-luan mei-k'uang* (Imperialism and the Kailan mines; Shanghai, 1954); Yang Lu, *K'ai-luan-k'uang li-shih chi shou-kuei kuo-yu wen-t'i* (The history of the Kailan mines and the problem of recovery; Tientsin, 1932).

61. Carlson, pp. 65–67; Hsü Keng-sheng, p. 7.

62. Carlson, pp. 96, 154.

63. H. Y. Hsieh, p. 34.

64. For the history of the Hanyehp'ing Company, see Ch'üan Han-sheng, "Ching-mo Han-yang t'ieh-ch'ang" (The Han-yang iron and steel works, 1890–1908), *She-hui k'o-hsüeh lun-ts'ung* (Journal of social sciences), 1:1–33 (Apr. 1950); Sun Yu-tang, II, 743–892.

65. The Hanyehp'ing Company became entirely a private enterprise.

66. For a list of such loans, see Wang Ching-yu, II, 121.

67. Remer, *Foreign Investments*, p. 510.

68. For the agreements, see MacMurray, II, 1077–1083.

69. *Chung-kuo k'uang-yeh chi-yao*, p. 93.

70. Wu Ching-ch'ao, "Han-Yeh-P'ing kung-ssu ti fu-ch'e" (The Lesson of the Hanyehp'ing Company), *Hsin ching-chi* (New Economy; Jan. 1, 1939), p. 106.

71. *Chung-kuo k'uang-yeh chi-yao*, pp. 100–102.

72. *Ibid.*

73. MacMurray, I, 793–795.

74. Hsu Ken-sheng, p. 223.

75. *Ibid.*, pp. 225–226.

76. *Ibid.*, pp. 220–221.

77. *Chung-kuo k'uang-yeh chi-yao*, pp. 100–102.

78. For a list, see Sun Yu-tang, I, 234–241.

79. *Ibid.*, p. 113.

80. Note that the important foreign newspapers in China were founded before 1894, such as the following: *North China Herald*, 1850 (Shanghai); *Shen-pao*, 1872 (Shanghai); *Shanghai Mercury*, 1879; *Chinese Times*, 1885 (Tientsin).

81. Sun Yu-tang, II, 1201.

82. For a list of foreign manufacturing firms established in China between 1895 and 1913, see Wang Ching-yü, I, 7-11. A computation by the same author of the total investment by 37 leading foreign manufacturing firms in China in 1913 reveals the following distribution among various fields: machines and ship-building — Chin.$8.9 million; textiles — 10.8 million; food and drink — 13.2 million; others — 5 million. See *Ibid.*, I, 18–25.

83. See Table 3.
84. Table 18 does not include Manchuria. According to *The Japan-Manchoukuo Yearbook, 1939*, p. 812, the percentage distribution of "capital investment outstanding in manufacturing industry in Manchuria" was as follows:

Manufacture	1931	1935	1936
Textile	7.5	3.0	4.5
Metal refining	27.7	30.7	25.0
Machine and tool	2.4	2.7	2.8
Ceramics	3.4	4.8	3.9
Chemical	14.8	13.3	13.4
Food and drink	22.1	8.4	8.0
Electricity	1.5	29.8	24.0
Gas	11.0	2.6	1.9
Lumber and woodworking	5.3	1.6	1.5
Miscellaneous	3.5	2.9	15.6

85. A. Wright, ed., *Twentieth Century Impressions of Hongkong, Shanghai and Other Treaty Ports of China* (London, 1908), pp. 196–198.
86. Sun Yu-tang, I, 1–43.
87. Tōa kenkyūjo, *Shozai koku no tai-Shi tōshi*, II, 35.
88. Allen and Donnithorne, p. 168.
89. Up to 1938, the Taikoo Dockyard and Engineering Company had built 78 vessels with a total tonnage of 141,000; the Hong Kong and Whampoa Dock Company had built 96 vessels with a total tonnage of 150,000; the Shanghai Dock and Engineering Co. (and its predecessors) had built 58 vessels with a total tonnage of 73,000; and the New Shipbuilding and Engineering Works had built 28 vessels with a total tonnage of 22,000. The largest ship ever built, between 7,000 and 8,000 tons, was built by the Taikoo shipyard. See Tōa kenkyūjo, *Shozaikoku no tai-Shi tōshi*, II, 29–30.
90. *Ibid.*, Vol. 2.
91. Sun Yu-tang, I, 44.
92. *Ibid.*, II, 1182.
93. "Chinese Eggs and Egg Products," *Chinese Economic Journal*, 14.2:157–199 (Feb. 1934).
94. The largest was the Nisshin mill, founded at Dairen in 1907 with a capital of 3,750,000 yen. See W. H. Wang, "Japanese Manufacturing Industries in Manchuria," *Chinese Economic Journal*, 5.6:1105–37 (Dec. 1929).
95. Fang Hsien-ting (H. D. Fong), *Chung-kuo kung-yeh tzu-pen* (Industrial capital in China; Changsha, 1939), p. 51. This book is an expansion of the author's "Industrial Capital in China," *Nankai Social and Economic Quarterly*, 9.1:27–94 (Apr. 1936).
96. Allen and Donnithorne, p. 80.
97. Z. T. Kyi, "Matchmaking Industry," *Chinese Economic Journal*, 4.4:305–311 (Apr. 1929); "Match Industry in China," *Chinese Economic Journal*, 10.3:197–211 (Mar. 1932).
98. Yen Chung-p'ing, *Mien-fang-chih*, p. 98.

99. Allen and Donnithorne, p. 195.
100. Yen Chung-p'ing, *Mien-fang-chih*, p. 151.
101. Sun Yung-tang, I, 148–152.
102. Allen and Donnithorne, p. 172.
103. Wang Ching-yü, I, 206–234.
104. Allen and Donnithorne, p. 171.
105. Wang Ching-yü, I, 234–235.
106. Foreign population in China increased from less than 3600 in 1875 to nearly 164,000 in 1913, 220,000 in 1917, and 302,000 in 1927. *China Yearbook*, various years.
107. The Shanghai Electric Co., after an unsuccessful start, was reorganized in 1888 into the New Shanghai Electric Company, which was then purchased in 1893 by the Municipal Council of the International Settlement in Shanghai. In 1929 some American and British interests took over the concern and changed its name to the Shanghai Power Company. In 1937 it had a generating capacity of 183,500 kilowatts — about 70 per cent of the total in Shanghai. Allen and Donnithorne, p. 145.

CHAPTER 5

1. Remer, Foreign Investments, pp. 164, 165.
2. See Reubens, "Foreign Capital and Domestic Development in Japan," and William W. Lockwood, "The Scale of Economic Growth in Japan, 1868–1938," both in S. Kuznets, W. E. Moore, and J. L. Spengler, eds. *Economic Growth: Brazil, India, Japan* (Durham, N.C., 1955); Bruce F. Johnston, "Agricultural Productivity and Economic Development in Japan," *Journal of Political Economy*, 59:498–513 (Dec. 1951).
3. Reubens, p. 185.
4. *Ibid.*, p. 186. The actual yield to Japan was substantially reduced by discounts and commissions. The actual yield from the various categories of loans is calculated by Reubens at ¥1,762 million.
5. *Ibid.*, p. 187
6. *Ibid.*, p. 188.
7. *Ibid.*, p. 189.
8. Allen and Donnithorne, p. 264
9. The Japanese population is taken to be 64,448,000 and the Chinese population 450,000,000 in 1930. Thus per capita foreign investment in Japan was US$21, while in China it was US$7.2.
10. See Chong-su, *The Foreign Trade of China* (New York, 1919), p. 395.
11. For 1897 and 1917, see *ibid*. For 1930, see Remer, *Foreign Investments*, p. 363.
12. Remer, *Foreign Investments*, p. 166.
13. The annual earnings of Great Britain from her foreign investments were, on the average, about £100 million, of which about £60 million were used to finance imports in excess of exports and £40 million were reinvested. See Arthur Salter, *Foreign Investment* (Essays in International Finance No. 12; Princeton University, Feb. 1951), p. 3.
14. Article 13 of the resolutions reads as follows: "Whenever a British subject has reason to complain of a Chinese he must first proceed to the Consulate and state his grievance. The consul will thereupon inquire into the merits of the case, and do his utmost to arrange it amicably. In like manner, if a Chinese has reason to complain of a British subject, he shall no less listen to his complaint and en-

deavour to settle it in a friendly manner . . . If, unfortunately, any disputes take place of such a nature that the consul cannot arrange them amicably, then he shall request the assistance of a Chinese officer, that they may together examine into the merits of the case, and decide it equitably. Regarding the punishment of English criminals, the English Government will enact the laws necessary to attain that end, and the consul will be empowered to put them in force; and regarding the punishment of Chinese criminals, these will be tried and punished by their own laws, in the way provided for by the correspondence which took place at Nanking, after the concluding of the peace." Quoted from *Customs Treaties*, I, 386, in Willoughby, II, 558–559.

15. The most-favored-nation clause was not extended to extraterritorial provisions of the treaties, so that these rights were not exactly the same for all powers. The extraterritorial countries were: Great Britain (1843), U.S. (1844), France (1844), Norway (1847), Sweden (1847), Russia (1860), Germany (1861), Denmark (1863), Netherlands (1863), Spain (1864), Belgium (1865), Italy (1866), Austria-Hungary (1869), Japan (1871), Peru (1874), Brazil (1881), Portugal (1887), Congo Free State (1898), Mexico (1899), and Switzerland (1918). Germany and Austria-Hungary lost their rights in 1917 when China declared war against them. Russia lost her rights in 1917 when she no longer had consuls in China whose authority was recognized by China. Belgium, Italy, Denmark, Portugal, and Spain abandoned their rights in 1928, and Great Britain and the U.S. in 1943.

16. For the scope of British extraterritorial jurisdiction in China see, for instance, G. W. Keeton, *The Development of Extraterritoriality in China* (London, 1928), II, 571.

17. Willoughby, II, 599–600.

18. Chu Ch'i, *Chung-kuo tzu-shui wen-t'i* (China's taxation problem; Shanghai, 1936), p. 170.

19. *Ibid.*, pp. 484–488.

20. For a list of such ports, see Yen Chung-p'ing, ed., *Tung-chi tzu-liao*, pp. 41–48.

21. In the Treaty of Tientsin of 1858 the rights of aliens in China were broadened by a provision permitting them to travel for pleasure or trade to all parts of the interior under passports issued by their consuls and countersigned by local authorities. After the Sino-Japanese Treaty of 1915 foreigners in South Manchuria were given many rights that were extended elsewhere only in the open ports. Article 3 of the treaty reads: "Japanese subjects shall be free to reside and travel in South Manchuria and to engage in business and manufacture of any kind whatsoever." These rights extended to the nationals of all other treaty powers by operation of the most-favored-nation clause. Willoughby, II, 734, 736, and 737.

22. *Ibid.*, I, 134.

23. Great Britain and Germany had previously come to an understanding with regard to the rights of the former in the Yangtse Valley and the latter in Shantung.

24. By a convention signed July 30, 1907, it was made clear that Japan and Russia had decided to cooperate in Manchuria, each to support the other within its respective sphere.

25. The new rates (for imports) were considerably lower than the previous ones, which had been 24 percent for raw cotton, 13.4 percent for cotton yarns, and 15 to 33 percent for various cotton cloth. Yen Chung-p'ing, ed. *Tung-chi tzu-liao*,

p. 59. However the old rates reported by Yen included all dues and levies imposed on imported articles.

26. According to one calculation, the effective rate for imports varied from 3.1 to 3.9 percent for the years from 1903 to 1928. The effective rate for exports was from 217 to 4.5 percent for the same period. See Yen Chung-p'ing, ed. *Tung-chi tzu-liao*, p. 61.

27. Calculated by Cheng Yu-kwei, p. 57. Cheng also calculates the tariff rates for the different groups of commodities and concludes that the primary purpose of the Chinese tariff was the increase of revenue, whereas protection of domestic industries was of secondary concern.

28. For a detailed analysis, see Lo Yü-tung, *Chung-kuo li-chin shih* (History of the likin in China: Shanghai, 1936).

29. After the Treaty of Tientsin the Chinese authorities tried to levy charges on imported and exported goods, which, though nominally not transit dues, had substantially the same incidence. As the result of protest by the powers, however, these charges were never as burdensome as the likin. See Willoughby, II, 752–758.

30. Inland navigation rights were discussed in Chapter 3.

31. China was among the very few countries where foreign direct investment constituted as high as nearly 80 percent of total foreign investment. The other countries were largely those in Southeast Asia where in 1930 direct investment accounted for 80 percent of the total. H. G. Callis, *Foreign Capital in Southeast Asia* (New York, 1942), p. 108. For the share of direct investment in total foreign investment in other underdeveloped countries, see Royal Institute of International Affairs, *International Investment*, p. 225. The favorable conditions of foreign investment in the treaty ports may have contributed in part to the predominance of direct investment in China.

32. For the original text of the regulations see the following: for 1898, 1899, and 1902, *Huang-ch'ao ch'ang-ku hui-pien* (A compilation of important events of the Ch'ing dynasty), ed. Sung Cheng-chih et al. (Shanghai, 1902), section on foreign affairs, 24:41–44, 60–62, 64–67; for 1904, *Tsou-ting kuang-wu chang-chang* (Mining regulations; 1904); for 1908, *Ta-Ch'ing fa-kui ta-ch'üan* (Complete laws and ordinances of the Ch'ing dynasty), section on industries; for 1914, *Fa-ling ta-ch'üan* (Complete laws and ordinances of the Republic of China; Shanghai, 1924); and for 1930, *Tsui-hsin kuo-min cheng-fu fa-ling ta-ch'üan* (Newest comprehensive compendium of laws and ordinances of the National government; Shanghai, 1932), section on mining laws.

For the English translation see the following: for 1898, 1899, and 1902, Rockhill, pp. 338–344, 373, 380–382. (Rockhill omits a few key words with regard to the tax on "net profit," which was to be computed after a deduction for interest and amortization on capital.) For 1904, E. T. Williams, *Recent Chinese Legislation relating to Commercial Railway and Mining Enterprise* (Shanghai, 1904), pp. 79–101; for 1914, *China Yearbook, 1921–1922*, pp. 181–192.

33. The 1930 regulations also stated that minerals such as iron, petroleum, copper, and coking coal were reserved for the Chinese government to mine. However, when the government organized a corporation to work such a mine, foreign investors were allowed to buy shares, not to exceed 49 percent of the total. If the government decided not to work such a mine, it could be leased only to Chinese citizens. Foreign capital was also denied participation in the "small" or "native" mines.

34. According to the 1902 regulations, the output tax was 5 percent for coal, iron, antimony, alum and borax; 10 percent for kerosene, copper, lead, tin, sulphur, and cinnabar; 15 percent for gold, silver, spelter, and quicksilver; and 25 percent for diamonds, crystals, and the like.

35. The 1908 regulations stipulated a fixed amount for iron and coal, namely, one tenth of a tael per ton. In terms of the price of coal in 1916, this was equivalent to about 3 percent.

36. MacMurray, I, 350, 427–428. The unratified treaty of November 11, 1904, between Portugal and China had the same provision.

37. H. Y. Hsieh, pp. 16–17, 53. This venture was abandoned in 1917.

38. Yen Chung-p'ing, *Mien-fang-chih*, p. 63.

39. It is assumed that each ratio represents one business firm; the actual number of firms involved is smaller than that of the ratios, since many firms published financial statements (included here) in more than one year.

40. Remer, *Foreign Investments*, p. 294.

41. *Ibid.*, p. 294.

42. The actual rate should be lower because the profit figures were at current prices, which were rising during the period, whereas capital investment was most probably valued on the basis of the original cost.

43. The dividend payments of the company may also be noted. The Japanese government guaranteed payment up to 6 percent for the publicly held shares, which formed half of the total capital of the company, while the other half was owned by the Japanese government. The publicly held shares received a 6 percent dividend for the first fiscal year in 1907; this was gradually increased to 11 percent in 1928 and then reduced to 8 percent in 1930. The Japanese government received 4.3 percent on its holding from 1921 to 1927. The rate reached a peak of 5 percent in 1928 but was down to 4.4 percent in 1938. See *Japan Manchoukuo Year Book, 1939*, p. 893.

44. The profit rates are the income-to-capitalization ratios before federal income tax, as noted in Table 26. When the tax is taken into consideration, the situation remains essentially the same. For instance, for 1924–1928 the average profit-to-total-capital ratio of the 2,046 manufacturing corporations was 10.4 percent before federal income tax, as noted in Table 26. It was 9.3 percent after the tax. See Ralph C. Epstein, *Industrial Profits in the United States* (New York, 1934), p. 56.

45. The profit rates reported here are not far from the interest rates that the Chinese industrial firms had to pay in China. For the interest rates, see Chapter 7, note 7.

46. As a comparison, the returns (received in the form of interest and dividends) on nominal capital of British long-term overseas investments are noted (in percent) in the table at the top of p. 251. See Royal Institute of International Affairs, *International Investment*, p. 160. No computation is made in this study regarding capital appreciation or depreciation; and return in the form of sinking funds, etc., is likewise disregarded.

47. See Chapter 9.

48. See Chapter 1.

49. Yen Chung-p'ing, *Mien-fang-chih*, p. 179.

50. On export development in China, more will be said in Chapter 9.

Type of investment	1907–1908	1930	1934
Government, etc.	4.0	4.5	4.1
Railroads	4.4	4.9	2.6
Public utilities, etc.	5.9	6.0	4.4
Shipping, etc.	—	8.9	12.3
Commerce and industry	5.7	7.0	4.9
Raw materials	10.6	9.0	7.7
Banks and finance	5.6	6.2	3.2
Other investments	—	5.7	4.3
Total	5.2	5.6	4.3

51. For a brief discussion of his activities, see Allen and Donnithorne, pp. 38, 83, 121, 124–125, 129–130, 158.

52. Remer, *Foreign Investments*, p. 165.

53. Liu Kwang-Ching, *Steamship Rivalry*, Chap. 1.

54. For a history of international capital movement, see C. K. Hobson, *The Export of Capital* (London, 1914); Herbert Feis, *Europe, The World's Banker, 1870–1914* (New Haven, 1930); Royal Institute of International Affairs, *International Investment;* Staley; and Cairncross.

55. Cairncross, p. 2.

56. United Nations, *International Capital Movements during the Inter-war Period* (New York, 1949), p. 2.

57. Royal Institute of International Affairs, *International Investment*, p. 4.

58. Ragnar Nurkse, "International Investment Today in the Light of Nineteenth-century Experience," *Economic Journal*, 64:744–758 (Dec. 1954): reprinted in Nurkse, *Equilibrium and Growth in the World Economy: A Collection of Economic Essays*, ed. Gottfried Haberler and Robert M. Stern (Cambridge, Mass. 1961).

59. This is a gross figure, since some of the migrants returned. *Ibid.*

60. *Ibid.* World distribution of the total long-term foreign investment in 1913 is as shown below. See United Nations, *International Capital Movements*, p. 2.

Area	US$ millions	Percent
Europe	12,000	27
North America	10,000	24
Latin America	8,500	20
Asia	6,000	13
Africa	4,700	11
Oceania	2,300	5
Total	44,000	100

61. Royal Institute of International Affairs, *International Investment*, p. 122.

62. Nurkse, "International Investment," p. 139.

63. United Nations, *International Capital Movements*, p. 17.

64. The annual flow of capital into the underdeveloped countries in the 1920's averaged not more than US$500 million. During 1926–1929 the annual outpayment of interest and dividends from these countries amounted to some US$1530 million. For statistical convenience, included in underdeveloped countries are all countries in Asia except Japan, all of Africa, all of Latin America, and Bulgaria, Greece, Hungary, Lithuania, Poland, Romania, and Yugoslavia. For the figure of interest and dividends, see League of Nations, *Balance of Payments, 1930*, pp. 10–15. The figure is derived by applying to all underdeveloped countries the ratio of interest and dividend outpayments to total foreign investments in the 14 underdeveloped countries that utilized more than 53 percent of total foreign investment in the underdeveloped world in 1938. For the figure of annual inflow of foreign capital, see United Nations, *Measures for the Economic Development of Underdeveloped Countries* (New York, 1951), p. 79.

65. This applied everywhere except in South Manchuria, where by the Sino-Japanese Treaty of 1915 foreign nationals could, by negotiation, lease land necessary for buildings, for trade and manufacture, or for agricultural enterprises.

66. For a collection of the material on foreign efforts to improve Chinese agriculture, see Chang Yu-i, ed., *Chung-kuo chin-tai nung-yeh shih tzu-liao, ti-erh chi, 1912–1927* (Source materials on the history of agriculture in modern China, Second collection, 1912–1927; Peking 1957), pp. 154–165, 494–503.

69. Ragnar Nurkse, *Problems of Capital Formation in Underdeveloped Countries* (Oxford, 1953), pp. 25–29. The manner in which international politics and internal political instability restricted foreign borrowing by the Chinese government was noted in Chapter 2.

CHAPTER 6

1. The extent of underdevelopment will be discussed in Chapter 8.

2. Franklin L. Ho and H. D. Fong (Fang Hsien-ting), *Extent and Effects of Industrialization in China* (Tientsin, 1929), p. 33.

3. See Chang Chi-hung, "Chung-kuo chiu-yeh jen-shu ti ku-chi" (An estimate of the working population of China), *She-hui k'o-hsüeh tsa-chih* (Quarterly review of social sciences), 9.2: 71–91 (Dec. 1947).

4. Ho and Fong, p. 5; *Chung-hua min-kuo t'ung-chi t'i-yao* (The statistical abstract of the Republic of China; 1948), p. 155.

5. Koh Tso-fan, (Ku Ch'un-fan), *Capital Stock in China* (New York 1942), p. 21 and Appendix E. The amount of annual growth, estimated from a straight secular trend, was £5.5 million. The secular trend equation is $Y = 69,001,547 + 5,518,969.3X$. The figure for 1938 does not include Manchuria. Koh does not say whether adjustment is made for price changes. According to Cheng Yu-kwei, pp. 31–32, all imported machinery amounted to 8 million Haikwan taels in 1913 and 38.5 million in 1936. (Manchuria is not included in 1936 figure).

6. Yen Chung-p'ing, ed., *T'ung-chi tzu-liao*, p. 190. Calculations based on H. Lin Cheng's data show slight differences from Yen's figures. In terms of the mileage of railroad that were completed and open to traffic the percentage share of those built with Chinese and foreign capital was as follows:

Year	Chinese capital	Foreign ownership	Foreign loans
1876	0.0	100.0	0.0
1895	100.0	0.0	0.0
1903	3.9	96.1	0.0
1911	3.5	45.9	50.6
1914	3.0	38.9	58.1
1920	6.2	32.7	61.1
1926	15.2	26.3	58.5
1934	22.8	23.8	53.4

See Cheng Lin, pp. 92–138.

According to another quite different estimate: "Out of the total mileage of 16,972 kilometers, 9.4 percent (1,594 kilometers) was owned by foreign interests and 11.9 percent (2,025 kilometers) was jointly owned and operated by Chinese and foreign interests, and the balance of 78.7 percent (13.353 kilometers) was owned by Chinese, mainly by the Chinese government. But 45.5 percent of the capital invested in this 13,353 kilometers of Chinese-owned railroads was financed by foreign loans . . . It is, therefore, safe to estimate that over half of the Chinese railway enterprises were also directly or indirectly under the control or influence of foreign capital." (This presumably refers to the situation in 1936, with Manchuria excluded.) See Cheng Yu-kwei, p. 41.

The basic difficulty in estimating the share of foreign capital in the railroads of China lies in the almost impossible task of estimating its share in those railroads that were constructed partly with foreign loans and partly with Chinese funds. Even for railroads that were originally constructed entirely with Chinese funds, there is still the difficulty of estimating the value of later additions to or expansions of these lines, financed with Chinese funds. Apparently, both Yen Chung-p'ing and Cheng Lin tried to avoid these difficulties by including in the foreign share the entire mileage for which foreign loans had been raised. A justification for this approach is that without foreign loans, the lines might never have been started. Cheng Yu-kwei does not say exactly how his estimates are made.

7. The Chinese share (including junks) in the total tonnage of ships (including foreign sailing vessels) that entered and cleared through Maritime Customs was:

Period	Total tonnage (in millions)	Percent
1880	15.9	30.4
1890	24.9	25.5
1900	40.8	19.3
1903–1913 (av.)	88.2	21.0
1925–1929 (av.)	137.4	21.8
1930–1934 (av.)	145.8	23.9
1935	144.0	29.1
1936	145.0	30.5

For 1880–1900, see F. Otto, "Shipping in China and Chinese Shipping Abroad," *Chinese Economic Journal*, 5.2: 128 (Feb. 1930). For 1909–1936, see F. V. Field, ed., *An Economic Survey of the Pacific Area* (New York, 1942), Pt. 2, p. 39. Steamer tonnage entering Manchurian ports is not included for the years after 1932. (It amounted to 8.9 million tons for 1935 and 9.1 million tons for 1936; Japan owned more than two thirds. Hong Kong is not included. (Total tonnage of ships entered and cleared amounted to 21 million tons in 1935 and 20 million tons in 1936; Great Britain owned about 45–50 percent.)

8. Field, Pt. 2, p. 39. Manchuria not included after 1932.

9. Yen Chung-p'ing, ed., *T'ung-chi tzu-liao*, p. 104.

10. Ou's estimate may be compared with a recent estimate by Liu and Yeh with regard to the foreign share in manufacturing of the factory type (in terms of gross product) in 1933.

Manufacturers	Ou		Liu and Yeh	
	Chin$ millions	Percent	Chin$ millions	Percent
	China proper			
Chinese	1341.5	69.4	1771.4	78.1
foreign	590.7	30.6	497.4	21.9
Total	1932.2	100.0	2268.8	100.0
	Manchuria			
Chinese	74.0	29.1	—	—
foreign	180.1	70.9	—	—
Total	254.1	100.0	376.7	
Grand total	2186.2		2645.5	

For Ou, see Table 29. For Liu and Yeh, see Liu Ta-chung and Yeh Kung-chia, assisted by Twanmo Chong, *The Economy of the Chinese Mainland: National Income and Economic Development, 1933–1959* (Princeton, 1965), p. 588. In this study factory is defined as a manufacturing establishment using mechanical power regardless of the number of workers employed (p. 590). Water and electricity, included in manufacturing by Ou, are not included by Liu and Yeh.

11. See Introduction.

12. While research into the quantitative share of foreign capital in the entire modern sector of the Chinese economy remains to be made, an estimate appears in the table on p. 255.

13. This is the Lou-chih (drain) argument, meaning that profits made by foreigners were a drain of wealth from the Chinese economy.

14. For a study of this system see for instance Feuerwerker.

15. The most important companies under the Kuan-tu shang-pan arrangement

See note 12. Total modern industrial capital in China, excluding Manchuria, 1936 (Chin$ millions; percent in parentheses).

Use	Domestic capital	Foreign capital	Total
Manufacturing	627.8 (36.8)	1076.7 (63.2)	1704.5
Public utilities	0.0	277.7 (100.0)	277.7
Mining	44.3 (33.5)	88.0 (66.5)	132.3
Transportation	315.3 (18.6)	1378.1 (81.4)	1693.3
Railroads	148.3 (13.4)	961.7 (86.6)	1110.0
Highways	117.0 (100.0)	0.0	117.0
Aviation	7.6 (64.4)	4.2 (35.6)	11.8
Shipping	42.2 (9.3)	412.3 (90.7)	454.5
Total	987.3 (25.9)	2820.5 (74.1)	3807.8
Total in US$ millions	296.5	847.0	1143.5

Source: Ku Ch'un-fan (Koh Tso-fan), *Chung-kuo kung-yeh hua tung-lun* (Industrialization in China; Shanghai, 1947), pp. 169–171. For an English version of a part of this book see Koh Tso-fan, *Capital Stock.*

were the China Merchant's Steam Navigation Company (1872), the Kaiping Coal Mines (1877), the Shanghai Cotton Cloth Mill (first planned in 1877, later changed to the Hua-sheng Cotton Mill, which began to operate in 1894), the Imperial Telegraph Administration (1881), the Mo-ho Gold Mines (1887), the Hanyang Ironworks (1896), the Ta-yeh Iron Mines (1896), the Imperial Bank of China (1896), and the P'ing-hsiang Coal Mines (1898).

16. These estimates are based on: Sun Yu-tang, Chaps. 2 and 3. Wang Ching yü, Vol. 1, Chap. 2.

17. Lo Yü-tung, "Kuang-hsü ts'ai-cheng"; Chin Kuo-chen, *Chung-kuo ts'ai-cheng lun* (Public finance of China; Shanghai, 1931), pp. 79–97.

18. T. C. Smith, *Political Change and Industrial Development in Japan: Government Enterprises, 1868–1880* (Stanford, 1955), p. 69.

19. Feuerwerker, pp. 18, 26–28.

20. In 1867 the T'ung-wen kuan (College of Foreign Languages), which had been established in Peking in 1861, began to add to its curriculum such courses as mathematics, chemistry, physics, biology, mineralogy, mechanics, anatomy, physiology, political economy, and international law. Between 1872 and 1881 one hundred and twenty Chinese students studied in the United States, while a smaller number studied in France and England. Feuerwerker, p. 2. Also Knight Biggerstaff, *The Earliest Modern Government Schools in China* (Ithaca, 1961).

21. Thus, for the first time in China, a merchant from Szechwan obtained in 1901 a twenty-five year patent when he imitated a foreign method of manufacturing a chemical product. See Kung Chun, *Chung-kuo hsin-kung-yeh fa-chan-shih ta-kang* (Outline history of the development of modern industry in China; Shanghai, 1933), p. 61.

22. For example, the Wuhan Industrial Exposition was proposed in 1909, and

in 1910 the famous Wanyang Industrial Exposition was held in Nanking, for which various articles were gathered from different parts of the country. About Chin$1,500,000 were spent for the exhibit. See Kung Chun, p. 68.

23. For cotton textiles, woolen textiles, ironworks, and the like, the dividend was 6 percent; for silk, tea, and sugar manufacturing, it was five percent. Only firms whose paid-up capital was over Chin$700,000 for the first category and over Chin$200,000 for the second were eligible to apply for such a guarantee. Kung Chun, p. 97.

24. An interesting and useful sample study has recently been made by Albert Feuerwerker (pp. 18, 26–28). He attributes the failure of the kuan-tu shang-pan enterprises largely to bureaucratic management, official squeeze, and patronage, among other unfavorable traditional forces. He also reports the government gave substantial loans and other assistance to these enterprises, especially to the China Merchant's Steam Navigation Company, which was a typical kuan-tu shang-pan enterprise. This company apparently made handsome profits, although its accounting records remain to be analyzed. The stockholders received an annual dividend of about 15 percent on their investment for the period 1873–1914, plus a fivefold capital gain. It is questionable whether, from the viewpoint of the owners, this company can be called a failure.

25. For instance, in objecting to Western learning, Wo-Jen said this in 1867: "astronomy and mathematics are of very little use . . . If astronomy and mathematics have to be taught, an extensive search should find someone who has mastered the technique. Why is it limited to barbarians, and why is it necessary to learn from the barbarians? The only thing we can rely on is that our scholars should clearly explain to the people the Confucian tenets . . . Now if these brilliant and talented scholars, who have been trained by the nation and reserved for great future usefulness, have to change from their regular course of study to follow the barbarians, then the correct spirit will not be developed, and accordingly the evil spirit will become stronger. After several years it will end in nothing less than driving the multitudes of the Chinese people into allegiance to the barbarians." See Teng and Fairbank, p. 76.

26. Wang Ching-yü, II, 738.

27. D. K. Lieu (Liu Ta-chün), *The Growth and Industrialization of Shanghai* (Shanghai, 1936), pp. 31, 41, 43, 46, 52, 57.

28. In some cases foremen were enticed to join the Chinese enterprises and workmen were "kidnapped." See Akira Nagano, *Development of Capitalism in China* (Japan Council, Institute of Pacific Relations, 1931), p. 15: D. K. Lieu (Liu Ta-chün), *The Industrialization and Reconstruction of China* (Shanghai, 1946) p. 51.

29. Akira Nagano, p. 15.

30. For a general description of the comprador system, see, for instance, Sha Wei-k'ai, *Chung-kuo ti mai-pan chih* (The comprador system in China; Shanghai, 1934). As one writer observed, "the compradores possess a vast store of information, not only with regard to business in their own country, but conditions in the United States and England. They follow the American cotton market closely; they watch the course of exchange, because China's currency is on a silver basis; and they study world-wide commercial and political conditions, because all these matters have a direct or indirect bearing on the market in China. They know the requirements and the relative importance of the principal consuming districts in China and the exact kinds of goods which each district uses. It is doubtful if there

exists in any other country in the world such an excellent system for the dissemination of information and for the distribution of imports or the collection of goods for exports as China has in the institution of compradores." Quoted by Fang from Ralph M. Odell, *Cotton Goods in China* (Washington, D.C., 1916). Fang Hsien-ting (H. D. Fong), "Industrial Capital in China," p. 50.

31. Calculations on the percentage distribution of capital of modern enterprises founded in the nineteenth century will show that the bureaucrats and compradores had the largest share among all investors. See Yen Chung-p'ing. ed., *T'ung-chi tzu-liao*, pp. 96–99.

32. For an interesting discussion of the linkage effects, see Albert O. Hirschman, *The Strategy for Economic Development* (New Haven, 1958).

33. M. J. Levy and Shih Kuo-heng, *The Rise of the Modern Chinese Business Class* (New York, 1949). It was chiefly the growth of foreign trade that gave birth to the famous Kwantung plutocracy and the Chekian group. They were so named because they were from the Kiangsu, Chekiang, and Kwangtung provinces, which were located near to the open ports.

34. See the statistics for this and other fields already given above.

35. Yen Chung-p'ing, ed., *T'ung-chi tzu-liao*, p. 131.

36. The history of the individual cotton mills in China has been briefly presented in Yen Chung-p'ing, *Mien-fang-chih*, appendices. For the Chinese mining enterprises, see *Chung-kuo kuang-yeh chi-yao*, various issues.

37. Based on a survey, Fang has estimated the relative size of the Chinese and foreign cotton mills in China in 1930 as follows:

Per mill: mean	Chinese mills	Japanese mills	British mills
Net worth (Chin$ millions)	1.7	3.5	4.2
Yarn spindles (thousands)	29.9	39.9	51.1
Workers (thousands)	2.2	1.8	4.3
Electric power (thousand watts)	1.2	1.5	—
Looms	500.0	758.0	633.3
Cotton consumption (thousand piculs)	74.9	70.9	151.1
Yarn output (thousand bales)	21.1	19.7	43.2
Cloth output (thousand bolts)	236.6	543.6	—

In 1930, 123 cotton mills were in operation in China: Chinese, 77; Japanese, 43; British, 3. The mean averages given above were representative to the extent that they were not distorted by extreme values. See Fang Hsien-ting, *Mien-fang-chih*, Chap. 5 and p. 105.

38. In an attempt to compare the efficiency of Chinese and Japanese cotton mills in China in 1930, Fang made the estimates shown in the table on p. 258. See Fang, p. 107. These statistics suffer from the fact that Chinese mills concentrated on coarse yarns whereas Japanese mills concentrated on finer yarns. In what way the difference in specialization should alter the interpretation of the above statistics cannot be ascertained.

39. Yen Chung-p'ing, *Mien-fang-chih*, p. 218.

See note 38.

Item	Chinese mills		Japanese mills	
	Mean	No. of mills	Mean	No. of mills
Spindle per worker	16.1	42	24.1	28
Power required per worker (watts)	530.0	73	828.0	28
Power required per spindle (watts)	35.5	42	36.1	28
Cotton used per spindle per year (piculs)	2.45	71	1.81	42
Cotton used per worker per year (piculs)	34.6	42	43.0	28
Yarn output per worker per year (bales)	9.85	42	11.95	28
Yarn output per spindle per year (bales)	0.692	71	0.501	42

40. Annual interest rates charged by modern banks in various cities around 1910 have been estimated as follows:

Cities	Interest rate (percent)
Ying-kou	9.6
Peking	6.6–12.0
Tientsin	8.4–9.6
Shanghai	7.2–9.6
Hankow	9.6
Chenkiang	8.4–9.6
Nanking	12.0
Wuhu	12.0
Kiukiang	9.6–18.0
Changsha	9.6–11.0
Hsiangtan	6.0–7.2
Shashih	12.0
Yi-chang	12.0–18.0
Chungking	10.0–12.0
Nanchang	11.0
Ningpo	6.0–20.0
Foochow	8.0–20.0
Amoy ·	10.0–25.0
Swatow	12.0
Wenchou	15.0–30.0
Canton	18.0–36.0
Wuchou	12.0–15.0
Average	12.5–14.8

See Wang Ching-yü, II, 1016. In the early 1930's Chinese owned cotton mills had to pay an interest rate of 10-12 percent at maximum and 7-8 percent at minimum. See Wang Tzu-chien and Wang Chen-chung, *Ch'i-sheng Hua-shang sha-ch'ang tiao-ch'a pao-kao* (Report of a survey of Chinese cotton mills in seven provinces; Shanghai, 1935), p. 221.

41. Yen Chung-p'ing, *Mien-fang-chih*, pp. 239–242.

42. Sun Yu-tang, I, 248; Wang Ching-yü, I, 355, 357, 372; also Ch'en Chen *et al.*, comps., *Chung-kuo chin-tai kung-yeh-shih tzu-liao, ti-erh chi: ti-kuo chu-i tui Chung-kuo kung k'uang shih-yeh ti ch'in-lüeh ho lung-tuan* (Source materials on China's modern industrial history, second collection: Imperialist aggression against and monopolization of China's industries and mines; Peking, 1958), pp. 854–935.

43. The guaranteed interest on capital ran from 7 to 10 percent in the years before the First World War. See Wang Ching-yü, II, 1011–1115.

44. *China Yearbook, 1925*, pp. 777–778.

45. This was not carried out until 1891. Teng and Fairbank, p. 111.

46. Yen Chung-p'ing, *Mien-fang-chih*, p. 220.

47. Ch'en Chen, *et al.* p. 148.

48. China: Ministries of Communications and Railways, *Chiao-t'ung-shih: Hang-cheng p'ien.*

49. C. F. Remer, *A Study of Chinese Boycotts* (Baltimore, 1933), p. 245.

50. *Ibid.*, p. 230.

51. *Nanyang hsiung-ti yen-ts'ao kung-ssu shih-liao* (Historical materials concerning the Nanyang Brothers Tobacco Co.), comp. Shanghai Economic Research Institute, Chinese Academy of Sciences, and the Economic Research Institute, Shanghai Academy of Social Sciences (Shanghai, 1958).

52. *Ibid.*, pp. 254, 255.

53. *Chin shih-wu-nien lai Shanghai chih pa-kung t'ing-yeh* (Strikes and lockouts in Shanghai since 1928; Shanghai: Bureau of Social Affairs, City Government of Greater Shanghai, 1933), pp. 41, 42.

54. The formation of the Fuchung Corporation was another case of eliminating competition between a British and Chinese mining concern.

55. R. H. Tawney, *Land and Labor in China* (London 1932), p. 13.

56. The share of these six cities in the total spindles of Chinese-owned mills were: 1890 — 100 percent, 1900 — 83.7 percent, 1910 — 63.0 percent, 1920 — 74.2 percent, 1930 — 67.2 percent. See Yen Chung-p'ing, ed., *T'ung-chi tzu-liao* pp. 107–109.

57. Recent attempts to explain the limited degree of economic development in China include: Teng and Fairbank; Marion J. Levy Jr. "Contrasting Factors in the Modernization of China and Japan" in Kuznets, Moore, and Spengler, eds., *Economic Growth: Brazil, India, and Japan* (also in *Economic Development and Cultural Change*, 2.3:161–197 [Oct. 1953]); Marion J. Levy Jr., "Some Aspects of 'Individualism' and the Problem of Modernization in China and Japan" in *Economic Development and Cultural Change*, 10.3:225–240 (Apr. 1962); Mary Clabaugh Wright, *The Last Stand of Chinese Conservatism* (Stanford, 1957); Feuerwerker; Kwang-Ching Liu, *Steamship Rivalry;* Kwang-Ching Liu, "Steamship Enterprise in Nineteenth-Century China," *Journal of Asian Studies*, 18.4:435–455 (1959); John K. Fairbank, Alexander Eckstein, and L. S. Yang, "Economic Change in Early Modern China: An Analytic Framework," *Economic Development and Cultural Change*, 9.1:1–26 (Oct. 1960); Edwin O. Reischauer and John K. Fairbank, *East Asia: The Great Tradition* vol. 2 (Boston, 1965).

58. Hu Shih, *The Chinese Renaissance* (Chicago, 1934), pp. 9–10.

59. *Ibid.*, pp. 7–8.

60. *Ibid.*, p. 9.

61. In a brief, remarkable account of China's modern history, Tsiang Ting-fu shared Hu shih's view. In suggesting that from 1842 to 1862 China lost twenty of the most precious years in her modernization efforts, Tsiang singled out one important factor — namely that the statesmen at the time, like Lin Tse-hsü, were too weak or powerless to make their views prevail in the conservative court. Tsiang T'ing-fu, *Chung-kuo chin-tai shih* (History of modern China; Changsha, 1938), Chap. 1.

62. For agrarian policies in the 1860's, see Mary Clabaugh Wright, pp. 157–167; Li Wen-chih, ed., *Chung-kuo chin-tai nung-yeh-shih tzu-liao, ti-i chi, 1840–1911* (Source materials on the history of agriculture in Modern China, First collection, 1840–1911; Peking 1957), Chap. 8.

63. Hu Shih, p. 24.

64. *Ibid.*, p. 25 and Chap. 6. Hu lists a number of changes in various areas: establishment of gigantic factories and trading companies; new ways of transportation and communication; new forms of financial organization; modern education; political revolution; rearrangement of social classes; breakdown of the old family; migration of people; transmission of new manners and ideas, etc. He recognizes that not all the transformations touched the vast hinterland of China; they took place only in the cities. However, the following three helped to spread the effects of the other changes far and wide: the migration to the cities, the founding of new schools, and the political revolution.

65. See, for instance, H. W. Singer, "Economic Progress in Underdeveloped Countries" *Social Research*, 16:1–11, March 1949.

66. A sophisticated version of this thesis is presented by Harvey Leibenstein, *Economic Backwardness and Economic Growth* (New York, 1957).

67. Hou Chi-ming, "The Critical Minimum Effort Thesis: A Critique," *Tsing Hua Journal of Chinese Studies*, New Series, 3.2:87–109 (June 1963).

68. J. L. Buck, *Land Utilization in China* (Shanghai, 1937), p. 197.

69. For an evaluation of China's population data, see Ho Ping-ti, *Studies on the Population of China 1368–1953* (Cambridge, Mass., 1959).

70. Tseng K'un-hua (1924 ed.), pp. 420–424; Hsieh Pin, *Chung-kuo t'ieh-lu shih* (History of Chinese railroads; Shanghai, 1929), pp. 20–26.

71. During the period 1904–1911, only about four hundred miles of railroads were built with private capital. Chang Chia-nau, p. 39.

72. In the rural sector where risks were high and the market was more imperfect, interest of 40 to 80 percent was common, while a rate of 150 to 200 percent was not unknown. Tawney, p. 62. According to Buck, the rate of interest averaged 32 percent per year for the entire rural sector in 1929–1933. Buck, p. 463. Interest rates charged by Chinese modern banks were not this high; they ranged from 12 percent to 15 percent around 1910. Wang Ching-yü II, 1016.

In the case of share rent, the most common rate was from 40 to 50 percent of the total crop, depending upon the amount of assistance given by the landlord in the form of seeds, implements, etc. In the case of cash rent, it averaged 46 percent of the gross product. However, in terms of the value of land the average crop rent was 13 percent, the average cash rent was 11 percent, and the average share rent was 14 percent. (All these figures refer to the 1930's.) Ch'iao Ch'i-ming, *Chung-kuo nung-ts'un she-hui ching-chi-hsüeh* (The economics of Chinese rural society; Chung-king, 1945), pp. 242–246.

73. Tawney, p. 11.

74. Entire Anhwei, Southern Kiangsu, Northern Chekiang, Northern Kiangsi, parts of Hupei, Southern Honan, Western Shantung. See Ho Ping-ti, Chap. 10.

75. *Ibid.*

76. *Ibid.*

77. Some nineteenth-century Western observers estimated that China lost between 20 and 30 million people during the Taiping Rebellion. Though largely in the nature of guesswork, such estimates can hardly fail to indicate the serious effect of the war on population. Losses due to the civil war between the Nationalists and Communists up to July, 1934, according to *Chiang-hsi nien-chien, 1937* (the Kiangsi yearbook) were: about 279,800 homes destroyed; property valued at Chin$582 million damaged; and about 568,000 people killed. For a useful study of the effects of civil war and natural calamities on population in China, see Ho Ping-ti, Chap. 10.

CHAPTER 7

1. While this definition is generally followed in this chapter, some exceptions are made. Because of availability of data, included in handicrafts are small-scale workshops producing new commodities that were never produced in "traditional" China, such as electrical instruments, cigarettes, etc. These exceptions were not significant enough to alter the conclusions. Furthermore, these workshops were basically traditional in operation and organization.

2. A modern mine is one that uses machines of the Western type.

3. See Yen Chung-p'ing, ed., *T'ung-chi tzu-liao,* p. 104.

4. *Chung-kuo k'uan-yeh chi-yao,* various issues.

5. Leonard G. Ting, "Chinese Modern Banks and the Finance of Government and Industry," *Nankai Social and Economic Quarterly,* 8.3:578–616 (Oct. 1935).

6. Yen Chung-p'ing, ed., *T'ung-chi tzu-liao,* p. 72.

7. Ou Pao-san (Wu Pao-san), "Chung-kuo kuo-min so-te i-chiu-san-san hsiu-cheng" (Corrections to China's National Income, 1933), *She-hui k'o-hsüeh tsa-chih,* 9.9:92–153 (Dec. 1947). According to Ou's estimates, the shares contributed by various industries to net national product are as follows: agriculture, 61.5 percent; mining, 1.1 percent; manufacturing, 9.2 percent; construction, 1.1 percent; transportation and communications, 4.5 percent; commerce, 12.4 percent; banking and finance, 1.0 percent; housing, 4.6 percent; professional services, .8 percent; domestic services, .7 percent; public administration, 3.1 percent.

8. Liu Ta-chung and Yeh Kung-chia, p. 89. The percentage distribution of net domestic products was as follows: agriculture, 65 percent; modern non-agricultural sectors, 12.6 percent; traditional nonagricultural sectors, 19.6 percent; government administration, 2.8 percent.

9. See Henry Rosovsky and Kazushi Ohkawa "The Indigenous Components in the Modern Japanese Economy," *Economic Development and Cultural Change,* 9.3:476–501 (Apr. 1961).

10. The computation is based on the quantity index of Chinese exports as published by the Nankai Institute of Economics. See *Nankai Social and Economic Quarterly,* 10.2:346–347 (July 1937). The equation of the trend of exports is $Y = 30.59 + (1.024)^x$ with the origin at 1866.

11. Yen Chung-p'ing, ed., *T'ung-chi tzu-liao*, p. 70.

12. The price index used is the index number of wholesale prices calculated by Franklin L. Ho and given in Yang Twan-liu, Hou Hou-pei *et al.*, p. 3. The base year of the index is 1913. The 1873 export figure is deflated by the 1874 index number, and the 1930 export figure is deflated by the 1928 index number.

13. The export figures were supplied by Theodore Herman of Colgate University who also generously shared with me his expert knowledge of Chinese handicrafts. The index number used for deflation is Ho's, cited above. Herman defines a handicraft article as one in which most of the value and/or sales appeal of the end product results from the effort, skill, or artistry of one person or several people working closely together and using very little mechanical power. See his "An Analysis of China's Export Handicraft Industries to 1930," unpub. diss. (University of Washington, 1954).

14. P'eng Tse-i, ed., *Chung-kuo chin-tai shou-kung-yeh shih tzu-liao, 1840–1949* (Source materials on the modern history of Chinese handicrafts; Peking, 1957), Vol. 3, Appendix 3. Many items that are excluded by Herman's definition are included in this study such as tea and silk.

15. Calculations are based on figures given by Fang Hsien-ting (H. D. Fong), *Rural Industries in China* (Tientsin, 1933), p. 14. The trend line is fitted by the freehand method.

16. Yen Chung-p'ing, ed., *T'ung-chi tzu-liao*, p. 16.

17. *Ibid*.

18. It is assumed that in the long run the elasticity of aggregate supply was greater than zero — that is, an increase of production in the export and modern sectors does not require a declining availability of resources for development of the traditional sector.

19. For an interesting description of the Chinese junks, see G. R. G. Worcester, *The Junkman Smiles* (London, 1959).

20. Yen Chung-p'ing, ed., *T'ung-chi tzu-liao*, p. 103.

21. Based on data given in *ibid.*, pp. 134–135.

22. The value of the import of cotton goods is deflated by Ho's index, cited above. For import data on cotton yarn and cotton goods, see Yang Twan-liu, Hou Hou-pei *et al.*, pp. 20, 46.

23. For the Kao-yang area, see Wu Chih, *Hsiang-ts'un chih-pu kung-yeh ti i-ko yen-chiu* (A study of the rural cloth industry; Shanghai, 1936). For Ting-hsien, see Chang Shih-wen, *Ting-hsien nung-ts'un kung-yeh tiao-ch'a* (A survey on rural industries in Ting-hsien; Hopei, 1936).

24. The industry declined sharply in the Kao-yang area from 1929 to 1933, but whether this was a temporary decline or a new trend cannot be determined. No data are available for later development.

25. For the Nan-tung area, see Yen Chung-p'ing, *Mien-fang-chih*, pp. 260–261.

26. Odell observed: "The cloth that is woven on these [hand] looms is extremely popular among the natives, and although that sold in the market is often as expensive as similar foreign goods, it must be remembered that a large proportion of it is made in the homes of the people for their own use; and as long as they can buy raw cotton and spin it into yarn or buy foreign yarn at low prices for weaving into cloth in seasons when they are not occupied, in the fields, they will likely find this a more economical method of providing themselves with clothing than to buy foreign goods." See Odell, p. 193.

27. There is also evidence to show that new cloth-weaving workshops were constantly being established in various hand-weaving centers after the turn of the century. Such evidence, though suggestive of growth of the industry, cannot be considered conclusive, for failures must also have occurred from time to time. For the newly established workshops, see P'eng Tse-i, Vol. 2, Chaps. 12 and 15.

28. Yen Chung-p'ing, *Mien-fang-chih*, p. 334.

29. The cultivated area of cotton constituted respectively 11 percent, 14 percent, 18 percent, and 20 percent of total crop area in China for 1904–1909, 1914–1919, 1924–1929, and 1929–1933. See Buck, p. 217. Total crop area is estimated to have been the same during the period. See Yen Chung-p'ing, ed., *T'ung-chi tzu-liao*, p. 357. The reasons given by Buck for the increase in cotton acreage were high price and high yield.

30. The highest estimate of cotton production for 1913 in Table 37 is quite close to the 1127 million pounds that according to one estimate is the cotton production figure for 1918–1919. See Fang Hsien-ting, *Mien-fang-chih*, p. 26.

31. See Yen Chung-p'ing, ed., *T'ung-chi tzu-liao*, p. 130.

32. For Ou's figure, see Ou Pao-san *et al.*, *Chung-kuo kuo-min so-te i-chiu-san-san nien* (China's national income, 1933; Shanghai: Institute of Social Sciences, Academia Sinica, 1947), I, 24. Yen's figure is that of the National Agricultural Research Bureau, which made the following estimates of cotton production in China (in 1,000 piculs):

1931	14,570
1932	15,143
1933	16,595
1934	15,849
1935	14,338
1936	20,639

See Yen Chung-p'ing, *Mien-fang-chih*, p. 340.

33. Liu and Yeh, p. 300.

34. For the various estimates, see Ou Pao-san *et al.*, *Kuo-min so-te*, II, 96.

35. In 1929 hand-spun yarn still accounted for 40 percent of the total yarn consumption of the hand-weaving industry in Hopei. Yen Chung-p'ing, *Mien-fang-chih*, p. 256.

36. Ou Pao-san, "So-te hsiu-cheng," pp. 130–133.

37. Yen places the production of machine yarns in 1934–35 at 4,934,000 quintals and hand-spun yarn at 1,000,000 quintals (Yen, *Mien-fang-chih*, p. 309). After Yen's error in domestic cotton production is corrected, as noted in Table 37, hand-spun yarn production should be 2,635,000 quintals or about 35 percent of the total. According to Liu and Yeh, hand cotton yarn in 1933 also accounted for 20 percent of the total gross output, whereas machine cotton yarn accounted for 80 percent. (Liu and Yeh, pp. 426–428, 512–513.) Ou's percentages (in terms of gross output) are 10.4 percent for hand cotton yarn and 89.6 percent for machine cotton yarn.

38. Yang Twan-liu, Hou Hou-pei *et al.*, p. 46.

39. American cotton seeds were introduced to China in the 1860's perhaps first by foreign merchants and then by the imperial government. In the 1890's American cotton seeds were even forced upon some Chinese cotton growers by

Chang Chih-tung. An imperial edict was issued to improve cotton seeds and plantation methods in 1908. Further efforts were made from time to time, both by textile firms and the government. See Yen Chung-p'ing, *Mien-fang chih*, pp. 324–330.

40. For a brief discussion see, for instance, Charles P. Kindleberger, *Economic Development* (New York, 1958), Chap. 10.

41. G. H. Boeke, *Economics and Economic Policy of Dual Societies* (New York, 1953). For a discussion of Boeke's thesis, see B. Higgins, "The Dualistic Theory of Underdeveloped Countries," *Economic Development and Cultural Change*, 4.2:99–115 (Jan. 1956); and J. M. van der Kroef, "Economic Development in Indonesia: Some Social and Cultural Impediments," both in *ibid.*, pp. 116–133.

42. Max Weber, *The Religion of China*, tr. and ed. Hans H. Gerth (Glencoe, Ill., 1951).

43. Alpha C. Chiang, "Religion, Proverbs, and Economic Mentality" in *American Journal of Economics and Sociology*, 18:250–258 (Apr. 1961).

44. *Ibid.*, p. 260.

45. R. S. Eckaus, "The Factor Proportions Problem in Underdeveloped Areas," *American Economic Review*, 45:539–635 (Sept. 1955). A. O. Hirschman, "Investment Policies and Dualism in Underdeveloped Countries," *American Economic Review*, 47:550–570 (Sept. 1957).

46. For some of the scattered wage data available, see P'eng Tse-i, Vol. 2, Chap. 18 and Vol. 3, Chap. 21.

47. Yen Chung-p'ing, *Mien-fang-chih*, p. 255.

48. The conclusions will not change, although the diagramatic presentation will be complicated, if some degree of factor substitution is allowed; that is, there is more than one process in traditional or modern technology.

49. Ferdinand Freiherrn von Richthofen, *China* (Berlin, 1882), II, 146.

50. P'eng Tse-i, II, 143.

51. China: Maritime Customs, *Decennial Reports, 1922–1931* (Shanghai, 1933), I, 118.

52. *Ibid.*, p. 114, citing *Commercial Reports from British Consuls in China, 1874*, Shanghai, p. 116.

53. *Ibid.*, citing *Commercial Reports from British Consuls in China, 1877, Chefoo*, p. 37. According to an earlier observer: "The home-made cloth is of thrice the substance, and will last a Chinaman for at least two years. The British calico, washed in Chinese fashion by beating between stones, would wear out in six weeks." George Wingrove Cooke, *China: Being "The Times" Special Correspondence om China in the Years 1857–58* (London, 1859), p. 185.

54. China: The Maritime Customs, *Decennial Reports, 1922–1931*, p. 114, citing *Commercial Reports from British Consuls in China, 1879*, Chinkiang, p. 52.

55. *Ibid.*, p. 114.

56. Cheng Kuan-ying, *Sheng-shih wei-yen* (Warnings to a seemingly prosperous age; 1895), 7:20, as cited in P'eng Tse-i, II, 165.

57. P'eng Tse-i, II, 691.

58. *Ibid.*, II, 392, 403, 691; III, 72.

59. While there are no statistics to show the increase in China's internal trade, the ratio (by value) of interport movements of Chinese products carried on steam vessels to foreign imports and exports may be suggestive:

Year	Foreign imports	Foreign exports	Interport trade of Chinese products	Total
1913	49.6	35.1	15.3	100
1916	42.2	39.4	18.4	100
1920	45.6	31.9	22.5	100
1930	44.4	30.7	24.9	100
1936	33.1	24.8	42.1	100

See Cheng Yu-kwei, p. 36.

60. China: Maritime Customs, *Decennial Reports, 1922–1931*, I, 136.

61. Myrdal attempts to analyze the relationship between the developed and underdeveloped regions of a country. Since the modern sector of the Chinese economy was developed primarily in the coastal and riverine regions, Myrdal's analysis seems applicable. See Myrdal, *Rich Lands and Poor*. A. O. Hirschman addresses himself to the same problem in "Investment Policies and 'Dualism.' " His trickling-down effects are similar to Myrdal's spread effects, and his polarization effects similar to Myrdal's backwash effects, but his emphasis and conclusions are not quite the same.

62. Theodore Herman is making a study of the effect of modern economic activity on various zones of the country since the latter part of the nineteenth century.

63. The population of 33 cities increased from 7 million in 1904 to 13 million in 1931, or at an annual rate of 2.3 percent. The increase cannot be accounted for entirely by natural causes. For population data, see China: The Maritime Customs, *Reports and Returns of Trade*, and *Foreign Trade of China*, various years.

64. E.g., W. A. Lewis, "Unlimited Labor: Further Notes," *Manchester School of Economic and Social Studies*, 26.1:22–23 (Jan. 1958); H. G. Johnson, "Economic Expansion and International Trade," *ibid.*, 59:498–513 (May 1955).

65. Hirschman, *Strategy for Economic Development*, p. 189.

66. Commodity terms of trade of the Chinese farmers are estimated in the table on p. 266.

67. Li Wen-chih, Chap. 8. Chang Yu-i, Chaps. 2, 3, 4; also P'eng Tse-i, Vol. 2, Chap. 17.

68. Buck, pp. 316, 330.

69. China: Maritime Customs, *Decennial Reports 1882–1891*, pp. 620–621.

70. China: Maritime Customs, *Returns of Trade and Trade Reports, 1887*, Chefoo, p. 43.

71. It is also possible, however, that productivity in the traditional sector could have developed faster if the modern sector had not intruded and disrupted the economy.

72. In an unpublished memorandum, "Proposals for Industrial Research and Training: A Phase of Rural Reconstruction," prepared in 1933 by the Industrial Association of North China, it is estimated that in North China the idle time of farmers who did not have outside employment lasted from five to six months a year. For the whole country the idle time of farmers in the age group 15 to 54 is

See note 66.

Year	Index numbers of prices received by farmers for commodities sold (1926 = 100); P_r	Index numbers of retail prices paid by farmers for commodities purchased (1926 = 100); P_p	P_r/P_p (percent)
1906	39	71	54.9
1907	46	58	79.3
1908	49	57	86.0
1909	50	54	92.6
1910	53	57	93.0
1911	56	61	91.8
1912	55	65	84.6
1913	58	65	89.2
1914	59	64	92.2
1915	61	68	89.7
1916	65	71	91.5
1917	69	76	90.8
1918	69	79	87.3
1919	69	82	84.1
1920	80	85	94.1
1921	90	88	102.3
1922	92	91	101.1
1923	98	95	103.2
1924	97	101	96.0
1925	102	101	101.0
1926	100	100	100.0
1927	95	103	92.2
1928	106	109	97.3
1929	127	118	107.6
1930	125	126	99.2
1931	116	135	85.9
1932	103	127	81.1
1933	71	104	68.3

Source: Buck, p. 319.

estimated to have been equal to the full-time unemployment of 55 million farmers. See Fang Hsien-ting and Wu Chih, "Chung-kuo chih hsiang-t'sun kung-yeh" (Rural industries of China), *Ching-chi t'ung-chi chi-k'an* (Quarterly journal of economics and statistics), 2.3:617 (Sept. 1933).

In a study of 15,316 farms in 152 localities in 22 provinces, Buck reports that of the able-bodied men over 15 and under 60 years of age in 1929–1933, 35 percent were engaged in full-time work, 58 percent were engaged in part-time work, 1 percent had no work, 1 percent were sick throughout the year, 1 percent were sick part of the time, and 4 percent were partly idle, partly sick, and partly working. Idleness averaged 1.7 months per able-bodied man.

Other things being equal, there is doubt whether it would have been possible to withdraw some of the farmers from the farms and yet maintain the same level of agricultural production. According to the same study, 80 percent of the farmers' idle time occurred in the winter months of November, December, January, and February. In many places there was a shortage of labor during the period of harvest and, to a lesser extent, during the period of cultivation. In a survey of 260 localities in 1929–1933, nearly two thirds of the units reported a scarcity of labor at harvest time, over one fourth reported a scarcity at planting time, and one eighth reported a shortage for irrigation. See Buck, pp. 294, 299.

CHAPTER 8

1. For both 1933 and 1936 Manchuria is included. Cheng Yu-kwei, p. 198 and Appendix 1.

2. Manchuria is included. Total foreign trade in 1933 is computed as follows (in Chin$ millions):

Trade	China	Manchuria	Total
Exports	612	310	922
Imports	1346	359	1705
Total	1958	669	2627

For China, see Yen Chung-p'ing, ed., *T'ung-chi tzu-liao*, p. 64. For Manchuria, see Cheng Yu-kwei, p. 198. (US$1 = Chin$3.2, average for 1933–1936). National income for 1933 is assumed to be Chin$29,000 million (Liu Ta-chung and Yeh Kung-chia, p. 66. If the figure for net domestic product estimated by Ou Pao-san is used (Chin$20,320 million), the foreign-trade-to-national-income ratio is 10 percent.

3. The ratio for 1933 appears to hold for other years before 1936.

4. For a discussion of the trade-income ratio and a graphic presentation of the imports as a percentage of national income of the underdeveloped countries in 1953, see Kindleberger, *Economic Development*, pp. 121–123.

5. For the percentage distribution of China's imports and exports, 1842–1931, see China: Maritime Customs, *Decennial Reports, 1922–1931*, pp. 120, 180–181, 190. For the period 1932–1936, see Yen Chung-p'ing, ed., *T'ung-chi tzu-liao*, p. 76.

6. H. B. Morse, *The Trade and Administration of China* (London, 1913), pp. 289–304.

7. In terms of groups, the share of raw materials including cotton and tobacco increased from 1913 to 1936, while semimanufactured goods decreased. The share of manufactures remained constant, although producer's goods and finished goods for construction gained in relative importance. Cheng Yu-kwei, p. 35.

8. The total export of China is assumed to be US$360.7 million in 1936, Manchuria included. The total export of beans and bean cakes is assumed to be US$80.2 million, with Manchuria accounting for US$75.2 million. See Yen Chung-p'ing, ed., *T'ung-chi tzu liao*, p. 76; Cheng Yu-kwei, p. 201, and Appendix 1. (1 Haikwan Tael = US$0.463).

9. United Nations, *Relative Prices of Exports and Imports of Underdeveloped Countries* (New York, 1949), p. 36.

10. Tsai Chien and Chan Kwan-wai, *Trend and Character of China's Foreign Trade, 1912–1931* (Shanghai, 1933), p. 10.

11. *Ibid.*

12. Ou Pao-san, "So-te hsiu-cheng," pp. 130–133.

13. United Nations, *Instability in Export Markets of Underdeveloped Countries* (New York, 1952), p. 10. The periods covered for various commodities differ, but they all fall within the period 1900–1950. The year-to-year fluctuation is measured the same as in Table 39.

14. *Ibid.*, pp. 31, 40.

15. Note that the proceeds of exports are in Haikwan taels. Therefore, they reflect not only the basic supply and demand conditions of the exports but also the exchange rate between silver and gold. To observe the effect of export instability on domestic economic changes, it is more appropriate to render the value of exports in Haikwan taels than in a foreign currency, such as pound sterling or American dollars.

16. The year-to-year fluctuation in the proceeds of the tea export was only 2.5 percent in 1901–1913, but gained after 1914. For the period 1901–1950 it was 24.7 percent, while the year-to-year fluctuation in volume was 22 percent. For China's cotton export (1904–1944) the year-to-year fluctuation in proceeds was 33 percent and that in volume was 29 percent. For carpet wool, feathers, and weasel fur (undressed) the year-to-year fluctuation in price (1922–1949). was 20 percent or more. United Nations, *Instability in Export Markets*, pp. 36–39.

17. It appears to have been generally true in the United States (1890–1936) that when there was a fall in the wholesale commodity price index, there was also a fall in the purchasing power of silver. See Cheng Yu-kwei, Appendix 3. For the relationship between the purchasing power of silver and China's exports, see section on China's terms of trade.

18. For instance, the average annual export of coal in 1928–1931 was 3,744,000 tons, whereas the average annual coal production of modern mines was 19,455,000 tons. Therefore, total export was about 19 percent of the production of modern mines and about 15 percent of the production of all mines. The export figure is from China: Maritime Customs, *Decennial Reports 1922–1931*, pp. 185–193. The production figures are from Yen Chung-p'ing, ed., *T'ung-chi tzu-liao*, pp. 123–124.

19. The figures in Table 40 may exaggerate the situation somewhat, inasmuch as Ou's output estimates are generally on the lower side and the exports in 1928–1931 were on fairly high levels.

20. D. K. Lieu, *The Silk Industry of China* (Shanghai, 1941), p. 27.

21. Unless otherwise specified, the terms of trade referred to are the net barter or commodity terms.

22. Franklin L. Ho, *Index Numbers of Quantities and Prices of Imports and Exports in China* (Tientsin, 1930).

23. Ho Lien (Franklin L. Ho) "Chung-kuo chin-ch'u-k'ou mao'i wu'liang chih-shu wu-chia chih-shu yü wu-wu chiao-i-lü chih-shu pien-chih chih shuo-ming" (Index numbers of quantities and prices of imports and exports of China, an explanation), *Ching-chi t'ung-chi chi-k'an*, 1.1:128–149 (Mar. 1932); "Min-kuo erh-shih nien chih Chung-kuo tui-wai mao-i" (China's foreign trade during 1931), *ibid.*, 1.4:741–810 (Dec. 1932).

24. Wu Ta-yeh and Hu Yuan-chang, "Min-kuo erh-shih nien chih Chung-kuo tui-wai mao-i" (China's foreign trade during 1935), *Cheng-chih ching-chi hsueh-pao* (Quarterly journal of economics and political science), Vol. 5, No. 1 (Oct. 1936).

25. Tientsin, 1937.

26. Perhaps the fact that the revisions have never appeared in English has led Theodore Morgan to complain that "the series (for 1867–1928) of these two publications [as cited in Fn. 22 and 25] for unexplained reasons march off in opposite directions; one shows China's terms of trade improving, the other shows deteriorating, though the dates are supposedly identical." Theodore Morgan, "The Long-Run Terms of Trade between Agriculture and Manufacturing," *Economic Development and Cultural Change*, 8.1:8–9 (Oct. 1959).

27. Remer, *Foreign Investments*, p. 197.

28. C. M. Li, "China's International Trade Statistics: An Evaluation," Nankai Social and Economic Quarterly, 10.1:12 (Apr. 1937).

29. John B. Condliffe, *China Today: Economic* (Boston, 1932), p. 183.

30. China: Ministry of Industries, *Silver and Prices in China* (Report of the Committee to Study Silver Values and Commodity Prices; 1935), p. 14.

31. Wu Ta-yeh, who was also in charge of the preparation of the Nankai series, made some necessary adjustments in his article, "Chin-yin pen-wei kuo chien chin-yin huo liu-tung ti yuan-tse chi Chung-kuo chin-yin huo chin-ch'u k'ou ti chieh-shih" (Principles governing the movement of gold and silver between gold standard and silver standard countries), *Chin-chi t'ung-chi chi-k'an* 2.2:351–381 (June 1933). However, the figures for the years 1904–1914 of the final Nankai series were from the 1932 revision, in which no adjustment had been made for the change in the valuation method in 1904. Otherwise Wu would not have found it necessary to make the adjustment in his 1933 article. Mr. Wu concurred in correspondence with me.

32. It is clear that the Nankai series, after adjustment, is reasonably reliable and may be used although it does not avoid the shortcomings that are inherent in any long-run terms-of-trade index. The change in quality of goods and services is not recognized. The weighting problem can not be solved to complete satisfaction when there is significant change in the composition of trade or when a great number of new products are introduced over the years. When unit value is used to represent price, it is valid only when the commodity class is completely homogeneous which is not usually the case. When there is no complete homogeneity, changes in unit value may reflect changes in the composition of the class as well as in price. See C. P. Kindleberger, *The Terms of Trade, A European Case Study* (New York, 1956), p. 317; also, comments by G. Haberler in the "Introduction" to *Review of Economics and Statistics*, Vol. 40 supplement (Feb. 1958), p. 5.

33. The trend is $Y = 76.0027 + 0.4442X$ with origin at 1866. The trend line of the unadjusted Nankai series ·is $Y = 87.9451 + 0.4438X$ with origin at 1866. This means that at the end of the period a given quantity of exports could pay for 74 percent of the imports that it could have bought at the beginning of the period. The trend line would appear slightly different if the catastrophic 1930's were disregarded. The United Nations study, *Relative Prices of Exports and Imports of Underdeveloped Countries*, indicates that from the 1870's to the eve of the Second World War there was a secular downward trend in prices of primary goods relative to prices of manufactured goods. On an average, a given quantity of primary exports could pay at the end of this period for only 60 percent of the quantity of

manufactured goods that it could have bought at the beginning of the period.

34. The seven cycles, if counted from trough to trough, are as follows:

$$1876 - 1886 - 1891$$
$$1891 - 1895 - 1899$$
$$1899 - 1904 - 1906$$
$$1906 - 1912 - 1913$$
$$1913 - 1920 - 1926$$
$$1926 - 1927 - 1929$$
$$1929 - 1933 - 1936$$

35. For the price index of bar silver in London (1867–1934), the index of wholesale prices in England (1867–1934), the index of purchasing power of silver in London (1867–1934), and the corresponding indexes for the United States, see China: Ministry of Industries, *Silver and Prices in China*, pp. 2–8. For a discussion of the mechanism of adjustment under the silver standard, see C. F. Remer, "International Trade between Gold and Silver Countries: China, 1885–1913," *Quarterly Journal of Economics*, 40:597–643 (Aug. 1926); Li Choh-ming "The Theory of International Trade Under Silver Exchange," *ibid.*, 53:491–521 (Aug. 1939); W. Y. Lin, *The New Monetary System of China* (Chicago, 1936).

36. Li has suggested that "due to the sluggishness of the cost structure, the export and the domestic prices are not expected to rise immediately to the same extent as the import prices do," but quickly added that "if there should be any lag in the rise of exported prices . . . it must be very short." Li Choh-ming, "The Theory of International Trade under Silver Exchange," p. 518. If Li's "very short" period was within one year, his conclusion would be the same as mine, for the terms of trade are measured on the basis of yearly data.

37. See Chong-su; also Pan Shu-lun, *The Trade of the United States with China* (New York, 1924).

38. Pan Shu-lun, p. 129.

39. Yen Chung-p'ing, ed., *T'ung-chi tzu-liao*, p. 82.

40. W. S. and E. S. Woytinsky, *World Commerce and Government* (New York, 1955), p. 145.

41. *North China Herald* (May 26, 1888), p. 589.

42. C. F. Remer, *Foreign Trade of China* (Shanghai, 1926), p. 85.

43. *Ibid.*, p. 141.

44. Woytinsky, p. 156.

45. *Ibid.*, p. 144.

46. In the field of commercial policy, China did not seem to adopt any policy that would affect the terms of trade significantly. The effective rates of tariff (on both imports and exports) underwent some changes, but they were very small before 1929, when China regained her tariff autonomy.

47. The index of total gain from trade is calculated by multiplying the net barter terms of trade (the ratio of export to import prices) by an index of the total quantity of trade (exports plus imports). Since no total quantity index is available for China's external trade, the weighted average of the quantity index of imports and that of exports is used. For data, see Table 52. Of the index of total gain from trade, Viner has this to say: "One advantage of a total gain index over a unit gain index would be that it would clearly show that the increase in the total amount of gain from trade was consistent with an unfavorable movement in the

index of unit gain from trade if the unfavorable change in the latter was associated with an increase in the volume of trade." J. Viner, *Studies in the Theory of International Trade* (New York, 1937), pp. 563–564. See also R. F. Harrod, *International Economics* (Cambridge, England, 1933), p. 32 ff.; and A. H. Imlah, "The Terms of Trade of the United Kingdom, 1789–1913," *Journal of Economic History*, 10:170–194 (Nov. 1950).

48. The income terms of trade are defined as: $(P_{e1}Q_{e1}/P_{e0}Q_{e0})/(P_{i1}/P_{i0})$, where P_{e0} is the merchandise export price index for the base year and P_{e1} that for the given year; P_{i0} and P_{i1} are corresponding import price indexes; and Q_{e0} and Q_{ei} are corresponding quantity indexes. For the Chinese data of various indexes, see Table 52. For a discussion of the concept of the income terms of trade, see G. S. Dorrence, "The Income Terms of Trade," *Review of Economic Studies*, 16.1:50–56 (1948).

49. Viner, pp. 559–561.

50. According to one estimate, transportation costs in China before 1937 were as follows:

	Freight rate per ton-km. (Chin$)
Land	
Railroads	.010
Auto trucks	.100
Carts (animal-drawn)	.100
Wheelbarrows	.200
Pack animals (data unsatisfactory)	.300
Human porterage	.450
Water	
Junks, upstream	.022
Junks, in interior canals	.019
Yangtze River, upper	.116
Yangtze River, lower	.020
Coasting steamers	.024

	Passenger rate per passenger-km. (Chin$)	
	First Class	Third Class
Land		
Railroads	.045	.015
Auto buses	—	.020
Rickshas	—	.060
Sedan chairs	—	.110
Water		
Junks, upstream	.020	.006
Yangtze River, lower	.070	—
Coasting steamers	.060	—

See Arthur M. Shaw, "Transport Trends in China," *Quarterly Review of Chinese Railways* (Jan. 1937), p. 146.

51. Consumption goods constituted over 90 percent of total imports before the turn of the century. Afterwards the proportion steadily declined, but it was

still more than 70 percent in 1930. In 1936 it dropped to 56 percent. See Yen Chung-p'ing, ed., *T'ung-chi tzu-liao*, p. 73.

52. Cheng Yu-kwei, p. 88.
53. *Ibid.*, p. 90. Investment figures are Remer's.
54. *Ibid.*, p. 92. Breakdown figures are as follows (in US$ millions):

Period: cumulative to and including	Great Britain		Japan		U.S.	
	Import excess[a]	Investment in China	Import excess[b]	Investment in China	Import excess[a]	Investment in China
1914	735.2	607.5	434.0	219.6	0.6	49.3
1930	1451.1	1189.2	987.2	1136.9	353.4	196.8

[a] Including trade via Hong Kong.
[b] Including trade from Korea and via Hong Kong.

55. Yang Twan-liu, Hou Hou-pei *et al.*, p. 1 (1 Haikwan tael = Chin$1.5).
56. See Chapter 5.
57. Remer, *Foreign Investments*, p. 174.
58. Tōa kenkyūjo, *Rekkoku tai-Shi tōshi to Shina kokusai shūshi*, pp. 215–216. According to this source, total capital-inflow in 1937 was Chin$168.4 million, of which Chin$59 million were due to direct investments.
59. For comparison, the following investment service ratios may be noted:

Japan   (1905–1913): 10–15 percent
Argentina (1881–1900): 30–40 percent (height of 66 percent in 1889)
           (1926–1938): 20–30 percent in most years
Indonesia (1925–1939): 22 percent in most years
India   (1930–1933): about 20 percent
           (1934–1938): 14–18 percent

See David Finch, "Investment Service of Underdeveloped Countries," *International Monetary Fund, Staff Papers*, 2:60–85 (Sept. 1951).

BIBLIOGRAPHY

GLOSSARY

INDEX

BIBLIOGRAPHY

Akira Nagano. Development of Capitalism in China. Japan Council, Institute of Pacific Relations, 1931.

Allen, G. C. and A. G. Donnithorne. Western Enterprise in Far Eastern Economic Development: China and Japan. London, 1954.

Bank of China. An Analysis of the Accounts of the Principal Chinese Banks, 1921-1931. Shanghai, 1933.

------Chinese Government Foreign Loan Obligations. Shanghai, 1935.

------Ch'üan-kuo yin-hang nien-chien 全國銀行年鑑 (Bankers' yearbook). 1937.

Baylin, J. R. Foreign Loan Obligation of China. Tientsin, 1925.

Biggerstaff, Knight. "The Secret Correspondence of 1867-1868: Views of Leading Chinese Statesmen regarding the Further Opening of China to Western Influence, " Journal of Modern History, 22. 2:122-136 (June 1950).

------The Earliest Modern Government Schools in China. Ithaca, 1961.

Boeke, G. H. Economics and Economic Policy of Dual Societies. New York, 1953.

Buck, J. L. Land Utilization in China. Shanghai, 1937.

Cairncross, A. K. Home and Foreign Investment, 1870-1913. Cambridge, England, 1953.

Callis, H. G. Foreign Capital in Southeast Asia. New York, 1942.

Carlson, Ellsworth C. The Kaiping Mines, 1877-1912. Cambridge, Mass. , 1957.

275

Chang Chi-hung 章季閬．"Chung-kuo chiu-yeh jen-shu ti ku-chi" 中國就業人數的估計 (An estimate of the working population of China); She-hui k'o-hsüeh tsa-chih 社會科學雜誌 (Quarterly review of social sciences), 9.2:71-91 (Dec. 1947).

Chang Chia-hsiang 張家驤．Chung-hua pi-chih shih 中華幣制史 (History of the monetary system in China). Peking, 1926.

Chang Chia-nau (Chang Kia-ngau). China's Struggle for Railroad Development. New York, 1943.

Chang Shih-wen 張世文．Ting-hsien nung-ts'un kung-yeh tiao-ch'a 定縣農村工業調查 (A survey of rural industries in Ting-hsien). Hopei, 1936.

Chang Yu-i 章有義，ed. Chung-kuo chin-tai nung-yeh shih tzu-liao, ti-erh chi, 1912-1927 中國近代農業史資料.第二輯 (Source materials on the history of agriculture in modern China, Second collection, 1912-1927). Peking, 1957.

Chao Feng-t'ien 趙豐田．Wan-Ch'ing wu-shih-nien ching-chi ssu-hsiang shih 晚清五十年經濟思想史 (Economic thought during the last fifty years of the Ch'ing period). Peking, 1939.

Chen Kuang-fu 陳光甫．"Chan-shih t'ing-chih hou yin-hang chieh chih hsin shih-ming" 戰事停止後銀行業之新使命 (The new mission of Chinese banks after the war); Yin-hang chou-pao 銀行週報 (Bankers' weekly), 16.13:1-6 (Apr. 12, 1932).

Chen, P. T. Recent Financial Developments in China, 1934-1936. Nanking, 1936.

Ch'en Chen 陳真 et al., comps. Chung-kuo chin-tai kung-yeh-shih tsu-liao, ti-erh chi: Ti-kuo chu-i tui Chung-kuo kung k'uang shih-yeh ti ch'in-lüeh ho lung-tuan 中國近代工業史資料，第二輯. 帝國主義對中國工礦事業的侵略

276

和藝断 (Source materials on China's modern industrial history, second collection: Imperialist aggression against and monopolization of China's industries and mines). Peking, 1958.

Cheng Kuan-ying 鄭觀應. Sheng-shih wei-yen 盛世危言 (Warnings to a seemingly prosperous age). 1895.

Cheng Lin. The Chinese Railways, Past and Present. Rev. ed.; Shanghai, 1937.

Cheng T'ien-shou 程天綬. "Kuo-ch'ü shu-shih-nien chih hua-ch'a ch'u-k'ou chia-ko" 過去數十年間之華茶出口價格 (The prices of tea exports in the past few decades); Kuo-chi mao-i tao-pao 國際貿易導報 (Foreign trade journal), Vol. 1, No. 5 (1930).

Cheng Yu-kwei. Foreign Trade and Industrial Development of China. Washington, D.C., 1956.

Ch'i Shu-fen 漆樹芬. Ching-chi ch'in-lüeh hsia chih Chung-kuo 經濟侵略下之中國 (China under economic exploitation). Shanghai, 1925.

Chia Shih-i 賈士毅. Min-kuo ts'ai-cheng shih 民國財政史 (The financial history of the Republic of China), Vol. 2. 2 vols.; Shanghai, 1917.

------ Min-kuo hsü ts'ai-cheng shih 民國續財政史 (The financial history of the Republic of China, Supplement), Vol. 4. 7 vols.; Shanghai, 1932-1934.

Chia Te-huai 賈德懷. Min-kuo ts'ai-cheng chien-shih 民國財政簡史 (An outline of the financial history of the Republic of China). Shanghai, 1946.

Chiang, Alpha C. "Religion, Proverbs, and Economic Mentality," American Journal of Economics and Sociology, 18:250-258 (Apr. 1961).

Chiang-hsi nien-chien, 1937 江西年鑑 (The Kiangsi yearbook).

Chiang Kai-shek. China's Destiny, tr. Wang Ch'ung-hui. New York 1947.

Ch'iao Ch'i-ming 喬啟明. Chung-kuo nung-ts'un she-hui ching-chi hsüeh 中國農村社會經濟學 (The economics of Chinese rural society). Chungking, 1945.

Chin Kuo-chen 金國珍. Chung-kuo ts'ai-cheng lun 中國財政論 (Public finance of China). Shanghai, 1931.

Chin Kuo-pao 金國寶. Chung-kuo mien-yeh wen-t'i 中國棉業問題 (The cotton industry in China). Shanghai, 1936.

Chin Lu-ch'in 金侶琴. "Ch'ü-t'i wai-ch'ao wen-t'i" 取締外鈔問題 (The problem of abolishing foreign banknotes); Ying-hang chou-pao, 11.13:1-19 (Apr. 12, 1927). 銀行週報

Chin shih-wu-nien lai Shanghai chih pa-kung t'ing-yeh 近十五年來上海之罷工停業 (Strikes and lockouts in Shanghai since 1918). Shanghai: Bureau of Social Affairs, City Government of Greater Shanghai, 1933.

China, Maritime Customs. Decennial Reports 1882-1891.

------Maritime Customs. Decennial Reports 1922-1931, Vol. 1. Shanghai, 1933.

------Maritime Customs. Foreign Trade of China.

------Maritime Customs. Reports and Returns of Trade.

------Maritime Customs. Returns of Trade and Trade Reports, 1887, Chefoo.

------Ministries of Communications and Railways. Chiao-t'ung shih 交通史 (History of communications). 37 vols.; Nanking, 1930 ff. Hang-cheng p'ien 航政編 (Section on shipping), Vol. 6 (1931); Lu-cheng p'ien 路政編 (Section on railroads and motor roads), Vol. 1.

278

------Ministry of Industries. Chung-kuo shih-yeh chih 中國實
業誌 (China's industries). Shanghai, 1933.

------Ministry of Industries. Silver and Prices in China. Report of
the Committee to Study Silver Values and Commodity Prices;
1935.

------Ministry of Railways. Statistics of Chinese National Railways.
Issued annually after 1915.

China Yearbook, The. 1921-1922, 1925, 1936, 1938, 1940-1941.

"Chinese Eggs and Egg Products," Chinese Economic Journal,
14.2:157-199 (Feb. 1934).

Chinese Yearbook, The. 1936-1937 and 1940-1941.

Chu Ch'i 朱偰. Chung-kuo tzu-shui wen-t'i 中國租稅問題
(China's taxation problem). Shanghai, 1936.

Chu, T.H. Tea Trade in Central China. Shanghai, 1936.

Chung-hua min-kuo t'ung-chi t'i-yao 中華民國統計提要
(The statistical abstract of the Republic of China). 1948.

Chung-kuo k'uang-yeh chi-yao 中國礦業紀要 (General statement
on the mining industry). Special reports of the Geological
Survey of China.

Ch'üan Han-sheng 全漢昇. "Ch'ing-mo Han-yang t'ieh-ch'ang"
清末漢陽鐵廠 (The Han-yang iron and steel works,
1890-1908); She-hui k'o-hsüeh lun-ts'ung 社會科學論叢
(Journal of social sciences), 1:1-33 (Apr. 1950).

Clark, Grover. Economic Rivalries in China. New Haven, 1932.

Condliffe, John Bell. China Today: Economic. Boston, 1932.

Cooke, George Wingrove. China: Being "The Times" Special
Correspondence from China in the Years 1857-58. London, 1859

Coons, A.G. The Foreign Public Debt of China. Philadelphia, 1930.

Dorrence, G. S. "The Income Terms of Trade," Review of Economic Studies, 16.1:50-56 (1948).

Eckaus, R. S. "The Factor Proportions Problem in Underdeveloped Areas," American Economic Review, 45:539-635 (Sept. 1955).

Epstein, E. I. and R. A. Gordon. "Profits of Selected American Industrial Corporations, 1900-1914," Review of Economic Statistics, 21:122-128 (Feb. 1939).

Epstein, Ralph C. Industrial Profits in the United States. New York, 1934.

Fa-ling ta-ch'üan 法令大全 (Complete laws and ordinances of the Republic of China). Shanghai, 1924.

Fairbank, John K., Alexander Eckstein, and L. S. Yang. "Economic Change in Early Modern China: An Analytic Framework," Economic Development and Cultural Change, 9.1:1-26 (Oct. 1960).

Fang Hsien-t'ing 方顯廷 (H. D. Fong). Rural Industries in China. Tientsin, 1933.

------Chung-kuo chih mien-fang-chih yeh 中國之棉紡織業 (China's cotton textiles). Shanghai, 1934.

------"Industrial Capital in China," Nankai Social and Economic Quarterly, 9.1:27-94 (Apr. 1936).

------Chung-kuo kung-yeh tzu-pen 中國工業資本 (Industrial capital in China). Changsha, 1939.

Fang Hsien-t'ing and Wu Chih 吳知. "Chung-kuo chih hsiang-ts'un kung-yeh" 中國之鄉村工業 (Rural industries of China); Ching-chi t'ung-chi chi-k'an 經濟統計季刊 (Quarterly journal of economics and statistics), 2.3:555-622 (Sept. 1933).

Feis, Herbert. Europe, The World's Banker, 1870-1914. New Haven 1930.

Feuerwerker, Albert.   China's Early Industrialization: Sheng Hsuan-
huai (1844-1916) and Mandarin Enterprise. Cambridge, Mass.,
1958.

Field, F. V. , ed.   An Economic Survey of the Pacific Area.
New York, 1942.

Fieldhouse, D. K.   "Imperialism: An Historiographical Revision, "
Economic History Review, 14.2:187-209 (Dec. 1961).

Finch, David.   "Investment Service of Underdeveloped Countries, "
International Monetary Fund Staff Papers, 2:60-85 (Sept. 1951).

Fong, H. D. , see Fang Hsien-ting.

"Foreign Banks in Shanghai, " Chinese Economic Journal, 16.1:63-95
(Jan. 1935).

"Foreign Banks in Tientsin, " Chinese Economic Journal, 17.4:399-405
(Oct. 1935).

Frankel, H.   Capital Investment in Africa. London, 1938.

Haberler, Gottfried.   "Critical Observations on Some Current Notions
in the Theory of Economic Development, " L'industria, No. 2
(1957).

------Introduction to Review of Economics and Statistics, Vol. 40
(Feb. 1958), Supplement, pp. 3-9.

------International Trade and Economic Development. Cairo, Egypt,
1959.

Harrod, R. F.   International Economics. Cambridge, England, 1933.

Herman, Theodore.   "An Analysis of China's Export Handicraft
Industries to 1930. " Ph. D. thesis; University of Washington,
1954.

Higgins, B.   "The Dualistic Theory of Underdeveloped Countries, "
Economic Development and Cultural Change, 4.2:99-115
(Jan. 1956).

Hirschman, Albert O. "Investment Policies and Dualism in Underdeveloped Countries," American Economic Review, 47:550-570
(Sept. 1957).

------The Strategy for Economic Development. New Haven, 1958.

Ho, Franklin L. (Ho Lien 何廉). Index Numbers of Quantities and
Prices of Imports and Exports in China. Tientsin, 1930.

------"Chung-kuo chin-ch'u-k'ou mao-i wu-liang chih-shu wu-chia
chih-shu yü wu-wu chiao-i-lü chih-shu pien-chih chih shuo-ming"
中國進出口貿易物量指數物價指數與
物物交換率指數編製之說明 (Index numbers of
quantities and prices of imports and exports of China: An
explanation); Ching-chi t'ung-chi chi-k'an, 1.1:128-149
(Mar. 1932).

Ho, Franklin L. and H. D. Fong. Extent and Effects of Industrialization
in China. Tientsin, 1929.

Ho Lien, see Franklin L. Ho.

Ho Ping-ti. Studies on the Population of China, 1368-1953.
Cambridge, Mass., 1959.

Hobson, C. K. The Export of Capital. London, 1914.

Hou Chi-ming, "The Terms of Trade of China, 1867-1936," in Carl J.
Friedrich and Seymour E. Harris, eds., Public Policy, 1961,
pp. 341-365. Cambridge, Mass., 1962.

------"The Critical Minimum Effort Thesis: A Critique," Tsing Hua
journal of Chinese studies, New series, 3.2:87-109 (June 1963).

Hsieh, H. Y. Foreign Interest in the Mining Industry in China.
Shanghai, 1931.

Hsieh Pin 謝彬. Chung-kuo t'ieh-lu shih　中國鐵路史 (History
of Chinese railroads). Shanghai, 1929.

Hsien K'o 獻可. Chin pai-nien ti-kuo chu-yi tsai-Hua yin-hang
fa-hsing chih-pi kai-k'uang 近百年來帝國主義在

華銀行發行紙幣概況 (A general account of the issuance of paper currency in China by imperialist banks in the past hundred years).

Hsü Chi-ch'ing 徐寄廎. Tsui-chin Shang-hai chin-yung shih 最近上海金融史 (A recent history of banking and finance in Shanghai). Shanghai, 1932.

Hsü Keng-sheng 徐梗生. Chung-wai ho-pan mei-t'ieh-k'uang-yeh shih-hua 中外合辦煤鐵礦業史話 (Histories of Sino-foreign jointly managed coal and iron mines). Shanghai, 1946.

Hu Shih. The Chinese Renaissance. Chicago, 1934.

Huang-ch'ao chang-ku hui-pien 皇朝掌故彙編 (A compilation of important events in the Ch'ing dynasty), ed. Sung Cheng-chih 宋澄之 et al. 60 vols.; Shanghai, 1902.

Imlah, A. H. "The Terms of Trade of the United Kingdom, 1789-1913; Journal of Economic History, 10:170-194 (Nov. 1950).

Japan Manchuoukuo Yearbook, 1939, The.

Japan Yearbook, 1943-1944, The.

Johnson, H. G. "Economic Expansion and International Trade," Manchester School of Economic and Social Studies, 59:498-513 (May 1955).

Johnston, Bruce F. "Agricultural Productivity and Economic Development in Japan," Journal of Political Economy, 59:498-513 (Dec. 1951).

Kann, E. "On the Refunding of China's Foreign Loan Obligations," Chinese Economic Journal, 11.1:33-39 (July 1932).

Kao P'ing-shu. Foreign Loans to China. New York, 1946.

Keeton, G. W. The Development of Extraterritoriality in China. London, 1928.

Kent, P. H.   Railway Enterprise in China: An Account of its Origin and
  Development. London, 1907.

Kindleberger, Charles P.   The Terms of Trade: A European Case
  Study. New York, 1956.

------Economic Development. New York, 1958.

Koh Tso-fang (Ku Ch'un-fan).   Capital Stock in China. New York, 1942.

Kroef, J. M. van der.   "Economic Development in Indonesia: Some Social
  and Cultural Impediments," Economic Development and Cultural
  Change, 4.2:116-133 (Jan. 1956).

Ku Ch'un-fan 谷春帆 (Koh Tso-fan).   Chung-kuo kung-yeh hua tung-lun
  中國工業化通論 (Industrialization in China). Shanghai,
  1947.

Ku Yuan-t'ien 谷源田. "Chung-kuo chih kang-t'ieh kung-yeh" 中國
  之鋼鐵工業 (Iron and steel industry in China); Ching-chi
  t'ung-chi chi-k'an, 2.3:693-728 (Sept. 1933). 經濟統計季刊

Kung Chun 龔駿. Chung-kuo hsin-kung-yeh fa-chan-shih ta-kang
  中國新工業發展史大綱 (Outline history of the development of modern industry in China). Shanghai, 1933.

Kuo Hsiao-hsien 郭孝先. "Shang-hai ti wai-kuo yin-hang" 上海
  的外國銀行 (Foreign banks in Shanghai); Shang-hai-shih
  t'ung-chih-kuan ch'i-k'an 上海市通志館期刊 (Journal
  of the Shanghai Gazetteer Office), 2.2:547-602 (Sept. 1934).

------"Shang-hai ti chung-wai ho-pan yin-hang" 上海的中外合
  辦銀行 (Sino-foreign banks in Shanghai); Shang-hai-shih t'ung-
  chih-kuan ch'i-k'an, 2.4:1339-54 (Mar. 1935).

Kyi, Z. T.   "Matchmaking Industry," Chinese Economic Journal,
  4.4:305-311 (Apr. 1929).

League of Nations. Balance of Payments, 1930.

Lee, F. E.   Currency, Banking and Finance in China. Washington,
  D. C., 1926.

Leibenstein, Harvey. Economic Backwardness and Economic Growth. New York, 1957.

Levy, Marion J. Jr. "Contrasting Factors in the Modernization of China, " in S. Kuznets, W. E. Moore, and J. J. Spengler, eds., Economic Growth: Brazil, India, and Japan. Durham, N. C., 1955; also in Economic Development and Cultural Change, 2.3:161-197 (Oct. 1953).

------"Some Aspects of 'Individualism' and the Problem of Modernization in China and Japan, " Economic Development and Cultural Change, 10.3:225-240 (Apr. 1962).

Levy, Marion J. and Shih Kuo-heng. The Rise of the Modern Chinese Business Class. New York, 1949.

Lewis, C. The United States and Foreign Investment Problems. Washington, D. C. 1948.

Lewis, W. A. "Unlimited Labor: Further Notes, " Manchester School of Economic and Social Studies, 26:1-32(Jan. 1958).

Li Ch'ang-lun 李昌隆. Chung-kuo t'ung-yu mao-i lun 中國桐油 貿易論 (A study of China's tung-oil trade). Shanghai, 1934.

Li Choh-ming. "China's International Trade Statistics: An Evaluation, " Nankai Social and Economic Quarterly, Vol. 10, No. 1 (Apr. 1937).

------"The Theory of International Trade under Silver Exchange, " Quarterly Journal of Economics, 53:491-521 (Aug. 1939).

Li Wen-chih 李文治 , ed. Chung-kuo chin-tai nung-yeh-shih tzu-liao, Ti-i chi, 1840-1911 中國近代農業史資料第一 輯 (Source materials on the history of agriculture in modern China, First collection, 1840-1911). Peking, 1957.

Lieu, D. K. (Liu Ta-chün). The Growth and Industrialization of Shanghai. Shanghai, 1936.

------The Silk Industry of China. Shanghai, 1941.

------The Industrialization and Reconstruction of China. Shanghai, 1946.

Lin, W. Y. The New Monetary System of China. Chicago, 1936.

Liu Kwang-Ching. "Steamship Enterprise in Nineteenth-Century China,"
Journal of Asian Studies, 18. 4:435-455 (1959).

------Anglo-American Steamship Rivalry in China, 1862-1874.
Cambridge, Mass. , 1962.

Liu, S. Y. "China's Debts and Their Readjustment," Chinese Economic
Journal, 5. 3:735-749 (Sept. 1929).

Liu Ta-chung and Yeh Kung-chia. The Economy of the Chinese Mainland:
National Income and Economic Development, 1933-1959.
Princeton, 1965.

Liu Ta-chün, see D. K. Lieu.

Lo Tsung-yü 羅從豫. "Wo-kuo t'ieh-lu chai-k'uan kai-yao" 我 國
鐵 路 債 欵 概 要 (A general statement on China's railroad
loans); Chung-hang yüeh-k'an 中 行 月 刊 (Bank of China
monthly review), 14. 5:1-14 (May 1937).

Lo Yü-tung 羅 玉 東 . "Kuang-hsü ch'ao pu-chiu ts'ai-cheng chih
fang-ts'e" 光 緒 朝 補 救 財 政 之 方 策 (The governmental
policies for meeting the financial crisis during the Kuang-hsü
period); Chung-kuo chin-tai chin-chi-shih yen-chiu chi-k'an
中 國 近 代 經 濟 史 研 究 集 刊 (Studies in the modern
economic history of China), 1. 2:189-270 (May 1933).

------Chung-kuo li-chin shih 中 國 釐 金 史 (History of the likin
in China). 2 vols.; Shanghai, 1936.

Lockwood, William W. The Economic Development of Japan.
Princeton, 1954.

------"The Scale of Economic Growth in Japan, 1868-1938," in S.
Kuznets, W. E. Moore, and J. L. Spengler, eds., Economic
Growth: Brazil, India, Japan. Durham, N. C. , 1955.

MacMurray, John V. A., ed.   Treaties and Agreements with and
   concerning China, 1894-1919.   2 vols.; New York, 1921.

Mao Chung-hsiu 繆鐘秀. "Erh-shih nien-lai chih ts'an-ssu yeh"
   二十年來之蠶絲業 (The silk industry in the past
   twenty years); Kuo-chi mao-i tao-pao, Vol. 2, No. 1 (1931).

Mao Tse-tung, "The Chinese Revolution and the Communist Party," in
   Selected Works of Mao Tse-tung, Vol. 3.   Bombay, 1954.

"Match Industry in China," Chinese Economic Journal, 10.3:197-211
   (Mar. 1932).

"Min-kuo erh-shih nien chih Chung-kuo tui-wai mao-i" 民國二十
   年之中國對外貿易 (China's foreign trade during 1931);
   Ching-chi t'ung-chi chi-k'an, 1.4:741-810 (Dec. 1932).

Morgan, Theodore. "The Long-Run Terms of Trade between Agriculture
   and Manufacturing," Economic Development and Cultural Change,
   8.1:1-23 (Oct. 1959).

Morse, H. B.   The Trade and Administration of China.   London, 1913.

------The International Relations of the Chinese Empire, Vol. 3: The
   Period of Submission, 1894-1911.   London, 1918.

------The Chronicles of the East India Company Trading to China,
   1635-1834, Vol. 4.   Oxford, 1926.

Moulton, H. G.   Japan: An Economic and Financial Appraisal.
   Washington, D. C.,1931.

Myrdal, Gunnar.   Rich Lands and Poor: The Road to World Prosperity.
   New York, 1957.

Nan-kai ching-chi yen-chiu so 南開經濟研究所 (Nankai Institute
   of Economics). Nan-kai chih-shu tzu-liao hui-pien 南開指數
   資料彙編(Collection of Nankai's indices).   Peking, 1958.

Nanyang hsiung-ti yen-ts'ao kung-ssu shih-liao 南洋兄弟煙草公
   司史料 (Historical materials concerning the Nanyang Brothers
   Tobacco Company), comp. Shanghai Economic Research Institute,

Chinese Academy of Sciences, and the Economic Research Institute, Shanghai Academy of Social Sciences. Shanghai, 1958.

North China Herald, The.

Nurkse, Ragnar. Problems of Capital Formation in Underdeveloped Countries. Oxford, 1953.

------"International Investment Today in the Light of Nineteenth-Century Experience, " Economic Journal, 64:744-758 (Dec. 1954).

------Equilibrium and Growth in the World Economy: A Collection of Economic Essays, ed. Gottfried Haberler and Robert M. Stern. Cambridge, Mass. , 1961.

Odell, Ralph M. Cotton Goods in China. Washington, D. C. , 1916.

Otto, F. "Shipping in China and Chinese Shipping Abroad, " Chinese Economic Journal, Vol. 5, No. 2 (Feb. 1930).

Ou Pao-san (Wu Pao-san) 巫寶三 et al. Chung-kuo kuo-min so-te i-chiu-san-san nien 中國國民所得，一九三三年 (China's national income, 1933; Monograph ser. [ts'ung-k'an 叢刊] of Institute of Social Sciences, Academia Sinica, No. 25.) 2 vols.; Shanghai¦ 1947.

------"Chung-kuo kuo-min so-te i-chiu-san-san hsiu-cheng" 中國國民所得，一九三三修正 (Corrections to China's National Income , 1933); She-hui k'o-hsüeh tsa-chih, 9. 2:92-153 (Dec. 1947).

Overlach, T. W. Foreign Financial Control in China. New York, 1919.

Pan Shu-lun. The Trade of the United States with China. New York, 1924.

"Paper Currency in China, " Chinese Economic Journal and Bulletin, 18. 4:545-558 (Apr. 1936).

Parkinson, Hargreaves. "British Industrial Profits, " The Economist (Dec. 17 , 1938), pp. 597-603.

Peng Hsüeh-p'ei 彭學沛. Chung-wai huo-pi cheng-ts'e 中外
貨幣政策 (Chinese and foreign monetary policies).
Shanghai, 1931.

P'eng Tse-i 彭澤益, ed. Chung-kuo chin-tai shou-kung-yeh shih
tzu-liao 1840-1949 中國近代手工業史資料
(Source materials on the modern history of Chinese handicrafts).
4 vols.; Peking, 1957.

Prebisch, Paul. "Commercial Policy in the Underdeveloped Countries,"
American Economic Review, Papers and Proceedings,
49:251-273 (May 1959).

Pritchard, Earl H. The Crucial Years of Early Anglo-Chinese Relations
1750-1800. Washington, D.C., 1936.

Remer, Carl F. "International Trade between Gold and Silver
Countries: China, 1885-1913," Quarterly Journal of Economics,
40:597-643 (Aug. 1926).

------Foreign Trade of China. Shanghai, 1926.

------A Study of Chinese Boycotts. Baltimore, 1933.

------Foreign Investments in China. New York, 1933.

Reubens, Edwin P. "Foreign Capital and Domestic Developments in
Japan," in Simon Kuznets, W. E. Moore, and J. L. Spengler,
eds., Economic Growth: Brazil, India, Japan. Durham, N.C.,
1955.

Richthofen, Ferdinand Freiherrn von. China, Vol. 2. Berlin, 1882.

Rockhill, W.W. Treaties and Conventions with or concerning China
and Korea, 1894-1902. Washington, D.C., 1904.

Rosovsky, Henry and Kasushi Ohkawa. "The Indigenous Components
in the Modern Japanese Economy," Economic Development
and Cultural Change, 9.3:476-501 (Apr. 1961).

Royal Institute of International Affairs. The Problem of International
Investment. London, 1937.

Salter, Arthur. Foreign Investment (Essays in International Finance, No. 12). Princeton University, Feb. 1951.

See Chong-su. The Foreign Trade of China. New York, 1919.

Sha Wei-k'ai 沙為楷. Chung-kuo ti mai-pan chih 中國的買辦制 (The compradore system in China). Shanghai, 1934.

Shaw, Arthur M. "Transport Trends in China," Quarterly Review of Chinese Railways (Jan. 1937).

Singer, H. W. "Economic Progress in Underdeveloped Countries," Social Research, 16:1-11 (Mar. 1949).

------"The Distribution of Gains between Investing and Borrowing Countries," American Economic Review, Papers and Proceedings, 40:473-485 (May 1950).

Smith, Thomas C. Political Change and Industrial Development in Japan: Government Enterprises, 1868-1880. Stanford, 1955.

South Manchuria Railway Company. Reports on Progress in Manchuria.

Sprague, Charles E. Extended Bond Tables. 4th ed.; New York, 1920.

Staley, Eugene. War and the Private Investor. Garden City, N.Y., 1935

Stanley, C. John. Late Ch'ing Finance: Hu Kuang-yung As an Innovator. Cambridge, Mass., 1961.

Straight, Willard D. "China's Loan Negotiations," in George H. Blakeslee, ed., Recent Developments in China. New York, 1913.

Sun Yat-sen. The International Development of China. New York, 1922.

------San min chu i, tr. into English by Frank W. Price. Shanghai, 1928.

Sun Yu-t'ang 孫毓棠, ed. Chung-kuo chin-tai kung-yeh shih tzu-liao, 1840-1895 中國近代工業史資料 (Source materials on the modern industrial history of China, 1840-1895). 2 vols.; Peking, 1957.

Sun Zen E-tu. Chinese Railways and British Interests, 1898-1911. New York, 1954.

Ta-Ch'ing fa-kui ta-ch'uan 大清法規大全 (Complete laws and ordinances of the Ch'ing dynasty). 70 vols.

Tamagna, Frank M. Banking and Finance in China. New York, 1942.

T'ang Hsiang-lung 湯象龍. "Min-kuo i-ch'ien kuan-shui tan-pao chih wai-chai" 民國以前關稅擔保之外債 (The foreign loans secured on the Customs revenue before 1911); Chung-kuo chin-tai ching-chi-shih yen-chiu chi-k'an, 3.1:1-49 (May 1935).

------"Min-kuo i-ch'ien ti p'ei-k'uan shih ju-ho ch'ang-fu ti" 民國以前的賠款是如何償付的 (A study of the indemnity payments before 1911); Chung-kuo chin-tai ching-chi-shih yen-chiu chi-k'an, 3.2:262-291 (Nov. 1935).

Tawney, R. H. Land and Labor in China. London, 1932.

Teng Ssu-yü and John K. Fairbank. China's Response to the West: A Documentary Survey, 1839-1923. Cambridge, Mass., 1954.

Ting, Leonard G. "Chinese Modern Banks and the Finance of Government and Industry," Nankai Social and Economic Quarterly 8.3:578-616 (Oct. 1935).

------"The Coal Industry in China," Nankai Social and Economic Quarterly, Vol. 10, No. 1 (Apr. 1937).

Tōa kenkyūjo 東亞研究所 (East Asian Research Institute). Shogaikoku no tai-Shi tōshi 諸外國の對支投資 (Foreign investments in China). Tokyo: Vol. 1, 1942; Vols. 2 and 3, 1943.

------Nihon no tai-Shi tōshi 日本の對支投資 (Japanese investments in China). Tokyo, 1943.

------Rekkoku tai-Shi tōshi gaiyō 列國對支投資概要 (An outline of foreign investments in China). Tokyo, 1943.

------Rekkoku tai-Shi tōshi to Shina kokusai shūshi 列國對支投資と支那國際收支 (Foreign investments in China and China's balance of payments). Tokyo, 1944.

Tsai Chien and Chan Kwan-wai. Trend and Character of China's Foreign Trade, 1912-1931. Shanghai, 1933.

Ts'ai-cheng nien-chien 財政年鑑 (Public finance yearbook). Shanghai, 1935.

Tsao Lien-en. The Chinese Eastern Railway: An Analytical Study. China, Ministry of Industries, 1930.

Tseng K'un-hua 曾鯤化. Chung-kuo t'ieh-lu shih 中國鐵路史 (History of Chinese railroads). Peking, 1924; Shanghai, 1929.

Tsiang T'ing-fu 蔣廷黻. Chung-kuo chin-tai shih 中國近代史 (History of modern China). Changsha, 1938.

Tsou-ting kuang-wu chang-ch'eng 奏訂礦務章程 (Mining regulations 1904).

Tsui-hsin kuo-min cheng-fu fa-ling ta-ch'üan 最新國民政府法令大全 (Newest comprehensive compendium of laws and ordinances of the National government). Shanghai, 1932.

United Nations. The Economic Development of Latin America and Its Principal Problems. New York, 1949.

------International Capital Movements during the Interwar Period. New York, 1949.

------Relative Prices of Exports and Imports of Underdeveloped Countries. New York, 1949.

------Demographic Year Book 1949-1950.

------Measures for the Economic Development of Underdeveloped Countries. New York, 1951.

------Instability in Export Markets of Underdeveloped Countries. New York, 1952.

Viner, J. Studies in the Theory of International Trade. New York, 1937.

Wagel, S.R.   Finance in China. Shanghai, 1914.

Wang Ching-yü 汪敬虞 , ed.   Chung-kuo chin-tai kung-yeh shih
tzu-liao, ti-erh chi, 1895-1914 nien 中國近代工業史資料
第二輯 1895-1914 年 (Source materials on the modern
industrial history of China, 1895-1914), 2 vols.; Peking, 1957.

Wang Tzu-chien 王子達 and Wang Chen-chung 王鎮中 . Ch'i-sheng
Hua-shang sha-ch'ang tiao-ch'a pao-kao 七省華商紗厰
調查報告 (Report of a survey of Chinese cotton mills in
seven provinces). Shanghai, 1935.

Wang, W.H.   "Japanese Manufacturing Industries in Manchuria,"
Chinese Economic Journal, 5.6:1105-37 (Dec. 1929).

Weber, Max.   The Religion of China, tr. and ed. Hans H. Gerth.
Glencoe, Ill., 1951.

Wei Tsu-ch'u 魏子初 . Ti-kuo chu-yi yü K'ai-luan mei-k'uang
帝國主義與開灤煤礦 (Imperialism and the Kailan
mines). Shanghai, 1954.

Williams, E.T.   Recent Chinese Legislation relating to Commercial
Railway and Mining Enterprise. Shanghai, 1904.

Willoughby, W.W.   Foreign Rights and Interests in China.
Rev. ed.; Baltimore, 1927.

Worcester, G.R.G.   The Junkman Smiles. London, 1959.

Woytinsky, W.S. and E.S. Woytinsky, World Commerce and Government.
New York, 1955.

Wright, A., ed. Twentieth Century Impressions of Hongkong, Shanghai
and Other Treaty Ports of China. London, 1908.

Wright, Mary Clabaugh.   The Last Stand of Chinese Conservatism.
Stanford, 1957.

Wright, Stanley F.   The Collection and Disposal of the Maritime and
Native Customs Revenue since the Revolution of 1911.
Shanghai, 1927.

Wu Ch'eng-hsi 吳承禧. Chung-kuo ti yin-hang 中國的銀行
(Banking in China). Shanghai, 1934.

Wu Ch'eng-ming 吳承明. Ti-kuo chu-i tsai chiu Chung-kuo ti t'ou-tzu
帝國主義在舊中國的投資 (Investments of imperialistic
powers in Old China). Peking, 1958.

Wu Chih 吳知. Hsiang-ts'un chih-pu kung-yen ti i-ko yen-chiu
鄉村織布工業的一個研究 (A study of the rural cloth
industry). Shanghai, 1936.

Wu Ching-ch'ao 吳景超. "Han-Yeh-P'ing kung-ssu ti fu-ch'e"
漢冶萍公司的覆轍 (The lesson of the Hanyehp'ing
Company); Hsin ching-chi 新經濟 (New economy; Jan. 1, 1933),
pp. 103-109.

Wu Chüeh-nung 吳覺農 "Shang-hai ch'a-yeh kai-k'uang" 上海茶
業概況 (The tea market in Shanghai); Kuo-chi mao-i tao-pao,
Vol. 1, No. 2 (1930).

Wu Pan-nung 吳半農. Mei-k'uang chi shih-yu 煤礦及石油
(Coal and petroleum). Peiping, 1932.

Wu Ta-yeh 吳大業. "Chin-yin pen-wei kuo chien chin-yin huo liu-tung
ti yuan-tse chi Chung-kuo chin-yin huo chin-ch'u k'ou ti chieh-shih"
金銀本位國間金銀貨流動的原則及中國金銀貨進出口的解釋
(Principles governing the movement of gold and silver between gold-
standard and silver-standard countries); Ching-chi t'ung-chi chi-k'an
2.2:351-381 (June 1933).

Wu Ta-yeh and Hu Yuan-chang 胡元璋. "Min-kuo erh-shih-szu nien
chih Chung-kuo tui-wai mao-i" 民國二十四年之中國
對外貿易 (China's foreign trade during 1935); Cheng-chih
ching-chi hsüeh-pao 政治經濟學報 (Quarterly journal of
economics and political science), Vol. 5, No. 1 (Oct. 1936).

Wu Yu-kan 武堉幹. Chung-kuo kuo-chi mao-yi kai-lun 中國國際
貿易概論 (A study of China's foreign trade). Shanghai, 1930.

Yang Lu 楊魯. K'ai-luan-k'uang li-shih chi shou-kuei kuo-yu wen-t'i 開灤礦歷史及收歸國有問題 (The history of the Kailan mines and the problem of recovery). Tientsin, 1932.

Yang Ta-chin 楊大金. Hsien-tai Chung-kuo shih-yeh chih 現代中國實業誌 (Industries in China). Shanghai, 1938.

Yang Twan-liu, Hou Hou-pei et al. Statistics of China's Foreign Trade during the Last Sixty-Five Years. National Research Institute of Social Sciences, Academia Sinica, 1931.

Yang Yin-p'u 楊蔭溥. Chung-kuo chin-jung lun 中國金融論 (Money market and finance in China). Shanghai, 1931.

Yen Chung-p'ing 嚴中平. Chung-kuo mien-fang-chih shih-kao 中國棉紡織史稿 (A draft history of Chinese cotton spinning and weaving). Peking, 1955.

------, ed. Chung-kuo chin-tai ching-chi shih t'ung-chi tzu-liao hsüan-chi 中國近代經濟史統計資料選輯 (Selected statistics on the modern economic history of China. Peking, 1955.

GLOSSARY

Anshan 鞍山	Haikwan 海關
	Han Fu-chü 韓復渠
Chang Chih-tung 張之洞	Hanyehp'ing 漢冶萍
Ch'ien-chuan 錢莊	Hu-pu 戶部
Chihli 直隸	Hu Shih 胡適
Ch'ing 清	
Chung-Fu 中福	Jung Ts'ung-ching 榮宗敬
Chung-Yuan 中原	
	Kaiping 開平
Fa-pei 法幣	Kuan-hsi 官息
Feng-shui 風水	Kuan-tu shang-pan 官督商辦
Fuchung 福中	Kuang-hsü 光緒
Fushun 撫順	Kuping 庫平

Li Hung-chang 李鴻章
Likin 釐金
Liu Hsi-hung 劉錫鴻
Liu Ming-ch'uan 劉銘傳
Lou-chih 漏卮
Luta 魯大

Nanyang 南洋
Nien 捻

Penhsihu 本溪湖
P'iao-hao 票號

Shen-Hsin 申新

Ta-sheng 大生
Ta Tung 大通
Taiping 太平
Tang Ching-hsing 唐景星
Tayeh 大冶
Tso Tsung-t'ang 左宗棠
Tsungli Yamen 總理衙門
T'ung-wen kuan 同文舘
Tz'u-hsi 慈禧

Wang Chung-hui 王寵惠
Wo-Jen 倭仁

Yin-hao 銀號
Yu-Feng 豫豐
Yuan Shih-k'ai 袁世凱

Index

For Product Safety Concerns and Information please contact our EU
representative GPSR@taylorandfrancis.com Taylor & Francis Verlag GmbH,
Kaufingerstraße 24, 80331 München, Germany

Printed and bound by CPI Group (UK) Ltd, Croydon, CR0 4YY

08/05/2025

01864422-0002